Home from Siberia

HOME FROM SIBERIA

The Secret Odysseys
of Interned American Airmen
in World War II

BY OTIS HAYS, JR.

Texas A&M University Press
College Station

The paper used in this book meets the minimum requirements
of the American National Standard for Permanence of
Paper for Printed Library Materials, Z39.48-1984.
Binding materials have been chosen for durability.

LIBRARY OF CONGRESS CATALOGING-IN-PUBLICATION
DATA

Hays, Otis, 1915–
    Home from Siberia : the secret odysseys of
interned American airmen in World War II /
by Otis Hays, Jr. — 1st ed.
      p. cm. — (Texas A&M University mili-
tary history series ; 16)
    Includes bibliographical references.
    ISBN 0-89096-434-3 (alk. paper)
    1. World War, 1939–1945 — Aerial
operations, American. 2. Prisoners of war —
Russian S.F.S.R. — Siberia. 3. Prisoners of
war — United States. 4. Aeronautics —
Accidents. I. Title. II. Series.
D790.H39 1990
940.54′4973 — dc20   89-20569
                                     CIP

For Dutch

WHO SHARED THE BURNING OF THE MIDNIGHT OIL

Contents

Illustrations

Preface

During World War II, U.S. airmen flew countless missions over the Japanese homeland and territory controlled by the Japanese in the North Pacific and Manchuria. Coming from the carrier *Hornet,* the Aleutian Islands, and deep inside China, army and navy flyers in disabled bombers on occasion sought to land in nearby Soviet territory. Between 1942 and 1945, a total of 37 crews had this experience. In every case the Soviets took the crews into custody as soon as possible and eventually moved them thousands of miles to south-central Asia. For 36 of the crews, their internment camp was near Tashkent. After being held for up to 13 months, they all eventually made it home again, either through one of four clandestine "escapes" from the Soviet Union or through open release at the conclusion of the war.

Nearly a half century has elapsed since five separate groups of American airmen entered and were funneled across Asia in this way. No complete roster of the names and whereabouts of present-day survivors of these groups can be found. However, according to an unofficial but realistic 1988 estimate, about 60 percent of the original 291 interned men are still living, witnesses to a largely forgotten chapter of World War II history.

For many reasons, the story of the five wartime group odysseys has not been told in its entirety. The main reason, however, apparently stems from a secrecy pledge that was demanded from each of the men who escaped. Although the pledge was not binding indefinitely, its duration remained a moot question for some. One former internee, now a retired businessman, reported that during his interrogation at the Pentagon after his return to Washington, a four-star general told him that certain aspects of his escape could be revealed only on direct order of the president. Other internees, heeding an injunction to forget that particular episode in their lives, kept the secret by trying to block the details from their memories.

Pieces of the story found in official documents stored in various governmental archives were tardy in being declassified, some as late as 1986. The declassified documents were impersonal records. They noted generally when each crew arrived in Siberia and when each assembled group of airmen was allowed to leave. What happened to the internees during the time of entry and departure? In order to obtain some of the personal details of individual experiences, a search was begun to locate former internees. One of the early results of the search was the growth of an "internee telegraph," whereby one correspondent would supply the name and address of a fellow internee. Information was obtained not only from various archives but also through detailed questionnaires to which responses were made in writing or by cassette recording, and by both telephone and face-to-face interviews.

Each of the men who were contacted fell into one of three categories. Some, whether disinterested or for some other reason, did not respond to inquiries and thus kept their silence. Others stated openly that they either would not or could not try to remember what had happened. A typical response was, "I have forgotten about those days and do not want to jog my memory. I just put those days out of my mind." Others told how they were trying to relive the Siberian experience but found that "everything is so hazy." Fortunately, others — although some of them at first were reluctant to delve too deeply into what they considered a "can of worms" — cooperated fully. A retired professional man in the Midwest wrote, "I have never talked about my experiences about town, and would like not to have my name mentioned." He later changed his mind.

Some of the former internees who were retired career military officers decided to ask the Department of the Air Force whether they were free to discuss their wartime experiences in the Soviet Union. The bureaucracy concluded that the officers no longer had to remain mute.[1]

Even while the search for surviving former internees was under way, the attrition among their members continued relentlessly. At least four potential respondents died during the process.

The recounting of the internees' story was based mainly on what cooperating individuals were able to recall. Not all of the men who provided information remembered what happened in precisely the same way. In cases where there was honest disagreement as to what occurred to whom and when and in what sequence, a consensus was adopted so that the story's continuity was not seriously interrupted.

For many of the men, recall was a painful process. "Since you first contacted me," a New England businessman wrote, "I have had at least a dozen nightmares and have lain awake half of countless nights trying

1. Letter, Headquarters, Department of the Air Force, Washington, D.C., to Col. C. K. Hanner, Jr., USAF (Ret), January 12, 1987. Copy provided by C. K. Hanner, Jr.

to pull bona fide memories from my subconscious." A Minnesota engineer said, "It is now three o'clock in the morning, and I find that I cannot sleep. All I can think about is you, [because] I still owe you some answers."

Several internees covertly kept diaries. Fearful of possible retaliation if their records were discovered, the writers did not even reveal to one another what they were doing. A few of the diaries were either destroyed or confiscated before the writers left the Soviet Union, but others were smuggled past Soviet guards and avoided American security scrutiny. One man reported, however, that he did not try to conceal his diary. "No one asked me about it," he said, "and I didn't mention it." Originally crude notes scribbled on bits of rough toilet paper or other paper scraps, the diaries were hidden in linings of jackets or boots or, in one case, strapped to a man's leg near his groin. These notes were later expanded into readable documents. In one special instance, the widow of a former internee shared the notes that made up her husband's record of his experience. The diaries were undimmed mirrors reflecting the feelings of young men during their last combat mission against Japanese targets, their journey 6,000 miles across Siberia to internment camp, their inactivity and despair while in camp, and finally their escape or release into Iran.

Any story as complex as the odysseys of the American airmen in the Soviet Union during World War II can be written only with the help of individuals who either have lived through it or have access to records of the experience. I have many individuals to thank for their invaluable assistance in providing information about the American story.

Except as otherwise noted in the text, first-hand information about American airmen in the Soviet Union comes from former internees, who have kindly given permission to share their memories. The author communicated personally with thirty-seven former internees: Gilbert S. Arnold, Donnie L. Broadwell, Cyril J. ("Pat") Brown, Jackson W. Clark, Joseph A. Dunwoody, Robert G. Emmens, Richard E. Filler, Samuel Gelber, Gerald J. Green, Ralph W. Hammond, Charles K. Hanner, Jr., William W. Head, Jr., Anthony L. Homitz, Harry J. Koepp, Irwin L. Lans, Carl W. Lindell, Darryl F. McDonald, John B. McIntosh, Russell L. Manthie, John F. ("Butterfly") Mathers, Allen T. ("Red") Miller, Berwyn J. Miller, Jr., Byron A. Morgan, James R. O'Dair, F. Clark Ogden, David W. Pohl, Vladimir P. Sabich, Richard D. Salter, John R. Smith, John S. ("Jack") Smith, Edward F. Sorenson, John M. Taylor, John W. Tyler, John P. Vivian, Robert W. Wiles, Hubert B. Winter, and Robert B. Wolbrink.

Also providing important information were former Aleutian airmen Rhodes F. Arnold, William S. Boone, Ted C. Buszek, William F. Mahaffy, J. E. Mills, Lawrence Reineke, Robert E. Talley, John L. Tidball, and Irving Wadlington. Assistance was also provided by Mrs. Ernest A. Stifel,

Jr., who generously granted access to her late husband's records, and by George G. Kisevalter.

Many others were very helpful in providing information necessary for telling the whole story, including Amy Schmidt and William G. Lewis, National Archives and Records Center, Washington, D.C.; Bernard F. Cavalcante and Edward J. Marolda, Naval Historical Center, Washington, D.C.; Lester A. Sliter, historian, U.S. Air Force Historical Research Center, Maxwell Air Force Base, Alabama; John H. Cloe, historian, Alaskan Air Command, Elmendorf Air Force Base, Alaska; Richard Norton Smith, director, Herbert Hoover Library, West Branch, Iowa; Katherine H. Frankum, librarian, Lyndon Baines Johnson Library, Austin, Texas; Martin M. Teasley, assistant director, Dwight D. Eisenhower Library, Abilene, Kansas; Hilary Cummings, special manuscripts collection, University of Oregon Library, Eugene, Oregon; Robert E. McCabe, U.S. Military Mission to Moscow (World War II); and Donald P. Booth and John L. Bates, U.S. Persian Gulf Command (World War II).

Home from Siberia

1

American Internees in "Neutral Country"
1942–1945

On September 1, 1945, the last interned American airman to be repatriated from the Soviet Union during World War II arrived in New York City without fanfare. The odyssey of Ernest A. Stifel, Jr., across Siberia, like the secret odysseys of 290 other American flyers before him, was over.

For hundreds of years Siberia seemed an endless yet isolated land mass extending from the Ural Mountains in the West to the Pacific Ocean in the East. From the beginning, the very name *Siberia* conjured images of danger and mystery. Siberia and central Asia were separated from the Orient and the Middle East by a series of lofty mountain ranges. Through and behind this craggy fringe once came Alexander's armies, Genghis Khan's hordes, and merchant caravans before and after Marco Polo. To the north of this fringe, the only means of crossing thousands of miles of wilderness had been horseback, sledge, and raft. Russian adventurers, fur traders, and political exiles intermixed with native tribes. Then, nearly 100 years ago, czarist Russia awakened to realize that a trans-Siberian railroad from Moscow to Vladivostok could be used to unify the Russian Empire. In the 40 years before World War II, the Great Siberian Railroad opened and expanded a corridor across this vast area. Nonetheless, on the eve of World War II, the very size of this Asian land mass still made it the object of exaggerated tales of violence, intrigue, and even romance.

Siberia swallowed 291 American airmen between 1942 and 1945.[1] What happened to them became their own personal secret.

These airmen were from the crews of 37 American army and navy bombers disabled while on combat missions against enemy targets in Japan, Manchuria, and the Kurile Islands. These were young men. Less than 10 percent were over the age of 25, and most of them were much younger, between 19 and 22. Some were flying on their first combat mission when they ar-

---

1. See alphabetical roster at appendix C.

rived in Siberia. Others were veterans who had already faced the terrors of antiaircraft artillery near-misses and the onslaught of enemy fighters.

Since Siberia offered a safer alternative to ditching at sea or falling into the hands of the Japanese, the bomber crews nursed their fuel-starved or battered aircraft toward the nearest Soviet territory. When they failed to return to their bases, the flyers were officially reported to be missing in action.

At one time, seven bombers reached Siberia in a single day. In rare instances, two of the planes crash-landed almost simultaneously. In most cases, however, the bombers limped one at a time toward Siberia, weeks or even months apart.

The Soviet Union, citing the International Hague Rules of Air Warfare adopted in 1923, repeatedly protested the American intrusion of its airspace as American planes strayed or sought refuge there. Bombers often were greeted by Soviet antiaircraft fire. Late in the war, in 1945, a B-25 bomber was struck and destroyed by Soviet ground fire near Cape Lopatka at the southern tip of Kamchatka. Soviet fighters also intercepted incoming American planes but, instead of attacking, escorted them to landing fields.

During their premission briefings, most of the crews had been warned that they probably would be interned if they landed or crashed in Siberia. And so they were. The Soviet Union, having announced its neutrality in America's war with Japan, publicly adhered to international law.

From the start the internees told their Soviet interrogators that they had been on training missions when the Japanese attacked them.[2] In telling this story, the Americans hoped that the Soviets would agree to return them quickly to American control. That never happened. Rumors later persisted that American internees managed to reach American ships at the port of Murmansk on the Arctic Ocean, or that other internees were evacuated from Kamchatka and Vladivostok by American submarines and Soviet air transports to the Aleutian Islands or the Alaska mainland. All such rumors, like many of the rumors about Siberia itself, had no basis in fact.

The Americans were interned for an average of five months. For a few, the confinement was shorter, and for others, much longer. Except for those in the final group, released after the Soviet Union declared war on Japan,

2. U.S. Embassy Moscow message M-22159 to Joint Chiefs of Staff, December 26, 1944, U.S. Military Mission to Moscow—"Internees" files, Record Group 334, National Archives (hereafter cited as "Internees" files). The chief of the U.S. Military Mission recommended "that the crews should not report their flights to the Soviets as training flights but as operational." The message pointed out that any "statement that the flight is a training flight does not change the conditions of internment and is only annoying to the Russians when planes are obviously battle damaged." The recommendation came too late to alter the "training flight" statements of the first 23 Aleutian Islands–based crews to be interned.

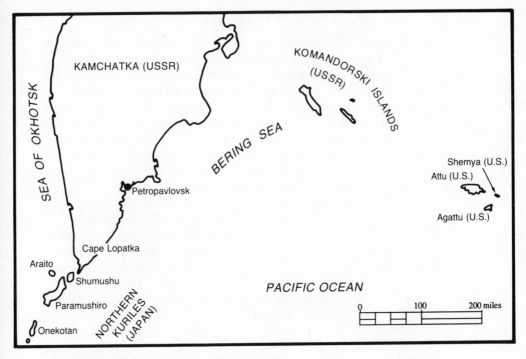

MAP 1. Scene of air activity in the North Pacific

the internees ended their odysseys across Asia by escaping, with the Soviet Union's clandestine help. When they departed, the internees did not go north, east, or west. Instead, they were sent south into Iran.

The Soviet Union assumed that Japan knew that American bomber crews had been interned after their disabled aircraft had landed in Siberia. It was uppermost on the Soviets' minds, however, that the Japanese must not learn that any of the internees had been released. Hints that Moscow may have violated its neutrality by freeing the airmen could have been considered by Tokyo as anti-Japanese provocations. The Soviet government, keeping a circumspect relationship with its old Pacific rival, wanted to avoid giving Japan an excuse for taking military action against the Soviet Far East.

Aware of this delicate situation, Washington in late 1942 nevertheless began negotiating with Moscow for the release of the first group of internees. In turn, Moscow in May, 1943, demonstrated that cooperation was possible by cautiously initiating the first escape.[3] On its part, Washington

3. Richard C. Lukas, "Escape," *Aerospace Historian,* Spring, 1969, 15. The article contains a declassified official postwar report by Gen. John R. Deane, summarizing Soviet-American efforts to execute Soviet plans that allowed American internees to escape.

made the first and all subsequent escapes official secrets. Realizing that the Soviets at any time could decide to adhere to the letter of international law and confine the American flyers for the duration of the war, Washington organized a concerted program to conceal the fact that American interned airmen were being smuggled from the Soviet Union to the United States. Any physical evidence—clothing, souvenirs, and other telltale objects—indicating that an airman had recently been in the Soviet Union was confiscated. The fact that the man had been interned in the Soviet Union was omitted from his personnel records. The man himself was gagged by threats of official retribution if the secret was disclosed.

The American Embassy's flow of information about and contact with the American internees came through two channels. For Ambassador William H. Standley (1942–43) and Ambassador W. Averell Harriman (1943–45), the channel was through the office of Foreign Minister V. M. Molotov. The U.S. military attaché, Brig. Gen. Joseph Michela (1942–43), and the chief of the U.S. Military Mission, Maj. Gen. John R. Deane (1943–45), were generally limited to the information supplied through the Red Army's Foreign Liaison Office, known as OVS.

Control of the internees was exercised by the People's Commissariat of Internal Affairs (Narodny Komisariat Vnutrennikh Del), referred to as the NKVD.[4] Consequently, the American Embassy was able to obtain only the information that the NKVD provided to the foreign minister's office and the OVS.

In addition to the bottleneck created by NKVD secrecy, at least two major obstacles contributed to slowing the process of identifying and locating missing American flyers whom the Soviets had interned. The first was the overloaded and inadequate communications facilities connecting the Soviet Far East and Moscow. Another was the inept deciphering of unfamiliar American names translated into Russian and then back into English again. The frustrated American Embassy therefore often waited weeks and even months before obtaining confirmed identifications that could be forwarded to Washington.

The long waiting period for learning what had happened to the missing men created unnecessary anxiety for the men's families. Among the parents, wives, and fiancées an informal network often helped to maintain a spark of hope. About 85 percent of the internees were from army and navy squadrons based in the Aleutian Islands, and censored letters from squadron mates of the missing airmen brought a measure of cheer to the waiting relatives.

Once Moscow confirmed to Washington that an airman was "safe and

4. Eugene K. Keefe et al., *Area Handbook for the Soviet Union* (Washington, D.C.: GPO, 1971), 143–44.

interned in a neutral country," the next-of-kin was informed by a visit from a military representative, an official telegram, or both. The representative and telegram warned against revealing the welcome news. Following the initial notification, an official letter from the Adjutant General's Office (army) or the Bureau of Naval Personnel (navy) reiterated that the news about the internment should be disclosed to the immediate family only. The letter insisted that public knowledge of the internee's status was not considered to be in the nation's best interest because such knowledge could hinder official efforts to obtain the internee's release. The army stated that the name of the neutral country where the internee was located "cannot be revealed." The navy admitted that the internee was "in Russia" but cautioned against public announcement.

Specific instructions were provided for sending letters and packages to the internee through Washington's military channels. All incoming mail was carefully censored by American authorities to eliminate any indication that the internee was in the Soviet Union. To families, this type of censorship seemed unnecessary because the map of Asia would show that the only neutral area within the range of bombers operating against Japanese targets was Soviet territory.

In 1942 one of the bombers from Doolittle's Tokyo raid landed near Vladivostok, and the Soviet internment of the five-man crew was later confirmed. A news leak in 1944 of the crew's escape from the Soviet Union caused diplomatic ripples in Soviet-American relations.[5] The news leak was quickly hushed.

After the war's end, the unofficial memoirs of General Deane mentioned the predicament of two other and larger groups of internees.[6] Related versions later emerged, but they were only portions of the whole story. Most of the disconnected fragments focused on the bizarre escapes of the first three groups into Iran.

In all, the Soviet Union interned five groups of American flyers.[7] Although several months separated the first two groups, the last three groups followed one another more closely. No one group came in contact with another, however, so the men in one rarely had any knowledge of the size or composition of groups ahead of or behind them.[8] Once repatriated, few of the former internees maintained contact with fellow escapees, except perhaps with some of their own crewmates.

5. Lukas, "Escape," 16.
6. John R. Deane, *The Strange Alliance* (New York: Viking Press, 1946), 59–63.
7. See summaries of groups interned in appendixes A and B.
8. Group No. 2 was an exception. Because of public knowledge that one crew from the Doolittle Tokyo raid had been interned, members of Group No. 2 speculated whether they would encounter the crew somewhere in the Soviet Union.

The war with Japan was only four months old when the first five American airmen were interned in Siberia. These men, after participating in the Doolittle raid on Tokyo, hoped that they could refuel their bomber at Vladivostok. This hope promptly faded. They finally escaped from the Soviet Union 13 months later, in May, 1943. At that time the Soviets may have thought that they had settled the problem created by the American violation of Soviet neutrality. Soon, however, the Soviets were faced with a much greater problem. Shortly after the Japanese lost their military toeholds in the outer Aleutian Islands in mid-1943, eight more American crews, all from Aleutian bases, made forced landings "in neutral country," this time on the remote Kamchatka Peninsula, north of Japan's Kurile Islands.

These latest internees as well as the 225 other flyers who followed them eventually were transferred by aircraft and trans-Siberian railroad to Uzbekistan in south central Asia. Here, outside the historic city of Tashkent near the village of Vrevskaya, the Soviets earmarked the grounds and buildings of a former school as an internment camp. The camp turned out to be large enough to accommodate the rising number of Americans arriving in Siberia during the war. The smallest group in the camp numbered 43 men, and the largest group, 130. The Soviets expected that the internment facility, thousands of miles from the Pacific war theater, would be remote enough to isolate the internees from the attention of the Japanese.

The camp's main building was a large E-shaped one-story structure, which became the barracks.[9] It was adapted to provide not only internee dormitory rooms but also a small dispensary, a disciplinary section for solitary confinement, a recreation hall, and sleeping quarters for some of the camp's staff, particularly the resident interpreters. The early internees recalled that the kitchen and dining room were also located in one wing of this building, but later internees reported that these facilities were relocated in a separate structure. Each dormitory room contained several cots and one or more small tables. Water troughs for face and hand washing were in the hallways outside the dormitory rooms, but these too were moved outdoors in 1944.

This large barracks, clean but damp at night, was made of whitewashed mud-and-straw adobe blocks with walls nearly two feet thick. The adobe material repelled some of the summer heat but, even when heating stoves built into the room partitions were used, turned the interior into an icebox in winter. Before the arrival of the first Americans, the occupants had been Polish displaced persons. Poles who had been unable to find shelter

9. Some of the men had difficulty in recalling the general appearance of the building. A few also remembered it as being U-shaped, and others as L-shaped.

in the building had lived in covered pits that they had dug in the surrounding grounds. Both the building occupants and the pit dwellers had been moved into abandoned structures in Vrevskaya when the Soviets made the decision to consolidate all American internees in one location.

A primitive outhouse, divided by a partition for the use of both men and women, was first located over a pit about 100 feet from the barracks. The outhouse arrangement was modified when later groups occupied the camp. Other adobe structures on the former school grounds included a horse stable, laundry, blacksmith shop, woodshed, and shelters for housing other members of the camp's staff. A food storage tunnel had been dug near the kitchen.

The grounds, several acres in size, were fenced on two sides by crumbling adobe walls and on the other two sides by waterways used for irrigation. One of these waterways was deep enough for summer swimming. The enclosed area was dotted with a few trees, mostly those similar to willow, locust, and elm. As each group of Americans passed through the camp, various portions of the grounds were converted into areas for playing games.

Although its hand was rarely revealed, the NKVD secretly kept its eye on the movement and activities of the internees. The Red Army, however, was given the responsibility for operating the camp and safeguarding the Americans interned there.

The camp commandant was a Red Army officer. Commandants were usually rotated when a group of internees escaped. When a new group of internees arrived, so did a new commandant. This officer as well as members of his military staff and the men of the camp's Red Army security unit were combat veterans who had been assigned to light duty because of war wounds or fatigue. The camp functioned with a domestic staff of cooks, waiters, housekeepers, and interpreters, nearly all of whom were women. The size of this domestic staff varied with the size of each internee group but averaged about 15. Except for the interpreters, there was a constant shifting of personnel. Familiar faces vanished, and new ones appeared. The reason for this gradual but constant turnover was never explained but apparently occurred due to individual staff members' becoming too friendly with Americans.

In addition to the 291 surviving Americans, 4 crewmen died while en route to, or soon after arrival in, Siberia. Three men suffered fatal combat or crash injuries, and their bodies were buried at Petropavlovsk. Another man drowned when his bomber ditched at sea off the Kamchatka coast. His body was never recovered. One writer lamented in his diary that the three buried men would "remain forever in Russia." After the end of the war, however, the three American bodies were exhumed and returned to

American graves registration officials in Japan for forwarding to final places of interment.[10]

Some of the men suffered battle wounds, and others were injured in crash landings and camp accidents. The crews of three bombers were forced to parachute from their disabled craft over Soviet territory, and another bomber burned after crashing. All four crews escaped alive.

Typhus fever, typhoid fever, and malaria were health hazards in Uzbekistan. Some internees contracted malaria but avoided the other two. However, they did not avoid dysentery, which, for most of the men, was recurring. An estimated one-third developed cases of athlete's foot because of a breakdown in bathhouse sanitation. Heads were often shaved to discourage lice infestation. Bedbugs were problems at Petropavlovsk and en route to Tashkent especially, but they were brought under control at the camp. Lacking customary hygienic supplies, internees developed dental problems. Emergency surgery performed at Petropavlovsk and Tashkent hospitals became ordeals because of Soviet wartime shortages of medical supplies and lack of adequate facilities with general anesthesia, sanitary bandages, and sterile operating areas. Recovery from surgery was sometimes slowed due to complications.

The men's physical problems were frequently serious, but the more enduring scars from their Siberian experience probably were psychological. Official records seemed to ignore the depression and frustration felt by the trained combat aircrews who were stunned by the realization that they could be interned for the war's duration. To the dejected men, this could seem to be forever. The men were grateful to be alive — but alive for what? Many related factors contributed to the weight of the men's depression, including the influences of diet, sanitation, clothing, worry about family, loss of communication with the outside world, and, worst of all, inactivity.

The first real shock that Americans felt after their arrival in "neutral country" was the sight and taste of the food. It was, simply stated, "different." The men suffered not so much from lack of food but rather from a diet that lacked variety and was probably vitamin deficient. The Soviets told the Americans that they, as interned military men, were being fed the regular Red Army ration. In wartime Soviet Union, the Red Army was given priority access to the nation's available food supplies. Granting that the internees' diet was more than adequate by wartime Soviet standards, most of the Americans nevertheless lost weight. The average reported loss was about 20 pounds per man, although a few reported no weight loss

10. War Department memorandum, undated, Missing Air Crew Reports, Record Group 92, report no. 14409, National Archives (hereafter cited as Missing Air Crew Reports, no. _____). The memorandum acknowledged the U.S. Army's receipt in postwar Japan of three bodies "from the Russians." The bodies were identified by tags on Sergeant Ring and Corporal Glodek and by markings on the box containing Sergeant Wutchic's remains.

whatsoever. Two men, however, claimed that when they were examined after repatriation, one had lost 75 pounds, and the other, 54.

Three meals were served daily at the camp. Breakfast was in midmorning, the second meal in midafternoon, and the last meal about eight o'clock in the evening. For breakfast, the men could expect *kasha* (a cooked ground grain that some called "mush" and others likened to Cream of Wheat) and tea (perhaps brewed from barley or from a locally grown source; one internee recalled having American Lend-Lease tea once). For lunch, they usually were served boiled cabbage or cabbage soup (potatoes or potato soup were substitutes), occasionally some meat (ground goat, ground mutton, or perhaps Lend-Lease canned Spam, but rarely beef or pork), black bread (the men liked the type with thick crust and moist center), and tea. For supper, the meal was a lighter version of lunch.

Borscht rather than cabbage soup appeared at times. Rice was a potato substitute, but not often. Lend-Lease sugar was rationed by the spoonful. The Uzbekistan agricultural area that surrounded the camp was irrigated for the production of cotton more than food. Few fresh vegetables reached the camp until near the final days of the war.

On special occasions such as holidays, canned fruit, white bread, or hard-boiled eggs might have been offered as treats. Beer, wine, spirits, or vodka also fell into the treat category. Several of the men, however, remembered only that the diet was a monotonous serving of soup, bread, and tea.

It was inevitable that some of the men filched food from the kitchen and food-storage tunnel or foraged for extra food items outside the camp. Also some of the foragers rescued pups to save them from the civilians' stewing pots. All four of the groups that passed through the camp cared for one or more dogs at any given time. The men pinched scraps of food from their own rations to feed the animals.

The internees were weakened to some degree by their diet but especially by dysentery, which few were able to escape. Dysentery probably was self-perpetuated by a sanitation breakdown. Flies were uncontrolled and, except during the coldest months, came from cesspits and other sources of filth to crawl on unprotected food in the camp's kitchen and dining areas. Feeble jokes were made about the speed records that were set on the 100-foot path to the outhouse. Rough toilet paper was a rare luxury, and pieces of the newspaper *Pravda* were often used as substitutes.

Dysentery made personal cleanliness a problem. Depending on camp conditions and the time of year, the frequency of bathing was flexible, but the average was three baths a month. Most of the men were issued standard Russian cotton underwear. A set of the garments consisted of two pieces — top and bottom with long sleeves and long legs. The camp housekeeping staff provided a laundered set of underwear after each bath.

After they arrived in Siberia, the men continued to wear their flight suits, which, for many of them, were their only clothing. The Soviets furnished the Doolittle flyers with heavy winter coats, felt boots, and work clothes. Men of the first group in the Vrevskaya camp were each provided a woolen shirt and trousers by the Soviets, and some piecemeal clothing issues were later made from American sources. For the most part, however, replacement clothing came only after the men escaped to Tehran, Iran.

The B-29 crews from China carried extra shoes in their emergency kits, but the navy and army crews from the Aleutian Islands had only their flying boots, most of which were eventually worn to a deplorable state. Internees reported that they were given standard Russian triangular footwraps to replace the airmen's rotting woolen stockings. A footwrap covered the foot's arch and toes but left the heel exposed. Wearing a footwrap was a painful experience until a callus developed on the unprotected heel.

Many of the men traveled across Siberia at times when the winter temperatures dropped to far below zero. The internment camp in Uzbekistan fortunately was located in a more temperate climate. Even so, the men who lived in the camp during portions of the 1943–44 and 1944–45 winter seasons said that they were "miserably uncomfortable." The stoves built into the interior walls of the barracks to heat the rooms were fired only when rationed fuel was available, and then only when specifically authorized by the commandant. Because wood or coal was always a scarce commodity, Uzbek villagers relied on dried cattle dung as a fuel substitute.

Finally, in December, 1944, General Deane in Moscow recommended to Washington that all aircrews operating in the North Pacific area near Soviet neutral territory should wear complete woolen uniforms and carry additional heavy winter clothing as well.[11] Before the recommendation could be fully implemented, the last of the American internees had arrived in Siberia between May and July, 1945.

The major problem causing the most stress among the internees was uncertainty about whether their families had been notified that they were safe. They had no personal knowledge of the manner in which the NKVD, the Red Army's OVS, and the American Embassy were involved in reporting their identities as men who were officially "missing in action." As far as the internees were concerned, the failure of the American Embassy to inquire about their well-being meant that they were still considered miss-

11. U.S. Embassy Moscow message M-22159 to Joint Chiefs of Staff, December 26, 1944, "Internees" files.

ing. Therefore, until they actually saw and talked with an American representative from the embassy, the internees were never certain that the authorities in Moscow, 2,000 miles away, were even aware that the airmen were in the Soviet Union.

Of course, the slow process of identifying the missing men as internees delayed the initiation of mail service. The only reliable means of sending mail from or receiving mail at the camp was via American military couriers from Moscow. These infrequent visitors were always officers who had been granted Soviet clearance to make the long trip to Tashkent in order to assess the physical and emotional health of the airmen. During the two-year period between September, 1943, and August, 1945, only six mail deliveries were made at the camp. With the arrival of the first letters from the outside world, the men were cheered by the realization that their families finally knew that they were alive. Nevertheless, they were consciously and constantly aware that they were separated by half a world and that the separation could be for a long time. The hope of future mail made acceptance of indefinite internment more bearable.

Families later reported that they also sent packages of personal items to the internees. Most of the packages never did arrive, probably because transportation for bulky objects from Washington to Moscow and Tashkent was slower than for letters. In addition, the men may have already secretly escaped before the packages could be delivered.

Even under more favorable conditions, the enforced idleness alone would have been enough to keep a pall of hopelessness over the camp. Some groups were more innovative than others in devising varied means for fighting boredom. Generally, however, daily camp routines of improvised sports, card games, and reading, although they quickly became monotonous, helped to fill the waking hours.

One diversion among the men of the earlier groups was plotting to escape. Soviet authorities warned repeatedly that any attempt to reach Iran to the southwest was foolhardy and likely to end disastrously. Nonetheless, several ill-conceived efforts were made, and all promptly failed. Surprisingly, Soviet reaction to the futile plots was mild, despite the fiasco in December, 1944. At that time, 34 frustrated men impulsively tried to vanish into the inhospitable Iranian borderlands. Most of them voluntarily returned within hours, and the others were later found by vigilant border guards.

Others in 1943–44 broke the monotony of camp routine by slipping past the camp guards at night to visit newfound friends in Vrevskaya and even in Tashkent itself. Although some were intercepted, many of the night-prowling Americans left and returned to the camp unnoticed. The guards during that time seemed more interested in protecting Soviet state property than in detecting and stopping the nocturnal stream of human traffic.

This story of the Americans' wandering through Siberia into Iran and beyond has now been stripped of its secrecy. Following chapters tell this amazing drama in detail, as recalled recently by the men involved.

2

The Soviet-American Connection
1917–1945

Take me over the sea
Where the Bolsheviks can't get at me;
Oh my, I don't want to die
I want to go home.
— U.S. Army barracks song,
Siberia, 1918–20

The relationship of the Soviet Union and the United States as adversaries dated from the beginning of the Red Revolution in Russia in 1917. Unrelenting mutual suspicion drew a curtain of shadows that kept both nations from viewing one another with clear eyes. Only briefly, from 1941 to 1945, was there respite in the antagonism. Germany was the bone over which the quarrel began in 1917, and Germany ironically was responsible for the unlikely alliance that temporarily changed the relationship a generation later during World War II.

As one of the Allies in World War I, Russia kept German and Austrian armies occupied on the Eastern Front while trench warfare raged on the Western Front during 1914–16. Neither the Allies nor their enemies gained decisive military advantage until finally the Russian army was exhausted. The government of Czar Nicholas II collapsed, after which the czar abdicated in early 1917. A new provisional Russian government was created. Still at war with Germany, the new government also collapsed when it found no support at home for continuing the fight. The Bolshevik wing of the Communist party seized power in late 1917. A few months later, in March 1918, while fresh American troops were beginning to bolster the Allied armies in France, the Bolsheviks and the Germans signed the Treaty of Brest-Litovsk. The treaty removed Russia from the war.

The Allies were faced with two momentous questions. First, would the German troops on the Eastern Front be moved in time to be a decisive factor on the Western Front? And second, would the Communist "disease," which had helped to destroy the Russian government, also spread among the war-weary people of other European countries and erode their governments as well?

Most of the Allies favored military intervention to overthrow the Bolsheviks. In so doing, they hoped to reestablish the Eastern Front. President Wilson demurred, then agreed to United States participation only in two separate limited Allied interventions.

In the first he ordered 500 soldiers to the Arctic port of Archangel. These troops were part of an Allied force to defend northern Russian ports from German seizure. The Americans remained in Archangel for a year, during which time their presence led inevitably to clashes with Bolshevik soldiers.

In the second, Wilson originally proposed that the United States and Japan each send 7,000 troops to Siberia in order to honor a pledge allowing the Czech Legion, which had fought the Germans on the Eastern Front, to be evacuated from Russia over the trans-Siberian railroad through Vladivostok.[1] Wilson, however, distrusted the motives of the Japanese government, which looked for opportunities to slice territory from the Siberian Far East.[2] Wilson, mindful that his major problem was how to limit the Allied intervention only to the Czech evacuation in the face of Japanese greed and the intrigues of other Allied powers, rushed two infantry regiments to Siberia. Shortly before the first American units began arriving at Vladivostok in August 1918, however, civil war erupted in Russia between the Bolshevik "Red" armies and the anti-Bolshevik "White" armies. The civil war produced chaos.

Maj. Gen. William S. Graves, commander of the American military force, had imprecise orders. He was broadly instructed to cooperate in the evacuation of the Czechs via the railroad between Lake Baikal and Vladivostok but otherwise not to interfere in Siberian political or military affairs.

As it pushed across Siberia, the Czech Legion clashed with Bolshevik troops and soon found itself fighting side-by-side with anti-Bolshevik units. At the same time, confusion and anarchy were compounded by Japanese-sponsored Cossack armored trains that ranged along the railroad.

However determined he was to maintain a neutral stance in compliance with Wilson's desires, General Graves nevertheless was accused of aiding the anti-Bolshevik struggle because of his association with the Czechs. Slowly the Bolsheviks gained strength. In late 1919, the White Army in Siberia started to disintegrate, and American units in the Lake Baikal area began to withdraw along the railroad toward Khabarovsk and Vladivos-

    1. Betty M. Unterberger, *Intervention against Communism* (College Station: Texas A&M University Lecture Series, 1986), 10–11.
    2. Ibid., 11.

tok. The Czechs also successfully moved ahead of the advancing Bolsheviks toward the evacuation port.

The American departure from Vladivostok commenced in January 1920 and was completed in April. The American soldiers' mournful wish ("I want to go home") was coming true. In the meantime, Wilson was determined to ensure that the Japanese, who had a far larger force than the Americans in Siberia, did not fulfill their intentions to occupy Siberia permanently, and he was able through negotiation to set the stage for the reluctant Japanese withdrawal from Siberia in 1922.[3]

Historians have disavowed Soviet allegations that Wilson took the lead in promoting hostile action against the Soviet Union in an effort to destroy the Soviet state at birth. Quite the contrary, they have argued. Wilson did his best at all times to keep the American action in Siberia from assuming the form of an interference in Russian internal affairs.[4]

Soviets apparently have not accepted the American view. For example, Soviet Intourist guides conducting tours in the city of Khabarovsk, north of Vladivostok, point to a monument honoring the Red Army heroes of the Revolution. "Many of these heroes," a guide has been heard to explain, "died at the hands of American and Japanese soldiers."[5]

In July, 1921 — a year after the last American soldier sailed from Siberia — the Russian author Maxim Gorky appealed to Herbert Hoover for help to save millions of people from starving in the drought-stricken areas of the Volga River and in the Ukraine. Hoover was chairman of the American Relief Administration, a private organization that had performed food-relief miracles in war-torn Western Europe.

Subject to certain conditions to be met by the new Soviet government, Hoover offered to provide emergency assistance. After the Soviets agreed on August 20 to release 100 American prisoners and not to interfere with the food distribution, the meals began arriving, with the first served on September 21. The feeding continued until the winter of 1923. The two-year program, Gorky said, saved the lives of 10 million children and adults. Hoover was convinced, however, that the Communists believed that there was some sinister American purpose behind this generous humanitarian work.[6]

The postwar period continued to be one in which the United States was also concerned, sometimes to the point of near-hysteria, that the new Soviet Union could carry out its threat to foment world revolution. The ques-

3. Ibid., 22.
4. Ibid.
5. As related by an Intourist guide to the author during a visit to Khabarovsk in August, 1986.
6. Herbert Hoover, *The Memoirs of Herbert Hoover, 1920–33* (New York: Macmillan, 1952), 23–26.

tion of recognizing the Soviet government arose periodically during the eight years of the Harding and Coolidge administrations. Among those who urged recognition were businessmen who sought to establish a lucrative trade. "I have often likened the problem to having a wicked and disgraceful neighbor," Hoover said. "We did not attack him, but we did not give him a certificate of character by inviting him into our homes."[7]

During this time when the United States was maintaining a watchful eye on the Soviet Union and wishing that the Communist regime would simply vanish, the USSR was undergoing a massive program of consolidation first started by Lenin and continued by Stalin. After President Roosevelt was inaugurated in 1933, he fulfilled a campaign pledge by initiating formal United States recognition of the Soviet Union at last. The United States had tried to ignore the USSR for 15 years. Roosevelt was convinced that the Communist regime was not going to disappear and that therefore it was time to learn how to coexist. The new and cautious Soviet-American ties did not produce reassuring results during the following six years as ominous clouds of war gathered over Europe and Asia.

Stalin was suspicious of everybody and everything, including his own people. He viciously purged Soviet governmental officials and Red Army officers by the thousands. The Soviet Union's unsettled internal problems were so overwhelming that Stalin, while noting the rising international crises, needed to wait and see before getting the Soviet Union involved in any major war. The Western powers did not show any great interest in joining the Soviet Union in an anti-German alliance until the late date of 1939. The suspicious Stalin then surprised his future allies by agreeing instead to a Soviet-German nonaggression pact.

Oddly enough, Stalin allowed his suspicions of Germany's immediate intentions toward the Soviet Union to be lulled while the opening phase of World War II exploded and Hitler's military juggernaut raced over Western Europe. He, however, did not have any illusions about the stability of his long-term relationship with Hitler's Germany.

Stalin had inherited the leadership of the largest country on earth. The Soviet Union's land mass stretched for thousands of miles across Eastern Europe and Asia. On the southeastern edge of Siberia the Soviet Union's border—its precise location in dispute for 250 years—was with China's Manchuria. As a result of Japan's military excursion into China during the 1930s, Japan maintained a well-equipped and highly trained army in Manchuria. Japanese troops were deployed along the disputed Manchurian-Soviet border, and confrontations ranging from minor clashes to pitched battles with Red Army units were not uncommon.

Such was the general situation as the year 1941 began, a year of sig-

7. Ibid., 182.

nificant events that would directly and forever change the lives of the 291 Americans who would be the players in the coming "neutral country" drama. Up to 1941, most of the future internees had been high school or college students, and the early phases of World War II touched them only when the first peacetime military conscription law in American history was passed in 1940.

The 1941 historical events, like thunderclaps, came one after the other. Each was important in its own right, but put together they led the United States and the Soviet Union toward an unforeseen relationship of common interest.

Listed chronologically, the first event was White House approval on March 11 of the Lend-Lease Act. Proposed initially as an economic vehicle that would give military aid to beleaguered Great Britain, the Lend-Lease emergency legislation was broad in its application. If President Roosevelt considered the defense of any country to be vital to the defense of the United States, that country was eligible for American arms and supplies. In the long run, the Lend-Lease cornucopia benefited not only Great Britain but 32 other countries as well, including the Soviet Union.

The next event was the April 13 signing of a five-year Soviet-Japanese neutrality pact. The treaty was made at a time when Moscow was preoccupied with the spreading war in Europe yet never quite certain how to take advantage of it. Considering the strategic circumstances that existed in the spring of 1941, Moscow welcomed any opportunity to dampen the smouldering tinder along the Manchurian-Siberian frontier, where tense Japanese and Red Army troops stood face-to-face.

The third event was the German invasion of the Soviet Union on June 22. It came as a stunning surprise to Stalin only because of his doubts about the sincerity of the Western powers. Thinking that they were trying to destroy the German-Soviet alliance, Stalin refused to heed their warnings of imminent German attack.

The next event was the joint neutralization of Iran by Great Britain and the Soviet Union. In the summer of 1941, London and Moscow became concerned over the pro-German sentiment of the Iranian government. Iran, on the USSR's southwestern frontier, not only provided vital oil reserves for the Allies, but its strategic location was astride Britain's lifeline to India. A hasty plan of action was devised by London and Moscow. The shah of Iran was told, among other demands, to expel his German colony of advisers and technicians. The shah refused, whereupon British and Red Army troops occupied Iran in late August. The shah was deposed and promptly replaced with his cooperative young son, Mohammad Reza Pahlavi. Iran was divided into two main occupation zones by an east-west line running through Tehran. The zone to the north was Soviet-occupied, and the one to the south was British. A small area immediately surrounding Tehran remained under Iranian control.

In the meantime, Roosevelt asked Harry Hopkins to be his personal envoy and visit Stalin in July. Upon his return in August, Hopkins convinced Roosevelt and Churchill at the Atlantic Conference that, although in retreat, the battered Red Army was not on the verge of collapse. The Red Army, however, did require help, and urgently. Despite deep-seated doubts regarding the Soviet Union, the two leaders decided to send a joint mission to Moscow for discussions about the USSR's critical defense requirements.

Averell Harriman headed the American party. He and his British counterpart, Lord Beaverbrook, arrived in a war-gloomed Moscow in late September. Their talks with Stalin had hardly begun before Stalin again questioned the sincerity of the United States and Great Britain. His cautious stance was a forerunner of the skepticism that seemed to plague future Soviet-American relations. Fortunately, initial tensions eased somewhat, and the discussions produced an agreement, known as the Moscow Protocol, to provide the Soviet Union with $1 billion worth of arms, supplies, and food for one year. The Lend-Lease agreement was officially approved in Washington weeks later.

New annual protocols were signed in 1942, 1943, and 1944. An additional provision of the 1944 agreement was delivery of Lend-Lease items to be used specifically in the Far East when the Soviet Union would enter the war against Japan.[8]

The crowning event of 1941 was, of course, the December 7 attack by Japan at Pearl Harbor. The United States declared war on Japan the next day. Three days later both Germany and Italy declared war on the United States, and the American government reciprocated in kind.

Sharing a mutual determination to defeat Nazi Germany completely, the United States and the Soviet Union were now cautious allies. The glue that would hold the anti-German alliance together was America's Lend-Lease support.

The slashing German war machine plunged deeply into Soviet territory and inflicted fearful casualties and massive destruction. Instead of crushing the defenders' will to resist, however, the German ruthlessness sparked a new devotion by the Soviet people to save the fatherland. The struggle was called variously the Great Patriotic War and the Second War of the Fatherland, the first such war being the successful resistance to Napoleon's invasion of Russia in 1812.

The Western Allies—the United States and Great Britain—agreed to

8. John R. Deane, *Strange Alliance* (New York: Viking Press, 1946), 248.

give first priority to the defeat of Germany. Japan, they decided, would not feel the full weight of the war until Germany's surrender was assured. Germany's collapse, strategists reasoned, would be achieved only with the help of the Soviet Union's Red Army. Therefore, Roosevelt and Churchill in the last weeks of 1941 initiated the war policy that would guide the conduct of their relationship with Stalin: while the Red Army fought the Germans in the Soviet Union, the Western Allies would open a second front in Western Europe. The mounting of such a second front was not immediately feasible. Therefore, the flow of Lend-Lease arms and food to ensure the survival and resurgence of the Red Army was essential, and deliveries were scheduled.

How to deliver the earmarked Lend-Lease materials, especially with a worldwide Allied shortage of ships to meet the war's needs, became a major problem that would take time to solve. For nearly two years the promised aid, although massive, fell behind schedule. The suspicious Soviets, aroused by remarks of prominent anti-Communist Americans that the United States should "let Stalin and Hitler battle it out," accused the United States of deliberately allowing the Red Army to bear the whole brunt of the war against Germany. Where, the Soviets asked, was the second front? Where, they repeated, was all of the promised help?

Because of the eventual postponement of the second front until 1944, Lend-Lease assistance became the major link of consequence between the Western Allies and the Soviet Union. Fulfillment of Lend-Lease promises became an ultimate test of the good faith that Stalin had originally questioned.

Various routes were used to enhance the flow of Lend-Lease deliveries. The first, shortest, and most dangerous route was via Iceland across the Arctic Ocean to the Soviet ports of Murmansk and Archangel. Regardless of the danger, the shortness of the route proved to be the most practical for the shipment of heavy armaments and equipment. The longest and slowest route ran around Africa to the Persian Gulf and Iran. This route became speedier in 1943 when the Allies regained control of the Mediterranean Sea and access to the Suez Canal. The most productive route was the one used by Soviet reflagged Lend-Lease freighters, which crossed the North Pacific through Japanese waters to Vladivostok. However, on the basis of a secret Tokyo-Moscow understanding, the Vladivostok-bound vessels were restricted to cargos of nonarmaments. An Alaska-Siberian air-ferry route connected American aircraft factories with the war front. Two other limited routes were also employed: to Siberian Arctic ports via the Bering Strait (summertime only) and, late in the war, to Soviet Black Sea ports.

In all, 2,530 ships reached their destinations safely with 17 million tons of cargo. An additional 77 ships were lost en route. Nearly half of all

Lend-Lease goods — 8 million tons — passed through Vladivostok for shipment across Asia on the trans-Siberian railroad. Another 4 million tons were discharged at Murmansk and Archangel. Still another 4 million tons were transferred through Iran by rail and truck.[9]

Stalin seemed determined to maintain Soviet neutrality with regard to the war in the Pacific. He had good reason to fear the strength of the Japanese Army in Manchuria while the Red Army was preoccupied on the German front. With the devastating evidence of German duplicity and violation of the Soviet-German nonaggression pact constantly before him, Stalin remained aware of the possibility that the Japanese, if given an excuse, might also strike in Siberia without warning. Fighting for its very life, the Soviet Union desperately needed access to Lend-Lease nonmilitary supplies, raw materials, and food through Vladivostok — a funnel that Japan apparently tolerated because of the Soviet neutrality.

When Harriman negotiated the first Lend-Lease agreement with Stalin in 1941, Harriman suggested using Soviet air bases in Siberia for the delivery of Lend-Lease aircraft via Alaska. He further suggested that American airmen might ferry the planes across Siberia. Stalin objected, stating that it was too dangerous.[10] The Siberian terrain and weather were dangerous, of course, but Stalin obviously did not want an American presence there. Later, after Japan and the United States were at war, Soviet neutrality became the explanation for the American exclusion.

Although no early agreement was reached regarding the ferry route, both the Soviet Union and the United States began separate preparations for its eventual use. Weeks after Harriman's visit, the Soviets initiated the survey of an emergency line of air bases in remote Siberian areas from the Bering Sea westward. There were no roads to serve as reference points. Magnetic compasses were unreliable, and maps imprecise. However, since no other route seemed feasible to the Soviets, the survey was approved, and landing-field construction and supply stockpiling commenced at Anadyr, Seymchan, Yakutsk, Kirensk, and Krasnoyarsk.

At the same time, a ferry route from Great Falls, Montana, across western Canada to Fairbanks, Alaska, was surveyed by the Americans, and landing strips were built. In June, 1942, Soviet ambassador Litvinoff in Washington informed Harry Hopkins that the USSR favored the Alaska-Siberian (ALSIB) ferry route proposal. On being advised of the Soviet decision, Roosevelt in turn told Stalin that he was ready to order American flyers to deliver aircraft directly to Siberian airfields near Lake Baikal. Stalin's response was polite but negative: "As to whose pilots should fly

    9. Robert H. Jones, *The Roads to Russia* (Norman: University of Oklahoma Press, 1969), 290.
    10. W. Averell Harriman and Elie Abel, *Special Envoy to Churchill and Stalin, 1941–1946* (New York: Random House, 1975), 88.

the planes from Alaska, it seems to me that can be assigned to Soviet airmen."[11]

Ambassador Standley, acting on orders from Washington, met with Stalin in Moscow to discuss the future of the ALSIB. Stalin insisted that "the Soviet Union must be especially careful to maintain our neutrality in the Pacific area."[12] After voicing this concern, Stalin agreed to accept an American official to work on details of making the ALSIB a reality.

That official was Maj. Gen. Follett Bradley. He arrived in his converted B-24 bomber via Iran in early August. He faced weeks of Soviet obstruction, but his patient negotiation with the Soviets resulted in the final arrangement for the delayed birth of the 6,000-mile ALSIB delivery system in September and October, 1942. The Soviets steadfastly refused to authorize aircraft ferrying into Siberia by American crews. At first, the unyielding Soviet position was believed to reflect Soviet fear of antagonizing the Japanese. However, Harriman, who later became the last wartime American ambassador to Moscow, came to believe that the real reason was that the Soviets, because of traditional internal-security policies, wanted to keep Americans from mixing with the population.[13]

As finally agreed, American pilots flew the factory-new aircraft only to Fairbanks, and Soviet pilots from Fairbanks to Krasnoyarsk.[14] On arrival at Krasnoyarsk, the Lend-Lease planes were moved, either by onward flight or by rail shipment, another 2,800 miles to enter combat. Of the 14,000 Lend-Lease aircraft delivered to the Soviet Union, 7,925 arrived via the ALSIB.[15]

His mission completed, General Bradley with his crew departed for Washington in early November 1942. He flew over the new route that he had helped to create—the ALSIB. His bomber was the first of only a few American-manned planes to cross Siberia during the war.[16]

Iran, on the other side of Asia, had no connection with the war in the Orient. Nevertheless, Iran's location at the Soviet Union's underbelly was

11. Ilya Mazuruk, "Alaska-Siberia Airlift," *Soviet Life,* October, 1979, 30.

12. William H. Standley and Arthur A. Ageton, *Admiral Ambassador to Russia* (Washington: Regnery, 1955), 259.

13. Harriman and Abel, *Special Envoy,* 559.

14. David Smoilovich Sherl, "Let's Meet Again!" *Soviet Life,* April, 1988, 56–59. Eight Soviet veterans of the ALSIB recalled the time when Soviet and American airmen were comrades-in-arms during "those grueling but wonderful days." In an open letter they proposed "to our American counterparts—veteran flyers, aircraft mechanics, people who worked at the Nome and Fairbanks airfields during the war, anybody who was involved in any way or another with the . . . ferry route—let's meet again!"

15. Jones, *Roads to Russia,* 277.

16. Barbara Gamarekian, "Ex-Ambassador Flies World War II Route," *New York Times,* July 21, 1987, sec. A, 16. In 1942, Capt. Thomas J. Watson, Jr., was copilot of General Bradley's B-24. From 1979 to 1981 Watson was the U.S. ambassador to Moscow. In 1987, the

where it satisfied both Soviet and American needs. During the war, Iran became a two-way corridor. Lend-Lease supplies were moved overtly to the north into the Soviet Union, and American internees covertly escaped to the south from the Soviet Union.

Having been cleansed of visible Germans by British and Soviet occupation troops, Iran had the potential of being a major supply funnel to the Red Army. That potential was not quickly realized because of logistic and terrain problems. In 1941, the port facilities at the head of the Persian Gulf were primitive, the railroad and highway nets through Iran were both poor and scant, and the railroad and trucking equipment to move Lend-Lease materials was unreliable. The overall task, the Allies came to realize, was beyond the capability of British combat troops. Specialized service troops trained as stevedores, railroaders, and truckers were required to organize and operate the massive supply effort. Churchill and Roosevelt agreed that suitable American troops should assume the responsibility.

In December, 1942, Brig. Gen. Donald G. Connolly arrived to establish and direct the Persian Gulf Command. Connolly brought with him a conventional military staff, one section of which was devoted to intelligence (G-2). Upon arrival, however, in order to reduce Soviet suspicions about Connolly's mission, the staff G-2 function was eliminated, and the intelligence personnel returned to the United States.[17] Connolly's sole responsibility was to deliver as much Lend-Lease supplies and equipment as possible and to do it as quickly as possible.

Using 30,000 troops, Connolly by 1944 had made the "Iran connection" an efficient avenue for high-volume Lend-Lease shipments. Railroad trains and truck convoys from busy Iranian ports went through deserts and over mountain ranges in the southern British zone to reach established cargo transfer points in the northern Soviet zone.

The northbound railroad and truck routes passed near Tehran. On the outskirts of Tehran was Camp Amirabad, the nerve center for the Persian Gulf Command operations. To the east of Tehran in the northeastern corner of Iran was the city of Meshed (now Mashhad). Located in the Soviet zone, Meshed was not normally accessible to Americans. Both Meshed and Tehran (Camp Amirabad), nonetheless, played important roles in the final phases of various American internee odysseys.

Behind the scenes in Moscow, whenever Soviet intelligence networks suspected that German peace feelers were being extended to the Western Allies, the Kremlin's fears arose: Would the 1918 Allied intervention in So-

---

72-year-old retired businessman obtained Moscow's permission to fly his private jet aircraft over the former ALSIB route. The 1987 retracing of the pioneer 1942 flight was flown without mishap.

17. Statements to the author by Lt. Gen. Donald P. Booth and Col. John L. Bates, both

viet affairs be repeated? Would the Germans and the Allies together try to destroy Communism?[18] The Soviets were further agitated by the delay of the promised second front in Western Europe.[19] Therefore, at the Soviet-American diplomatic level, whenever American-projected requirements for a military presence in Siberia were presented, the air continued to be clouded by veiled Soviet distrust. As a result, periodic Soviet-American discussions of the need for American bases in Siberia became inconclusive sparring matches.

Even while American troops were Aleutian Island–hopping toward the Japanese bases on Kiska and Attu in late 1942 and early 1943, Lt. Gen. Simon B. Buckner, Jr., was looking toward a major military offensive against Japan by using a northern approach. He set his Alaska Defense Command staff to work on preliminary plans for initiating a campaign from the Aleutians. Such a plan of necessity would include an American land base on the Kamchatka Peninsula to support a drive down the Kurile Islands chain. Buckner urged Washington to negotiate with Stalin for base rights, which Stalin in the past had repeatedly turned aside.

In the meanwhile, the American offensive to dislodge the Japanese from Attu was successful. Within weeks, while preparations to seize Kiska were being made, the first bomber strikes against the northern Kurile Islands were mounted in July, 1943.[20]

In August, the Japanese garrison escaped from Kiska under the cover of fog. The outer Aleutians again firmly in American hands, forward bomber bases were improved or constructed on Attu and nearby Shemya. Another air raid was ordered against the northern Kuriles. One bomber was disabled and crash-landed on Kamchatka. The first of 32 crews of airmen from Aleutian air bases was promptly interned by the Soviet Union.

Buckner's plans for using the northern approach to Japan began to unravel, and some Eleventh Air Force squadrons were deployed to other areas. In September, 19 bombers from two squadrons were mustered for a major strike against enemy bases in the Kuriles. The alert Japanese defenses turned the raid into a disaster. Seven of the disabled American bombers managed to reach Kamchatka, where the crews were also interned.

In November, the decision was finally made; Washington killed, once and for all, Buckner's dream of a northern invasion of Japan. Even so, at the Tehran summit conference the following month, Stalin was asked again whether the Soviet Union would provide Siberian port and air-base

---

of whom were members of Connolly's Persian Gulf Command staff. Booth later succeeded Connolly as commander.

18. Phillip Knightley, *The Second Oldest Profession* (New York: Norton, 1987), 178.

19. Deane, *Strange Alliance,* 16–17.

20. John H. Cloe, *Top Cover for America* (Missoula, Mont.: Pictorial Histories Publishing, 1984), 123–24.

facilities in the event of an American offensive along the Kurile Islands. There was no direct answer from Stalin. However, he did confirm that the Soviet Union would enter the war against Japan after Germany was defeated.

In effect, Stalin was notifying his American ally that Siberia would remain a neutral territory in every respect until the Soviet Union declared war. The Soviet Union's closely guarded Asian neutrality therefore would endure for another 19 months, until August 9, 1945.

Once the Joint Chiefs of Staff had vetoed a northern invasion of Japan, the Alaskan mainland itself was literally removed from the war. It no longer was officially a military combat area. From air bases in the Aleutians, on the other hand, bombers continued to carry the war to the Japanese. Until Japan's surrender, the Aleutians were wrapped in a security cocoon so that no information leaked about American military plans and strength in the North Pacific. Slowly at first, then with increasing frequency, bombing raids were made to the Kuriles to assure the Japanese that the American military presence in the Aleutians was alive and dangerous.

The truth was that the number of Aleutian-based bombers had been drastically reduced. Only four operating bombardment squadrons — two army and two navy — were available for harassing the enemy at any one time. The two army squadrons flew combat missions for the remainder of the war. The navy used a rotation system so that two squadrons were rested periodically by two relief squadrons.

The Soviet-American alliance at best was a cautious one. Roosevelt hoped that the outpouring of American Lend-Lease help would reassure Stalin even to the point that the two nations could enter into a new, more relaxed relationship after the war's end. It was not to be. Taking into consideration the prewar history of mutual suspicion, Americans should not have been so surprised by Soviet skepticism and lack of enthusiastic cooperation.

On reflection, even the most radical of the similar skeptics in the United States realized that an Allied landing in Europe could not have succeeded without Soviet help. Had the Red Army collapsed before the Western Allies could launch the second front, the massed German armies would then have been waiting to defend the rim of Europe.

The Soviets were slow to show their appreciation for Lend-Lease support. They knew, however, that the Red Army's resurgence against the German invaders was due to some degree to the generosity of the United States.

When the Red Army took the initiative on the battlefield in 1943, the Western Allies also supported the war against Germany in other ways. They provided naval support to protect vulnerable Lend-Lease convoys to the

Soviet Union, and their strategic bombers from British and Italian bases hammered enemy targets.[21]

Although the United States pressed in vain for the establishment of American air bases in Siberia, it enjoyed a brief success in persuading the Soviets to permit American strategic bombers to land in the Ukraine. In the spring of 1944, three bases were hastily constructed southeast of Kiev at Poltava and two adjacent sites. Here, beginning on June 2, strategic shuttle aircraft that had bombed German targets landed when weather did not allow them to return to their home bases in the West. Three weeks later, on June 21–22, a devastating German air raid severely damaged both bombers and facilities at Poltava. Thereafter, only five more shuttle missions were flown because Red Army ground advances against the Germans made future shuttle bombing unnecessary.[22]

In general, the story of Soviet-American wartime collaboration contained a multitude of American proposals that could have been beneficial to Soviet and American alike. Most of the proposals were either obstructed or ignored.[23] In view of this frustrating Soviet behavior, who could have foreseen that the Soviets would select a risky enterprise—the secret evacuation of American internees—on which to cooperate?

The Soviet Union was officially neutral in the Pacific war. Under international law, American airmen arriving on Siberian soil should have been interned for the duration of America's war with Japan or until the time when the Soviet Union should itself become a belligerent. Yet, despite its delicate relationship with Japan, the Soviet Union at the request of the United States chose to wink at international law and jeopardize Soviet security. Why?

Perhaps the intriguing nature of the NKVD's clandestine arrangements for releasing the internees appealed to the Soviets' sense of the dramatic. Perhaps the Soviets merely wanted to rid themselves of the American presence. Or perhaps they wanted simply to demonstrate a rare but effective example of cooperation. Whatever the reason, the NKVD fashioned and executed four secret and intricate escapes for 239 American internees. Another 52 were freed after Japan surrendered.

21. Eugene K. Keefe et al., *Area Handbook for the Soviet Union* (Washington, D.C.: GPO, 1971), 578.

22. Deane, *Strange Alliance,* 107–23.

23. Richard C. Lukas, "Escape," *Aerospace Historian,* Spring, 1969, 14.

3

The First Escape
May, 1943

*I was in action just one day and [now] have to spend the
rest of the war staring at four walls.*
— David W. Pohl, Okhansk, Nov. 14, 1942

January 11, 1942: Capt. Donald W. Duncan, air officer on the staff of Adm.
Ernest J. King, chief of naval operations, locked himself in his office and
began writing a secret plan for a bombing strike against the Japanese heartland.[1] The Pacific war was only one month old, and the Japanese Navy
and Army were ranging swiftly down the Asian coast and among the island
nations. Japan was seeking a stunning victory before the Allies could react. Duncan's plan, when executed, was designed to shake Japanese confidence and inspire the Allies.

The plan called for a navy carrier task force to deliver 16 army medium
bombers to Japanese waters. Launched from a carrier, the army B-25 aircraft would bomb Tokyo and its environs, then try to reach safe haven in
China. Whether the bombers would have enough fuel for the onward flight
was a question mark.

The Soviet Union was beginning to receive American Lend-Lease aid.
Duncan suggested that the bombers be landed at Vladivostok as a Lend-
Lease delivery. If the Soviet Union agreed, the formidable risk in reaching
safe haven would be lessened.[2]

Realizing that the proposed operation had monumental built-in hazards of every kind, Admiral King nevertheless enthusiastically endorsed
the plan. He carried the idea to Gen. H. H. Arnold, army air chief of staff.
Arnold not only approved the plan but began immediately to earmark the
B-25 crews who would undertake the raid in mid-April.

---

1. James M. Merrill, *Target Tokyo: The Halsey-Doolittle Raid* (Chicago: Rand, 1964), 20.
2. Ibid., 21.

February 5, 1942: General Arnold selected Lt. Col. James H. Doolittle to train and lead the volunteer unit. Doolittle continued to refine Duncan's plan, now referred to as B-25 Special Project, and reiterated the suggestion that "should the Russians be willing to accept delivery of B-25 airplanes on Lend-Lease at Vladivostok," the Soviet Union was a logical place to land.[3] In the weeks that followed, the air crews were plunged into intensive secret training, and their bombers were tuned and modified to include special auxiliary fuel tanks.

April 1, 1942: Cranes at the Alameda (California) Naval Air Station lifted the 16 bombers, plus spares, to the flight deck of the carrier *Hornet.* They were securely tied down. At the same time, a five-man army crew for each bomber came aboard.

April 2, 1942: The task force, with the *Hornet* as its centerpiece, sailed from San Francisco Bay. At sea, the Doolittle crews learned for the first time that their secret destination was Tokyo and other Japanese heartland industrial targets.

Later, during his detailed briefings of his crews, Doolittle reported that the Soviet Union had refused the American request to land at Vladivostok.[4] Therefore, he pointed out, the use of Soviet landing facilities was now out of the question, and the distant China airfields became the only ones available. According to Doolittle's refined plan, the *Hornet* would approach within 500 miles of Japan, the bombers would be launched at dusk, they would reach their targets at night, and they would land in China the next day.

April 13, 1942: As scheduled, Vice Adm. William F. Halsey with the carrier *Enterprise* and escorts met with the *Hornet*'s task force and formed a single task force under Halsey's command. The rendezvous occurred north of Midway Island, after which the task force continued toward Japan. Halsey wanted to bring the *Hornet* as close as possible to Tokyo before being discovered and forced to launch the bombers.

April 18, 1942: Despite heavy seas, the task force was running a day ahead of schedule. However, in the early morning light a Japanese picketboat sighted and reported the American fleet. Halsey made the decision to launch the bombers immediately, even though they were 700, not 500, miles from Japan. Because of the greater distance, the crews would have to stretch their available fuel to the limit if their bombers were to have any chance of reaching their destinations in China.

Doolittle was pilot of the lead bomber, and one by one the other 15 aircraft cleared the *Hornet*'s flight deck. The eighth B-25, airborne at 8:35 o'clock, was piloted by Edward J. York. The rate of their fuel consump-

3. Carroll V. Glines, *The Doolittle Raid* (New York: Crown Publishers, 1988), 25.
4. Merrill, *Target Tokyo,* 44.

tion was uppermost on the crew's minds as their bomber headed toward Tokyo. "We figured," York said, "that the auxiliary gasoline should last through Japan and that we would have to go on the main tanks after that. About 45 minutes before we got there we had to go on the main tanks. . . . We checked and found that we used approximately 98 gallons an hour instead of the 72 to 75 gallons we were supposed to use."[5]

Too much fuel was being burned. By that time, despite Doolittle's earlier warning that Moscow had rejected the American request to make a Lend-Lease delivery, York knew that the only safe landing field they could reach would be Vladivostok.

"After making landfall," York continued, "we flew for about 30 minutes but we still hadn't spotted Tokyo itself. So I started looking for any suitable target."[6] In an area believed to have been north of Tokyo, the crew found a large factory and dropped their bombs. Then York turned northwest toward Vladivostok.

Late in the afternoon they made landfall again, this time east of Vladivostok. York said, "We turned inland [north], as I didn't want to go right over the city itself. At the second airdrome north of Vladivostok I circled and landed."

Ambassador Standley later reported to Washington:

> At the time of landing at a naval air base approximately 40 miles from Vladivostok, the bomber crew had enough gasoline for only 150 miles. The bomber was not fired upon while passing over Soviet territory nor did any of the crew notice anti-aircraft defenses in the Vladivostok region. The bomber was intercepted by one Soviet fighter but that plane merely followed the bomber until it landed at the naval airbase. . . . All crew members were treated courteously and accorded considerate treatment during their stay in the Soviet Far East.[7]

The Soviets at the air base were surprised to see the American bomber, York recalled. None of them spoke English, so a captain took the crew to an office where they sat for over two hours until an interpreter arrived to announce that something was being prepared for them to eat. Some Soviet pilots came in the office and pointed to a map on the wall. They wanted to know from what direction the Americans had come to Vladivostok. "We pointed generally in the direction of Alaska," York said.

Later a naval colonel who was the air-base commander accused the crew of having been a part of the raid on Japan. "I admitted that we had,"

    5. Assistant Chief of Air Staff, Intelligence, War Department, June 3, 1943, "Interview with B-25 Crew That Bombed Tokyo and Was Interned by the Russians," file 142.05-5, U.S. Air Force Historical Research Center, 1.
    6. Ibid., 3.
    7. U.S. Embassy Kuibyshev message 441 to War Department, May 25, 1942, Army Intelligence Documents, Record Group 319, file 383.6 — USSR, National Archives (hereafter cited as Army Intelligence Documents).

said York. "I asked him if he would fix us up with gasoline, and if he could, we would take off early the next morning and proceed to China. He agreed."

York asked the colonel to notify the American consul in Vladivostok that the American bomber was there and wished to see him. The colonel shook his head. "He wouldn't let us do that," York said. "He apparently was still hoping that he might be able to send us off. When we went to bed we were fully confident that we were going to leave [for China] the next morning."[8]

April 19, 1942: Their confidence was rapidly eroded. After breakfast, York stated, "we were placed aboard a Russian DC-3 and flown to Khabarovsk, which is about 400 miles north of Vladivostok. When we arrived there we were interviewed for a short time by the Chief of Staff [General Stern] of the Far Eastern Red Army." General Stern then informed them that they had been interned.

Why did the Soviets change their minds about supplying fuel and allowing the bomber to fly to China? In York's opinion, "it is characteristic of the Soviets that no one makes any decision without consulting someone. The colonel, after leaving us, apparently got in touch [with a superior] and his mind was changed."[9]

April 20, 1942: After they left the Vladivostok naval airbase, York's crew never saw their bomber again. Of the 16 B-25s that were launched from the *Hornet,* only the York aircraft landed intact. The other 15 crashed en route to or in China.

April 21, 1942: The Soviet Foreign Office notified the American Embassy that an American bomber had landed on Soviet territory and that the crew had been interned near Khabarovsk.[10]

April 23, 1942: Ambassador Standley had recently arrived in the Soviet Union to assume his duties. The American Embassy, as well as all other foreign embassies, had been relocated east of Moscow to Kuibyshev because of the danger that the German forces might overrun Moscow. Standley went to Moscow for his first audience with Stalin. The new ambassador was chided. The Americans should not have landed on Soviet territory, Stalin said, but having done so, the airmen would be interned in accordance with international law.

April 24, 1942: At Kuibyshev during a Soviet press conference for foreign correspondents, including both American and Japanese newsmen, one of the Americans astonished the Soviet spokesman by asking, "What would the Soviets do if one of the planes involved in the Doolittle raid

8. Air Staff, "Interview with B-25 Crew," 6.
9. Ibid., 10.
10. William H. Standley and Arthur A. Ageton, *Admiral Ambassador to Russia* (Washington: Regnery, 1955), 222.

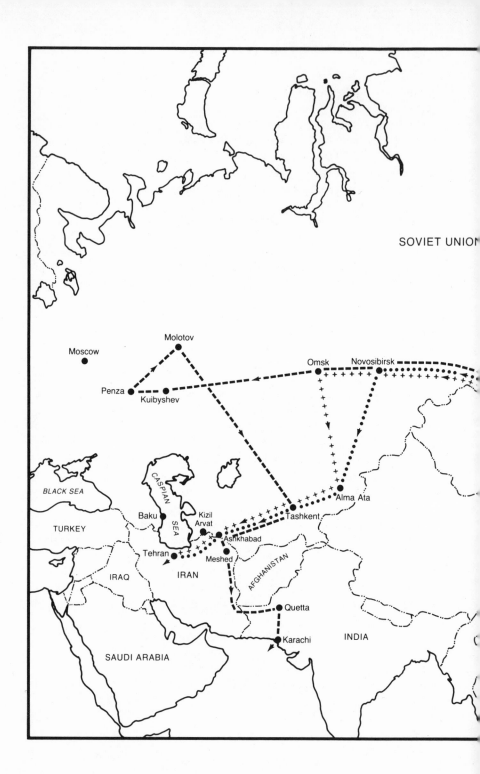

SOVIET UNION

Molotov

Moscow

Penza

Kuibyshev

Omsk

Novosibirsk

BLACK SEA

CASPIAN SEA

Baku

Kizil Arvat

Tashkent

Alma Ata

TURKEY

Tehran

Ashkhabad

Meshed

IRAQ

IRAN

AFGHANISTAN

Quetta

Karachi

SAUDI ARABIA

INDIA

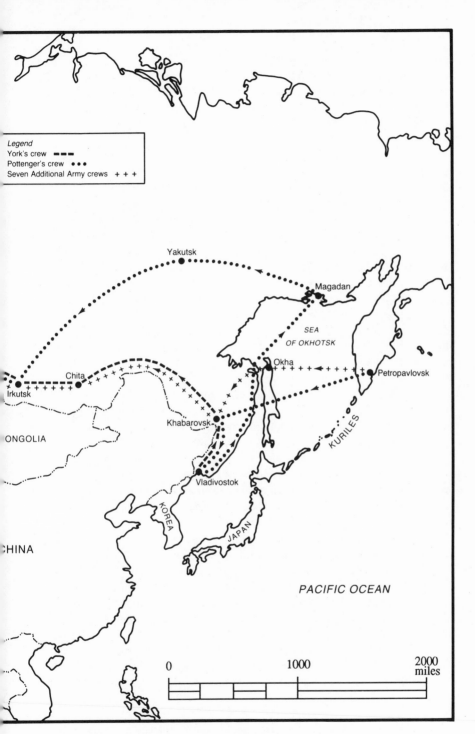

Yakutsk

Magadan

SEA
OF OKHOTSK

Okha

Chita

Petropavlovsk

Irkutsk

Khabarovsk

ONGOLIA

KURILES

Vladivostok

KOREA

JAPAN

CHINA

PACIFIC OCEAN

0   1000   2000
miles

MAP 2. Route of internee groups 1 and 2

on Tokyo landed in the Soviet Union?" The unprepared spokesman did not answer the question directly. The Soviet government immediately assumed, however, that the newsman had somehow learned that one of the bombers had indeed violated Soviet neutrality by taking refuge in the Soviet Far East. Therefore, the Soviets decided that a public acknowledgment of the landing must be made quickly.

April 25, 1942: For the first time, Soviet newspapers carried a story announcing that an American bomber, having lost its way after raiding Japan, had landed in the Soviet Maritime Province and had been interned. On the same day, Ambassador Standley met with Foreign Minister Molotov and listened to Molotov's complaints about the bomber. Molotov specifically asked that the United States government prevent any similiar incidents in the future. Such landings, he pointed out, would create embarrassing situations for the Soviet Union because of Soviet-Japanese relationships. [11]

When the announcement of the internment was made, York and his men were living, closely guarded, in a house about five miles from Khabarovsk. The Soviet guard detail was composed of three officers and two enlisted men. Whether deliberate or not, the one-to-one ratio of guard-to-internee seemed excessive. The only English-speaking member of the Soviet group was Lt. Mikhail Schmaring, familiarly called "Mike." He remained with the internees for nearly a year.

April 28, 1942: Late in the day, Mike returned to the house and announced that the internees were moving. They assembled their belongings, which earlier had arrived from Vladivostok, and were driven by automobile through the evening darkness to Khabarovsk. They were taken to a railroad siding where a lone railroad passenger coach was waiting.

The European-style arrangement inside the coach included a series of wooden-seated compartments that opened on an aisle running along one side of the car's full length. The coach was old, carpetless, and dark. The windows were covered with blackout curtains, and the car was lighted at night with candles. Each internees was given a separate compartment, and each was provided blankets and a pillow without linens.

The Soviet escorts were three officers, one of whom was Mike. The five Americans still did not know where they were going, and Mike was uncommunicative. When large quantities of food were loaded aboard the car, they began to suspect that the trip was going to be a long one. There were boxes of black bread, canned caviar, sausages, vodka, sugar, and tea. [12]

May 18, 1942: After a three-week railroad trip westward across Asia and the Ural Mountains into Europe, the internees' railroad coach finally reached Kuibyshev, where the American Embassy had been relocated. The

11. Ibid., 223.
12. Robert G. Emmens, *Guests of the Kremlin* (New York: Macmillan, 1949), 59–60.

airmen's original suspicions had been correct — the trip was tiring, depressing, and seemingly never-ending. Their private car had been coupled to the rear of various trains for the journey through Siberia. They had been locked in their car except for a few times when they were allowed to detrain and pace the length of the coach. Their longest outing was when they went to a track-side shower bath.

At Kuibyshev, Mike told them that they would not be permitted to visit the embassy because of the presence of Japanese diplomatic representatives and workmen in the city; the Soviets obviously did not want to risk having the Japanese learn the whereabouts of the Tokyo bombing crew.[13] In anticipation that the Soviets would advise the embassy of their arrival and that embassy personnel would come to the train, York and his men waited eagerly. As an extra precaution against a breakdown in diplomatic communication, they asked Mike himself to contact the embassy. Mike disappeared and was gone for hours. The helpless internees, locked in the railroad car while armed guards patrolled the outside platform, became both angry and frantic. When Mike finally returned in late afternoon, it was apparent that he had not gone to the embassy. After nightfall, the train continued to move westward.

May 19, 1942: The train stopped near the village of Okhuna. After their car had been uncoupled and shunted to a sidetrack, the five men were met by a Red Army officer welcoming party who drove them in automobiles to their new living quarters.

The internment facility, near the edge of the village, was a few miles from the town of Penza and located about 300 miles southeast of Moscow but west of the Volga River. The journey from Khabarovsk to Okhuna had taken 21 days to cover 5,000 miles. The average rate of travel was ten miles per hour. Some of the travel time had been spent on railroad sidings because of jammed train traffic.

May 21, 1942: Ambassador Standley was informed by the Soviet Foreign Office that the York crew had been transferred to Okhuna. He immediately arranged for Edward Page, embassy secretary, and Col. Joseph Michela, military attaché, to visit the men and report the situation that they found.

May 25, 1942: Page and Michela spent several hours with the internees on May 24. On the basis of their findings, Ambassador Standley sent a long message to Washington.[14] He pointed out that the flyers had not been

13. No documentary evidence can be found to indicate that the Japanese learned where the internees were located after they were removed from the Soviet Far East. The continued precautions taken by the Soviets, however, attested to their concern that the Japanese would try to trace the internees' movements.

14. U.S. Embassy Kuibyshev message 441 to War Department, May 25, 1942, Army Intelligence Documents.

permitted to report or contact the American consul at Vladivostok and, during their trip to Okhuna, were denied permission to talk with American embassy representatives in Kuibyshev. (In his memoirs, Standley wrote that when he learned of the Kuibyshev incident, he was furious but not surprised.) He advised Washington as follows:

> At this time the crew members are lodged in a large clean bungalow in a village approximately 10 miles outside of Penza. The bungalow is surrounded by lawns and gardens and adjoining a second house which contains the dining and recreation rooms and also houses three Soviet companions, one of whom is an interpreter.
>
> For recreation the Americans have been provided with books, billiards, athletic facilities and other distractions. All in all the Soviet authorities have been extremely considerate in providing for the crew.
>
> The food which the men receive is superior to that obtainable by the diplomatic corps at Kuibyshev and the men are allowed the same freedom of movement permitted to Chief of Missions at Kuibyshev. All men seem to be in excellent mental and physical condition. . . . There has been no illness among the crew. . . . At all times there is a Soviet doctor available.

During his visit, Colonel Michela brought a message to Robert Emmens (York's copilot), advising him that his son was born on May 18, the day when the frustrated internees were stalled in Kuibyshev.

May 26, 1942: Colonel Michela and Secretary Page had been gone 48 hours, time enough for the internees to reflect on what had transpired during the short visit. The official hosts for the meeting with the American Embassy representatives had been Red Army officers from the Penza Soviet Command, and they had managed to serve an unexpected banquet gleaned from a land at war. Even the sight and taste of such delicious foods, however, did not distract the flyers from asking the question that was uppermost on their minds: When were they going to be released?

Michela had explained the Soviet-Japanese relationship in the Far East and said that the Soviets were determined not to create an international incident by freeing the American internees. He hinted, nevertheless, that the American Embassy was working on a plan that might bear fruit. The hint buoyed the men's spirits.

Michela and Page had brought a few clothing items, cigarettes, soap, and magazines for the men. Michela promised to arrange for periodic shipment of items such as medical supplies, toilet articles, tobacco, and canned food. Now, two days later, the five internees were beginning to feel the gradual impact of what was suggested by that promise. "Periodic shipment" could mean that the American Embassy's plan for releasing them was a long time from realization. There was a dawning sense that repatriation probably would not be immediate. Never did they dream, however, that their year-long odyssey through the Soviet Union and the Middle East was only in its initial stage.

June 19, 1942: A month passed since their arrival at Okhuna, and the men heard no further news about their being released. They settled into a monotonous daily schedule, the pattern of which would become too familiar to the 286 airmen who would follow them into internment in 1943, 1944, and 1945.

The housekeeping staff, composed of seven women, outnumbered the internees, leaving the men without chores or other meaningful tasks to occupy their waking hours. They played volleyball, watched Soviet movies, and read and reread the magazines that the embassy had sent. They studied Russian and learned to play chess. They ate meals at precisely scheduled intervals, took walks inside the walled yard, and bathed three times weekly in a log bathhouse outside the yard. A guard walked with them whenever they went beyond the wall, even to bathe.

At first, they were shocked when they saw elderly prisoners in chains being marched past their bungalow morning and evening. The sight of the line of trudging prisoners, however, soon became a part of the internees' daily routine.

Nothing surprised them. Nothing changed. They were idle. They realized that they served no purpose.

July 20, 1942: Another month passed. Shortages began to develop in the food supplies—first meat, then vegetables. The shortages were not drastic but noticeable. However, black bread, cabbage, and tea were readily available. The cigarette supply was exhausted, but Mike found a source of loose Russian tobacco. The internees tore strips from the newspaper *Pravda* to hand-roll the tobacco into makeshift cigarettes.

The Soviet-German fighting was coming closer. The men could hear the explosions of antiaircraft shells that were fired from nearby Penza at German reconnaissance planes. Mike translated news stories from *Pravda* and radio broadcasts from Moscow and, using a map, showed where the front lines changed as the Red Army retreated to the east and southeast. He explained that the Soviet troops were withdrawing temporarily to more favorable terrain.

Mike delivered a package containing two sets of Soviet two-piece cotton underwear for each man. Although the internees' clothing supply was skimpy and the underclothing therefore appreciated, the clothing issue itself sobered them. They would not be receiving clothing, they reasoned, if the Soviets were planning to release them.

The men had not heard from the American Embassy since the visit by Colonel Michela and Edward Page. At that time, Michela had cheered them with a promise of frequent communication, but the promise had been unfulfilled. Even the men's inquiries to the embassy, hand-carried by Mike to Penza for transmission, had been unanswered.

August 15, 1942: During the morning Mike went to the Penza Soviet

Command headquarters, as he usually did each day. This time, his return was overdue. When the evening meal was served, he still had not appeared.

When he did arrive, it was with a rush. He burst into the dining room and announced, "We are leaving"—within two hours!

The internees collected their few possessions. In the meanwhile, York tried to question Mike. Where were they going? Mike ignored the question.[15]

Escorted by Mike, they were driven through the darkness to the village railroad siding, where, waiting for them, was an empty passenger coach identical to the railroad car that had carried them across Siberia in May. Soon a locomotive arrived to pull the car to Penza. There it was coupled to a waiting train. Mike continued to evade the question regarding their destination.

August 20, 1942: They traveled in their railroad car for three days in a northeasterly direction through Kazan until they reached the Kama River south of Molotov.[16] After detraining, they were put aboard a crowded river ferry. A slow voyage of two nights and a day down the river brought them to the remote, ramshackle village of Okhansk, on the western edge of the Ural Mountain foothills.

During the 600-mile trip, the men realized that they were not going in the direction of Moscow or Kuibyshev, where American authorities were located, but they had not completely abandoned the idea that perhaps the Soviets were releasing them. They were faced with reality, not conjecture, however, when they reached Okhansk and Mike announced that their journey was over. Okhansk may have been typical of villages in rural Russia, but to the internees the village was like something in a nightmare.

York confronted Mike and demanded an explanation. The German Army advance to Stalingrad had endangered the Americans, Mike said. Orders had been received to move them to a place of safety—Okhansk.

Not knowing whether the American Embassy was aware of their new plight, York asked Mike to arrange for the dispatch of a message to the embassy. Mike agreed. He later reported that the message had been sent.

August 27, 1942: According to Ambassador Standley, the first notification that the internees had been moved to Okhansk came from the Soviet Foreign Office.[17] What became of York's message addressed to the embassy on August 20?

September 1, 1942: The decision to move the internees had been made so abruptly that their new quarters were not ready for their use when they

15. Emmens, *Guests of Kremlin,* 113–14.
16. Molotov was the new name, announced in the early months of 1942, for the 160-year-old commercial and manufacturing city of Perm. The name change, however, was only temporary. Following the death of Stalin, the city again became Perm in 1958.
17. Standley and Ageton, *Admiral Ambassador,* 224.

arrived at Okhansk. As a consequence, they were put temporarily on the top floor of a crowded village building. A large room there contained six cots, one each for the internees and Mike.

Okhansk was 80 miles downstream from Molotov and was situated on high ground overlooking the Kama River. Occupied mostly by elderly people and children, the village had the appearance of fatigue and exuded an atmosphere of hopelessness. The water was contaminated, and the men were ill until Mike arranged for having the men's drinking water boiled.

Their new home was ready on August 30. It was a freshly whitewashed log house located between the river and the village's center. It contained a kitchen, dining room, four small bedrooms, and a toilet room. The toilet was basically the same as the usual outdoor toilet—simply a hole cut in the floor. Behind the house was a small log building containing a fire pit, rocks, a barrel of water, and a dipper—the furnishings of a typical Russian-style rural steam bath.

A staff of four women had been gathered to perform the housekeeping chores. Zietseva, an older woman, quickly asserted her dominance and assumed responsibility for the household operation.[18] The aggressive Zietseva made weekly visits to the food-distribution centers in Okhansk and occasionally as far as Molotov. Like Nona in the later internment camp at Tashkent, the neatly dressed Zietseva took a personal interest in the problems and welfare of the internees. She was the "mama" of the York crew.

Mike reminded the men that they were considered to be military personnel and therefore were authorized the same rations as those issued to the Red Army. The internees soon learned that, although authorized, the food supplies were not always available at Okhansk or even at Molotov.

September 9, 1942: Ambassador Standley wanted to make a personal visit with the internees. At the same time, Maj. Gen. Follett Bradley, who was temporarily in Moscow to help with the final planning for the ALSIB ferry route from Alaska across Siberia, already had obtained permission for a similar visit.[19] The Soviet Foreign Office suggested that the two men make a joint visit. General Bradley would fly from Moscow to Kuibyshev the next day.

September 10, 1942: Accompanied by Edward Page, Brig. Gen. Joseph Michela (recently promoted), a Red Army major, and four NKVD companions, Ambassador Standley met General Bradley at the Kuibyshev airport in the early afternoon. The combined party flew in a Soviet DC-3 type transport directly to Molotov. After being greeted by Soviet officials and senior military officers, the visiting group was escorted to a Kama

18. Emmens, *Guests of Kremlin,* 132.
19. Standley and Ageton, *Admiral Ambassador,* 225.

River boat landing where they boarded the provincial governor's official yacht. As the yacht began its voyage to Okhansk, a lavish Kremlin-style banquet was served, and vodka toasts continued far into the night.[20]

For over a week the internees had continued to be battered by events that alternately depressed and excited them. From the beginning, the promised ration supply was erratic. Since basic food items were often not available, makeshift meals quickly became commonplace. For a week the men's diet was limited to rice and cabbage with black bread and tea. They were measured for special clothing, which Mike said would be delivered before winter weather arrived. Did that mean that they would spend the winter at Okhansk?

Then came a bag of mail. Each man received letters, some of them months old. Except for the earlier news of the birth of Emmens's son, the letters provided the first personal contact from their families since the airmen boarded the *Hornet* on April 1.

Finally, Mike learned that a party of visitors, American as well as Soviet, was en route to Okhansk. Mike said that the commanding general of the Molotov Military District would be the host, but he did not know who the Americans were. Some of them were from Moscow, he said.

A flurry of preparation swept the internees' house. A wagon suddenly arrived at the kitchen door to unload supplies of beef and poultry and quantities of fresh vegetables, and the local military commander contributed vodka for the occasion. The men cleaned their uniforms and wrote letters to be given to the American visitors for posting.

September 11, 1942: At noon, the internees stood on the Okhansk heights overlooking the river and watched their visitors disembark from the yacht. Discovering that Ambassador Standley and General Bradley were in the American party was a surprise.

The Soviets allowed the Americans only a brief visit with the internees, who made their feelings known quickly. First, although General Michela brought a box containing shirts, toothpaste, magazines, and an English-Russian dictionary, the internees asked for other critical items. Michela asked that they provide him with a list. The items, he said, might be procured from American sources in Iran. Second, the York crew was concerned about overdue immunizations and requested a visit from an embassy doctor. Michela and the ambassador agreed to arrange for Dr. Fred Lang to come to Okhansk. Third, when York broached the subject of escape, both Michela and the ambassador discouraged the idea. And finally, assuming that there was no other recourse, the internees wanted to be relocated to

20. Ibid., 226–27.

a warmer climate and put to work. They were assured that the embassy would continue to use diplomatic pressure on their behalf.[21]

The restless Soviet host was anxious to return to Molotov, and having discussed the urgent topics with the internees, the ambassador and his party prepared to leave. York and his crew walked with them to the yacht at dockside, told them good-bye, and watched the yacht disappear upstream. They were alone again.

September 21, 1942: Going to Moscow, Standley met and talked with Foreign Minister Molotov. Standley requested that the American flyers be transferred from the frigid Ural Mountains area to a place where they could be given some sort of useful employment. Molotov listened but did not give the ambassador a direct answer.

Standley later asked Dr. Lang to plan an extended visit to Okhansk in order to give the internees any medical care and medicine that they needed. General Michela assigned Maj. Robert McCabe, assistant military attaché, to go with Dr. Lang. Both men waited while the Soviet bureaucracy considered the official American request to authorize the trip.

October 7, 1942: Several inches of snow fell on Okhansk. Ice began to form on the Kama River.

Discomforts such as bedbugs and diarrhea added to the men's state of depression. Weather permitting, the men walked through the village at will and, if they desired, watched Soviet movies, which were shown in an old barn. The bountiful foods that had been delivered to entertain the ambassador's party had been eaten long ago, and the rations again became scant. The meals reverted to servings of rice and cabbage and black bread and tea.

It had been nearly a month since the ambassador's visit. Where was the promised visit by the embassy doctor?

October 10, 1942: Ambassador Standley departed the Soviet Union and flew to Washington. He had been unexpectedly recalled for consultation and would be gone for three months.

October 16, 1942: Through the Okhansk Soviet Command Mike learned that "somebody from Moscow is coming." As was done for the ambassador's visit, special food arrived at the house. Somehow the local Soviet bureaucracy knew that the visitor, whoever he might be, was not as important as the ambassador because the preparations were not as extensive and the official atmosphere was more relaxed.

October 17, 1942: The men polished their footgear and cleaned their uniforms. They finished the letters that they had been writing. And they waited.

21. Ibid., 228–29.

More waiting. Then Mike received a report that "somebody" was in the village. In a few minutes a horse-drawn sleigh delivered two men — Dr. Lang and Major McCabe, both dressed in long sheepskin coats and felt boots. They had boarded a train at Moscow on October 13. After arriving at Molotov they had been snowed-in for nearly two days. When another train brought them from Molotov to a nearby village, they completed the final leg of the trip to Okhansk in the sleigh.

October 19, 1942: The two embassy representatives remained nearly two days and nights with the internees. During that time the doctor examined each of the men and found evidence of scurvy and pellagra. He promised to send them a supply of vitamin pills.

The visitors brought a large gift box containing shirts, magazines, books, cigarettes, aspirin, quinine, and three bottles of whiskey. In a planned effort to cheer the men, Dr. Lang and Major McCabe turned the two days into a continuous party with food and drink. The time passed quickly. It was a pleasant interlude for the internees, but it did not change anything. The two visitors climbed into their sleigh and, like Santa Claus, whisked away, leaving the five airmen isolated once more. They never saw another American in the Soviet Union.

October 24, 1942: Mike delivered five heavy coats for the men. These were the garments for which they had been measured in early September. The long coats were made of goatskins with the hair side used as the linings. Mike also had a pair of felt boots and a fur cap with earflaps for each of them. At that point, any hope that they would not be held in Okhansk for the winter evaporated.

The men wore their new Russian winter outfits during exercise walks through the village. Even though the temperature had turned bitter, the men were now more comfortably clad.

In the house, the stoves in the kitchen provided all the heat that was needed in the cooking area. Two other stoves were built into the dining room's thick walls, and they warmed the rest of the building. Wood was delivered from the village fuel supply center in the form of logs. For exercise the men cut and split the logs into size for stove use.

October 31, 1942: Aside from walking through the village and cutting wood, the men fought boredom by playing ceaseless games of cards and by studying Russian. The dictionary that General Michela brought to them served as guidance for the written language, but exchanging words and phrases with the household staff helped them to learn broken conversational Russian. York and Emmens especially made rapid progress. Nevertheless, the feeling that they had been abandoned could not be shaken.

November 4, 1942: The food allocation for November indicated that the supplies were not reaching the distribution center. The food situation, bad as it was in October, was now critical. Very little meat, poultry, or fish could be located. A barley-type cereal was issued as an emergency substitute, so the men ate three meals daily of barley and cabbage or sometimes only black bread and tea. Meanwhile, the use of the steam bath was reduced to once per week in order to conserve fuel.

November 6, 1942: His ALSIB ferry route mission completed, General Bradley, on the eve of his departure from Moscow, had not forgotten the predicament of the internees. In a message to Washington, he recommended that the secretaries of war and state officially request that the Soviet authorities allow the internees to engage in professional work while being on parole.[22]

November 14, 1942: Because of the food situation, Zietseva volunteered to make the 80-mile journey to Molotov in an effort to search for supplemental items at the district food distribution center. Her four-day trip in an open truck had some success. Half-frozen and exhausted, she returned with some meat, dried fish, and canned food, enough to bolster the internees' diet for a few days.

November 17, 1942: The men's spirits were lifted by the arrival of a bundle of mail, the second since their internment. The appearance of letters from the other side of the world refocused the internees' bitterness toward the American Embassy because of its silence and failure to deliver promised items of medicine, food, and clothing.

(Col. Robert McCabe, living in retirement, has written that he had no ready answers to questions about the embassy's lack of contact and its broken promises. "I do recall that General Michela was quite concerned about the York crew," he said, "and I must assume that he did everything possible to help the internees."[23] It was McCabe's impression that the ambassador — or, in the ambassador's absence, the chargé d'affaires — was constantly making requests for information about, contact with, or release of the internees.)

December 8, 1942: In Washington, the acting secretary of war, apparently reacting to General Bradley's plea from Moscow, signed a memorandum to the secretary of state: "In view of the changes that have taken place in the military situation and the existing relations between the United States and Russia, the War Department feels that it may be possible now, or at an early date, to effect the complete release of the [York] crew instead of their being merely permitted to work under parole. Strong representations

22. Bradley began his return trip to Washington on November 11, 1942.
23. Already frustrated by unproductive negotiations on a wide range of other Soviet-American problems, both Michela and Standley were especially distressed because of the lack of current information regarding the internees' situation. The NKVD controlled that information, McCabe said.

to the Russian Government at a suitable time will perhaps attain this highly desirable result."[24]

December 10, 1942: The temperature at Okhansk was below zero day and night. Under the snow the ground was frozen, and the Kama River was ice from bank to bank. At times the mercury dropped to 50 degrees below zero.

The food situation worsened again. The internees' diet was restricted to frozen potatoes, barley, and, of course, some bread and tea.

In a renewed search for edibles, Zietseva endured a cruel ride in an open truck to Molotov. She located six boxes of foodstuffs and started the return truck trip to Okhansk. En route there was a mechanical breakdown, so Zietseva found a horse-drawn sleigh whose driver preferred using the surface of the frozen river to travel toward Okhansk. When they were only a short distance from the village, however, the sleigh's driver, for some unexplained reason, refused to go any farther and abandoned Zietseva and her boxes. The determined Zietseva managed to reach the house and report what had happened. A mixed party of internees and women house servants was quickly organized to recover the boxes. Most of the trip up the river was made in icy darkness because of the short number of winter daylight hours. Fortunately, the party found the boxes intact and, with difficulty, carried them to the house. The boxes contained small amounts of essential rations, including dried beans and canned fat, the latter probably being *tushonka,* a Lend-Lease pork product seasoned with bay leaves.

December 19, 1942: Wood deliveries became infrequent. As one of the consequences, use of the steam bath was limited to twice monthly.

Faced with the growing wood shortage, the internees agreed to forage for fuel on the other side of the river. Two internees with two house servants were provided a horse and cart (with snow runners). They drove across the ice and into the forest. The expedition was a success. They returned with a load of logs that was converted into stove fuel. Thereafter, wood foraging across the river became a regular twice-weekly chore.

December 25, 1942: The internees had made no attempt to observe Thanksgiving, but Christmas could not be ignored, even though it would be a somber occasion. On one of the foraging trips across the river, the men found a small evergreen tree that they brought to the house and decorated with bits of cotton and paper. In the kitchen the cook attempted to prepare a special meal for them, but she really had no way to vary the plain menu. After dinner, the men concluded the observance by singing some Christmas carols.

24. Memorandum, OPD 336 Russia, from Acting Secretary of War to Secretary of State, December 8, 1942, Army Intelligence Documents. The communication was drafted at the behest of General Arnold, who from the beginning had maintained a continuing interest in what happened to the Doolittle bomber crews.

January 7, 1943: As far as the despondent internees were concerned, both Washington and the American Embassy had forgotten them. Living day by day with little hope in an isolated and harsh environment, the men decided to do the unthinkable—write an appeal to Stalin himself.

They rapidly drafted a letter to contain what they had on their minds. After the preliminary remarks, the letter went directly to the heart of the matter. First, they asked to be released. Because nearly nine months had elapsed since their internment, they believed that their release could be done in secret without any repercussions from Japan.

Alternatively, if a secret release could not be considered, then they requested that they be moved to a more moderate climate zone. They also wanted to end their idleness by working. They preferred to be employed in jobs where their knowledge of the B-25 bomber could be utilized. However, they would be willing to do any assigned job.

After they were satisfied with the English text, they used their English-Russian dictionary and enlisted Mike's help in preparing a Russian version of the letter. Then they sealed copies of both English and Russian versions in an envelope addressed to Stalin in Moscow.[25] Mike, at first astonished by the men's audacity, agreed to mail the letter.

January 10, 1943: The new year did not bring better conditions at Okhansk, and morale remained very low. The food situation was no better. Zietseva was able to go to Molotov again, but the rations that she managed to obtain were still far short of the internees' authorized food allowance.

January 12, 1943: Ambassador Standley had recently returned from Washington to his post. On his first visit with the foreign minister, Standley asked Molotov about the internees' situation. Molotov later told him that the York crew was still in Okhansk and was in good health.[26]

January 23, 1943: Mike Schmaring went to the Okhansk Soviet Command headquarters, as was his daily custom. Mike usually returned to the house in the evening before mealtime. Today he did not appear. The internees never saw Mike again. They never learned what happened to him.

Mike had been guard, guide, and interpreter from the time that the airmen had been interned at Khabarovsk in April, 1942. He was sullen and arrogant at times, but he was their link with the Red Army authorities. Now the link was gone.

No apparent effort was made to replace him. The puzzled internees seemed to have been cast adrift and were now dependent on Zietseva and on the Russian they had learned.[27]

25. Emmens, *Guests of Kremlin,* 212–13.
26. Standley and Ageton, *Admiral Ambassador,* 232.
27. Air Staff, "Interview with B-25 Crew," 13.

February 12, 1943: In response to an inquiry from Washington, General Michela in Moscow advised that "three visits by various members of the embassy have been made to [the internees] since their internment in April 1942 and the conditions under which they are cared for are satisfactory. At the present time they are being administered under the People's Commissariat of Defense. As to the costs of clothing, housing and subsistence, the Soviet authorities refuse to discuss the subject and have stated that such matters will be taken up at the end of the war."[28] The Michela report neglected to state that the third and last visit had been in October.

February 22, 1943: Milder weather arrived. There was a feeling that spring was not far away.

The internees were restless. Without guards or any visible monitors, they were determined to escape from Okhansk at the first favorable opportunity, possibly during the latter part of April, when the Kama River was clear of ice. According to their escape plan, they would travel 1,500 miles in two groups down the Kama River and on the Volga River in stolen boats, dress in stolen clothes, and survive on food stolen from spring gardens.

March 15, 1943: As winter began to moderate, the proposed escape down the river continued to be uppermost on the men's minds, and they discussed its pitfalls and chances of success. Since York and Emmens had the best command of Russian, they decided that one of them would go with each group.

Foodstuffs were beginning to be relocated from collective farm storage to riverbank storage for future barge shipment from Okhansk, so unfrozen cabbages and potatoes were now available to the men.

March 24, 1943: Zietseva went to Molotov by truck in an attempt to get a meat ration authorization. She promised to return the next day.

March 25, 1943: Before lunch, two well-dressed Red Army staff officers, a major and a captain, walked into the internees' house and assembled the startled, apprehensive men in the dining room. The major asked York, "Did you write this letter?" He showed York the letter that the men had written to Stalin two months earlier. York drew a deep breath and then answered affirmatively.

The tension in the room eased when the internees noticed that the major was relaxed. He began his explanation of his and the captain's mission. The men's letter, he said, had been received in the Red Army headquarters in Moscow. The letter's first request, that of secret release, was denied, but the Soviet government had decided to grant the second request,

---

28. U.S. Embassy Moscow letter from Military Attaché to Chief, Military Intelligence Service, War Department, subj: "U.S. Military Personnel Interned in USSR," February 12, 1943, Army Intelligence Documents.

that of moving to a warmer climate and having work to do.[29] Then the major asked the dumbfounded men if they were ready to leave.

They packed quickly, ate a snack, and told the three weeping housekeepers good-bye. They regretted not having an opportunity to see Zietseva, who had not yet returned from Molotov.

The exuberant men walked into the village, where the Red Army officers had automobiles waiting for them to begin a 12-hour drive to Molotov. Part of the trip was through a late winter snowstorm. At midpoint the automobile convoy encountered the Okhansk supply truck and Zietseva. She promptly abandoned the truck and returned to Molotov with them.

March 26, 1943: Immediately upon arrival at Molotov, the two escort officers took the men to a hotel. Here, the internees were sized for and given Red Army uniforms so that they would not be conspicuous and excite curiosity. Next, the major arranged for meals and even box seats for attending the local ballet. Finally, he allowed them to walk the city streets without accompanying them. Although they had been accustomed to freedom of movement at Okhansk, this latest gesture in Molotov pleased them. In the meantime, Zietseva came to their hotel to tell them that they were going to the extreme southern part of the Soviet Union. She never revealed where or how she obtained the information.

March 28, 1943: Zietseva was waiting at the Molotov airport to wave when the five men and the Red Army major boarded a DC-3 type transport plane. They flew through turbulent weather almost 500 miles due south in an all-day flight. They made one stop at Ufa, then continued to Chkalov.

At their Chkalov hotel the major told them that the remainder of their trip would be via train. He still did not reveal their destination to them.

March 29, 1943: In Washington, the Military Intelligence Service reported,

> This office has been informed by the United States Military Attaché in Moscow that the five U.S. aviators who have been interned since last April will be moved to Ashkhabad on the southern frontier where they will be given suitable clothing, rations and housing as well as an opportunity for professional work with the Civilian Air Fleet, which is a part of the Russian Air Force.
>
> This action by the Soviet authorities was the result of repeated requests by our Military Attaché and Ambassador to repatriate these personnel or to at least release them under parole for professional work.[30]

---

29. Emmens, *Guests of Kremlin,* 220.

30. Memorandum, Chief of Military Intelligence Service to Assistant Chief, Air Staff, A-2, War Department, subj: "U.S. Military Personnel Interned in Russia," March 29, 1943, Army Intelligence Documents.

March 30, 1943: At Chkalov, the internees and the major boarded a passenger train that also contained Soviet passengers. No effort was made to isolate the internees. The major took a compartment, four airmen were paired and assigned to two other compartments, but York himself was assigned to share a compartment with a Russian identified as Kolya.

Kolya said that he was an official of the Foreign Trade Ministry operating from offices in Ashkhabad, some 2,000 miles to the south. Kolya spoke understandable, heavily accented English. He quickly became a friend of York as well as of the remainder of the crew.[31]

April 4, 1943: The southbound train reached Tashkent, where the men were allowed to leave the train long enough to visit a bathhouse. They could not foresee that, six months later, the Soviets would establish a permanent camp near Tashkent for the other 286 American airmen who would be interned during the next two years. During the long trip between Chkalov and Tashkent, York found Kolya to be a sympathetic listener when York told him how much he and his men would like to leave the Soviet Union.

April 6, 1943: The escort major finally informed the Americans that the train would arrive at Ashkhabad the following day. This city, he said, was their destination.

Kolya appeared anxious to continue his relationship with his newfound American friends. He promised to contact them in Ashkhabad.

April 7, 1943: When the train arrived, the internees were greeted by officers of the Ashkhabad Soviet Command. Then they were driven in automobiles to the outskirts of the city, where there were rows of mud huts, each hut surrounded by a mud wall. The men were brought to one of these huts whose two rooms contained a table, five chairs, and five iron cots. An even smaller separate mud building housed a primitive kitchen with an elderly man assigned as cook. The internees, whose spirits had soared since they departed their wretched situation at Okhansk, were dismayed for a short time. They looked toward the distant mountains that marked the boundary between the Soviet Union and Iran. They relaxed. The mud hut and the living conditions were acceptable. Nolan Herndon, York's navigator, said, "We were on the way home as far as we were concerned."[32]

April 20, 1943: Quentin Reynolds, in the Soviet Union as an American news correspondent, also gathered material that he later incorporated into a book. In the book his notes datelined April 20 were devoted to the story of the five internees.

Reynolds tried to locate and interview the men, but he was blocked, he wrote, by the Soviet Foreign Office and by the American Embassy. Unable to talk with the men themselves, he nevertheless uncovered the story.

31. Emmens, *Guests of Kremlin,* 236.
32. Air Staff, "Interview with B-25 Crew," 24.

A bit of information from an RAF officer who knew about the internees, a scrap of news in one place, a hint in another — all from unofficial sources — and as a result Reynolds believed that he had one of the best stories of the war. Reynolds then related how the interned bomber crew was transferred from the Soviet Far East to Penza, Okhansk, and finally Ashkhabad, even though the men had arrived at Ashkhabad only two weeks earlier.[33]

May 10, 1943: Since their arrival at Ashkhabad on April 7, the internees were obsessed by one thought: escape! During the month they tried to adjust to their new situation as residents of Ashkhabad. The major who had escorted them from Okhansk promptly vanished and apparently returned to Moscow. Replacing him as their visible Soviet point of contact was a local officer who made short casual visits. They were given identification papers and Soviet work clothing so that they could begin their daily employment at an airport where airplanes used for training Soviet aviators were repaired. "It wasn't much of a job," Herndon conceded. "Fooling around with small airplanes — assembly and instruments, and so forth."[34]

Almost immediately Kolya found them. Night after night he either visited them or walked them to his home, where he entertained them. York privately continued to stress to him how desperately the Americans wanted an opportunity to go home. York left no doubt: he was enlisting Kolya's help to escape.

Kolya remained coy for a few days. Then he admitted that he knew a border smuggler who might be of assistance. Later Kolya arranged for York to meet the smuggler. In exchange for $250 (virtually every cent that the internees possessed among themselves), the smuggler agreed to take them by truck across the border to Meshed, Iran. Because there was no American Consulate in Meshed, Kolya suggested that the airmen go to the British Consulate instead, and he gave them a diagram showing its location in the city.

Shortly before midnight on May 10, the smuggler's truck arrived in front of the internees' walled hut to begin the journey. Suddenly beset with doubts regarding the success of their risky venture, York and Emmens both destroyed their detailed yearlong diaries, an action that they later regretted.[35] Climbing into the truck bed, the men hid themselves under a tarpaulin.

Kolya, waiting not far away, watched their departure. After a short but

33. Quentin Reynolds, *The Curtain Rises* (New York: Random House, 1944), 55–58. Reynolds apparently never learned the climax of the internees' odyssey, which was yet to come. The manner in which he collected and assembled the story from unofficial sources within the Soviet Union may explain the completeness of a similar story that Henry C. Cassidy wrote for the Associated Press in December, 1944, to the dismay of both the Soviet Union and the United States governments.

34. Air Staff, "Interview with B-25 Crew," 23.

35. Emmens, *Guests of Kremlin,* 268.

suspenseful delay caused by motor trouble, the truck traveled south through Ashkhabad to the 150-mile-long road leading to Meshed. Their major concern was getting past the Soviet border guards and the Soviet checkpoints in the Soviet occupation zone en route to their destination.

May 11, 1943: R. M. Hadow, British vice-consul at Meshed, reported that "on May 11 about 12 P.M., a pencilled chit was brought into my office saying that Major York and Lieutenant Emmens, U.S. Army, wished to see me. Two individuals were then ushered in looking more like down-at-heel Armenian or Russian lorry drivers than officers. I expressed pleasure at seeing American Army officers in Meshed and asked what we could do for them. They then apologized for their clothes and said they had just come from Russia."[36]

Hadow continued,

> They left Ashkhabad at midnight on May 10 and drove to about a mile or two from the frontier where they had to get down and walk across the hills with a guide. The most anxious moment of the whole escape was when they had to crawl across a ploughed strip marking the frontier line, in bright moonlight. This, however, they managed without mishap and rejoined the lorry on the road in Persia. They had no trouble at the Soviet posts [checkpoints] at Quchan, where they merely lay on the floor of the lorry while the driver talked his way through without search.

As the lorry approached the checkpoint post at the bridge just outside Meshed, the driver refused to take them further. Hadow related that York's three other crew members (Herndon, Laban, and Pohl) hid themselves and the crew's luggage in a nearby bomb crater while York and Emmens, dressed in their Soviet work clothing, boldly walked across the bridge with other pedestrians into Meshed. The guards at the bridge post made no attempt to stop them. Then, using the map furnished by Kolya, the two officers located the British Consulate.

"York then asked me to assist them in getting their baggage and the three other members of the party," Hadow explained. "In view of the extreme suspicion with which Consular cars are treated at the Russian posts, I decided that it was too dangerous to try and effect a rescue with one of our cars."

Instead, Hadow used a British Army lorry quite openly because British lorries were such common objects on the road that the Russian guards did not bother them. Hadow and the driver of the army lorry located the bomb crater and retrieved the men and baggage. According to Hadow:

---

36. U.S. Legation Tehran letter 573 to State Department, subj: "Escape of Five American Flyers from Russian Internment Camp," June 7, 1943, Army Intelligence Documents. The letter transmitted a dispatch from R. M. Hadow, the British vice-consul at Meshed, Iran, describing the steps taken by him in assisting the evacuation of the five American airmen.

Altogether we had only been out of sight of the [guard] post for three minutes behind a fold in the ground. The sentry . . . made no sign of trying to
stop us, and Stocken [the driver] decided to drive through the bridge at speed.
This he did most effectively, though we fully expected to hear the noise of
bullets whistling through the back of the lorry. However, nothing happened,
and the entire party was inside the Consulate in time for lunch.

We dispatched our telegram No. 149 to Tehran . . . and till orders were
received our only difficulty was in concealing our guests from chance visitors to the Consulate. This was satisfactorily achieved.

May 12, 1943: The American minister in Tehran, having been notified
by the British minister, advised the State Department in Washington of
the arrival of the five American airmen in Meshed.[37]

May 13, 1943: Vice-Consul Hadow in Meshed received orders from Tehran to make necessary arrangements to send the five Americans to India.

May 17, 1943: In Washington, the State Department notified the American minister in Tehran that army representatives in Karachi, India, had
been instructed to assist the former internees when they arrived in India.[38]

May 18, 1943: The men arrived in Quetta, India, after a five-day, 900-
mile trip from Meshed.

While secluded in the British Consulate in Meshed on May 11, the airmen happily discarded their Soviet work clothing, put on their army uniforms, and rested. Later, they waited impatiently for the completed arrangements to move them southward around the checkpoints in the Soviet
occupation zone and into the British zone. Hadow believed that there also
was another danger from attack by bandits from roving tribes.

On the morning of May 14, on Hadow's instructions, the airmen re-
sumed wearing their Soviet work clothing. Hadow loaded them into a small
Bedford lorry, which Hadow drove. He was accompanied by Attaché Khan
Sahib Sheikh Mohomed Ayub.

Hadow reported how he successfully managed to maneuver the group
past the Soviet checkpoints. "I then handed the lorry over to York to drive,
told the Khan Sahib to wire their safe arrival at Birjand [to the south] and
then saw them off down the road in good order," he concluded.

On May 16, together with Attaché Khan Sahib Fazal Haq and an armed
escort, the former internees drove to a British Army outpost near Zahedan,
where they stayed the night. On the following morning, May 17, they transferred to a British station wagon and, with a driver and Gurkha soldiers,
turned east to the Iranian-Indian border. Lacking official entry documents

37. U.S. Legation Tehran message 493 to State Department, May 12, 1943, Army Intelligence Documents.
38. State Department message 241 to U.S. Minister at Tehran, May 17, 1943, Army Intelligence Documents.

and not wanting to risk further delays at the border, they crashed through the wooden border barrier without stopping. They followed the road parallel to the Afghan border to another British Army outpost at Dolbedin. After overnighting, they continued toward Quetta.

May 20, 1943: American officials at Karachi, having been notified of the men's arrival at Quetta, sent an army DC-3 transport for them. By late afternoon the men were in Karachi.

May 22, 1943: The Military Intelligence Service in Washington advised the commanding general, Army Air Forces, that the five men departed Karachi for the United States via Accra on May 21.[39] "Secrecy regarding their former internment and escape is of vital importance," the notification read. "While authorities along their return route have been directed to instruct them to this effect, it is desired and requested that they be met at Miami and the urgency of complete security impressed upon them again."

May 23, 1943: Handled as high-priority passengers, the men were flown across the Middle East, North Africa, and the South Atlantic and, with only two rest stops, reached Miami. Here they were met by security officers.

May 24, 1943: After remaining overnight in a secure area outside Miami, they were escorted directly to Washington for debriefing in depth. Their odyssey, which began when they first boarded the carrier *Hornet,* had zigzagged them around the world in 14 months of high adventure, frustration, and puzzlement. For York and crew, the odyssey was ended at last.

When the five internees were leaving Okhansk in March, their euphoric state of mind overshadowed any notion that they might simply be pawns in an NKVD-orchestrated game. However, unlike earlier segregated travel arrangements, York was assigned on their southbound train to share a compartment with a Soviet civilian official — friendly, English-speaking Kolya. According to David Pohl in a letter written over 40 years later, "That was when our suspicions were aroused."

Pohl pointed out that the internees had been in the Soviet Union long enough to know that one unexplained action, however suspicious it might be, could be a simple coincidence. On the other hand, a series of conveniently related actions, such as those in Ashkhabad and en route to Meshed — could have occurred only with the knowledge and blessing of the NKVD.

"I now believe that our whole escape was engineered through the [Red Army] General Staff and the NKVD," Pohl wrote. The NKVD cover, he said, was so well concealed that some of the people involved "were either

39. Letter, Chief, Military Intelligence Service to Commanding General, Army Air Forces, subj: "Air Forces Personnel Formerly Interned in Russia," May 22, 1943, Army Intelligence Documents.

unaware of an NKVD guiding hand or were the best actors I have ever
seen. When we were crawling on our bellies across the mined border [be-
tween the Soviet Union and Iran], the guards in the towers may have had
the word, but our guide didn't. . . . He was as scared, if not more scared,
as we were."

Robert Emmens did not believe that anybody was play-acting. "Our escape was too real," he wrote recently. "It cost us every cent we had in
American money. York almost didn't make it — he got sick going up that
mountain [to cross the border] that night and wanted us to go ahead without him. We refused, of course. . . . Our contact in Ashkhabad [Kolya]
kissed each of us when we left him at midnight. He had tears in his eyes."

The deliberate NKVD game apparently began the moment that the internees began their long trip from Okhansk to the gates of Iran. As in
the cases of three other groups of American internees who escaped in
1944–45, selected NKVD players participated in the game. When the York
crewmen arrived at Ashkhabad, the internees were aware of the inviting
lofty borderlands to the south, and they could sense the nearness of freedom. The Soviet players had only to wait for the Americans to react. Because the Americans actions could be anticipated, the game was played
to its inevitable conclusion.

Whether the NKVD game plan was stimulated by the appeal in the internees' letter to Stalin was more difficult to say. The War Department
through the State Department and Ambassador Standley had made similar appeals to Foreign Minister Molotov at earlier times. Perhaps the Soviets reacted to a combination of the various approaches. It was apparent,
however, that the NKVD must have used the internees' letter as the convenient triggering mechanism to put the game into play.

Robert McCabe, the assistant military attaché who visited the York crew
at Okhansk in October, 1942, later figured prominently as the American
representative in the execution of NKVD plans for the escape of two other
internee groups in 1944. Colonel McCabe recently wrote, "I never received
any information concerning the departure of the York crewmen [from
Ashkhabad], nor do I believe that any such information was given to anyone in the Embassy. I believe that their departure was assumed when the
Soviets stopped giving us any information about them . . . and when we
no longer were asked by Washington about them."[40]

He estimated that it was mid-1943 when the subject of the York crew's
presence in the Soviet Union was dropped by the embassy for lack of pressure from the War Department. "In summary," McCabe said, "we had no

40. Standley and Ageton, *Admiral Ambassador,* 234. According to Standley, Molotov
was evasive and would give no information concerning the crew's whereabouts or the state
of the crew's health. Standley said, however, that he received an underground report that
the crew had "checked in" early in May at the British Consulate at Meshed.

information about the departure of the York crew or how it was accomplished. The crew's 'escape' of course was arranged and carried out by the NKVD up to the point that the crew was delivered to . . . British authorities. The crew had a cover story to tell about the departure and stuck with it."[41]

In his final official U.S. Military Mission report after the end of the war, General Deane gave credit to Ambassador Standley, whose conversations with Foreign Minister Molotov led to the "surreptitious evacuation" of the York crew into Iran. In January, 1944, while talking with Standley's replacement, Ambassador Averell Harriman, Molotov slyly made his admission: "You know, try as it can, the Soviet Government is unable to find in the Soviet Union the first group of five interned American aviators from the Tokyo raid."[42]

Nobody anticipated it at that time, but the general pattern had been set for the eventual escape of internees yet to come. York and his crew were the guinea pigs. "It is nice to know," David Pohl has concluded, "that we were instrumental in establishing an escape route [through Ashkhabad] and method used later for other airmen."

41. Letter, McCabe to author, July 6, 1986.
42. Quoted in Richard C. Lukas, "Escape," *Aerospace Historian,* Spring, 1969, 15.

4.

The Second Escape
February, 1944

*Dear Maw & Paw: You probably weren't alarmed at not
hearing from me, knowing my writing habits and all,
but this time it wasn't my fault. There isn't a lot I can
tell you about the present situation, but we were forced
down in a neutral country on our last flight.*
— A. T. Miller, Petropavlovsk, Sept. 24, 1943

May 29, 1943: The Japanese resistance on Attu Island at the western end
of the Aleutian Islands chain collapsed when the remnants of the Japanese defenders made their last desperate suicide charge. Bypassed Kiska
Island was still in Japanese hands. The American seizure of Attu and adjacent Shemya, however, freed those islands for the rapid construction of
bomber bases.

From these bases in 1943–45, American bombing raids and photo-
reconnaissance missions were mounted against Japanese installations on
the northern Kurile Islands. Most of the bleak story of sacrifice and death
in this North Pacific combat arena was heavily censored for wartime security reasons. Consequently, the North Pacific aerial war was swept into
the shadows of history, and with it were swept the personal stories of 242
American airmen. These men were the interned survivors of 32 crashes,
crash landings, and ditchings on or near the Soviet Union's Kamchatka
Peninsula.

So, with the conquest of Attu, American planners turned their attention to the northern island outskirts of the Japanese homeland — the forti-
fied islands of Paramushiro and neighboring Shumushu. Bringing these
enemy strongholds under air attack would be possible after a 750-mile
over-water flight. Immediately to the north and literally within sight of
these targets was the Soviet Union's Cape Lopatka on the southern tip of
Kamchatka Peninsula. The Soviets' main port and military base was Petro-

pavlovsk, located 175 miles up the Kamchatka eastern coast at the head of Avacha Bay. American bomber crews therefore would soon become familiar with a new set of unforgettable place-names.

Ironically, because the American commanders' attention had been focused on the effort to clear the Japanese from Attu and Kiska, planning for striking the Kurile targets was skimpy because of a lack of definitive intelligence.[1] Lawrence Reineke, an underemployed intelligence officer assigned to the 21st Bombardment Squadron on the eve of the assault on Attu, fortunately had the foresight to begin collecting neglected information on the Kurile bases. Without authorization he delved informally into the scattered bits and pieces of data in navy and army files. While Attu was being overrun and Kiska isolated, Reineke organized his data. The opporunity to present and use the data came quickly.[2]

July 10, 1943: From Washington came approval for the first bomber mission to the Kuriles. Six B-24s and eight B-25s were designated for making the raid. At the B-24 crew briefing, Reineke was asked to provide information about targets on Paramushiro. In addition, he furnished radio frequencies for and the location of Soviet landing fields on Kamchatka, including those at Petropavlovsk. His Soviet briefing material became the core of future detailed emergency instructions that crews of disabled American bombers could use for approaching the airspace over and landing sites on neutral Kamchatka territory.

While the six B-24s were enroute to the Kuriles, however, their mission was aborted so that the bombers could be diverted to new targets — Japanese cargo ships apparently trying to slip through the American blockade of Kiska. Meanwhile, the eight B-25s continued the long flight to Paramushiro. On arrival, the bomber crews found the island obscured by clouds. They dropped their bombs blindly through the overcast.[3]

July 18, 1943: Again, six B-24s were sent to Paramushiro on a more successful second mission. Caught by surprise, the Japanese defenders were able to resist only feebly.[4]

August 11, 1943: Thoroughly awakened to the American capability of sending bombers from the Aleutians, the Japanese were ready and waiting for the third raid on Paramushiro. A swarm of enemy fighters met nine B-24s over the target area.[5]

Irving L. Wadlington was one of the flight leaders. Before his death in 1987, he wrote: "I led the last [third] element, and one of my wingmen,

1. John H. Cloe, *Top Cover for America* (Missoula, Mont.: Pictorial Histories Publishing, 1984), 123.
2. Brian Garfield, *The Thousand-Mile War* (New York: Doubleday, 1969), 263.
3. Cloe, *Top Cover*, 123.
4. Ibid., 124.
5. Ibid., 124–25.

Captain Hoffman, was missing after the attack. . . . Our squadron was returned to the States shortly thereafter. I never knew whether Hoffman and his crew were interned in Russia." Forty-four years after the raid, Wadlington was advised that Hoffman never reached Kamchatka.

More fortunate was the crew of James R. Pottenger. For the historical record, these airmen became the first American flyers to crash-land on Kamchatka and the first Aleutian-based crew to be interned in the Soviet Union.

"We made the primary strike on the target and lost an engine on the bomb run," Navigator Charles K. Hanner, Jr., recalled. "We had been briefed to close formation on withdrawal, but due to the lack of power, we were unable to do so. Fighters attacked us as we dropped behind the formation. We had a second engine which started to run rough."

Frank Gash, the flight leader, reported that "30 to 40 minutes after the fighter attack started, Pottenger [by radio] said that he was unable to feather the prop on the engine which was out and that a supercharger was on fire." Pottenger was directed to go to the "alternate field," by which Gash meant, and believed Pottenger understood to be, Petropavlovsk.[6]

James Dixon (radio operator) said that 11 Japanese fighters attacked and pursued the crippled bomber for nearly one hour as Pottenger nursed the plane on a course parallel to the Kamchatka east coast toward Petropavlovsk. After Thomas Ring (waist gunner) shot down one of the fighters, the Japanese finally broke off the pursuit.[7]

Hanner said that "when the fighters turned away, we discussed whether to set a new course for the Aleutians. Then we lost the second engine. We headed for a landfall at a point about 25 miles from Petropavlovsk." Steadily losing altitude, the struggling bomber made a soft crash landing in a coastal swamp, according to the Soviets, near Kalaktyrka, north of Petropavlovsk.

August 12, 1943: Having earlier crossed the international date line en route to the Kuriles, Pottenger and his crew approached the neutral territory of Kamchatka on August 12. After Pottenger alerted the men that a crash landing was imminent, Robert Wiles (bombardier) moved from the bomber's nose to the waist area. He threw his bomb sight into the ocean and then joined other members of the crew who braced their backs against the forward bulkhead.

When the B-24 plowed into the swamp, the bomb-bay doors were ripped off, and a loose machine gun, torn from its waist mount, struck several of the huddled men. The bomber settled in shallow water.

Thomas Ring's hip and pelvis were broken. Dixon remembered that

6. Delayed eyewitness statement by Frank T. Gash, March 22, 1945, Missing Air Crew Reports, no. 13041.
7. Delayed eyewitness statement by James P. Dixon, October 18, 1945, Missing Air Crew Reports, no. 13041.

"when we pulled him from the airplane, he was moaning and could not walk." A life raft was inflated, and Ring was carried in it.[8]

Donald Dimel suffered internal injuries. Hanner said that "none of us realized how serious his condition was." Richard Varney had a knee injury, and Robert Wiles a cracked shoulder blade.[9]

Straggling from the marsh, the crew was met by several curious Red Army soldiers. Unable to communicate, the soldiers and the Americans waited for about one hour to be evacuated. Morphine was administered to Ring to ease his pain. He later lapsed into unconsciousness. Ring, Dimel, and Varney were taken to a military hospital near Petropavlovsk, and the other eight men to a log house, where they were confined. Like it or not, they were interned.

Back at their Aleutian base, the Pottenger crewmen were now listed officially as missing in action.

August 13, 1943: Lt. Mikhail ("Mike") Dondekin, who spoke Russian, Chinese, and German as well as English, arrived at the internees' house to serve as their interpreter. Mike had suffered a head injury from a landmine explosion while serving on the Manchurian border in 1940. His injury resulted in his being perpetually palsied. The trembling interpreter would also become a familiar figure to many future internees who would crash-land on Kamchatka.

The airmen were individually interrogated by Soviet officers. The Americans answered the Soviet questions by reciting their name, rank, and serial number, as instructed in their premission briefing. They admitted that they were from the Aleutians but said that they had become lost while on a training mission. Their responses irritated the Soviets, who urged cooperation because "we are allies." Having reached an impasse, the Soviets finally abandoned their effort to extract information from the men.

The internees learned little about their new surroundings because they were not allowed any freedom of movement outside of their living quarters. They were escorted once to a ship anchored in the harbor so that they could use the ship's bathing facilities, and some of the men (again, under escort) visited the injured men in the hospital.

August 14, 1943: Hanner reported that the medical treatment, despite the absence of basic equipment and supplies, seemed to be unusually good. "I cannot recall the name of the doctor," he said, "yet I have thought of him often over the years and remembered, admired, and respected him as a man of exceptional medical skill and great empathy and a wonderful person."

8. Delayed eyewitness statement by Donald L. Dimel, October 18, 1945, Missing Air Crew Reports, no. 13041.

9. Wiles was not examined for a possible fractured shoulder until the crew later arrived at Tashkent.

James Pottenger's B-24 crew after their repatriation. *Front row:* Richard Varney, Anthony Homitz, Peter Bernatovich, Charles Day, and James Dixon. *Back row:* James Pottenger, Charles K. Hanner, Jr., Richard Filler, and Robert Wiles. Other members of the original crew were Donald Dimel, who was hospitalized by crash injuries, and Thomas Ring, who suffered fatal injuries in the crash. Photograph courtesy Charles K. Hanner, Jr.

The doctor's exploratory operation on Dimel found the cause of Dimel's intense pain—a ruptured spleen, which the doctor removed. Loss of blood due to preoperative internal bleeding and the surgery resulted in a critical need for transfusions. Dimel's fellow crewmen with the same blood type were taken to the hospital, where blood was transferred by means of a crude emergency apparatus directly from donor to patient. The doctor also used cord and large stones to fabricate a makeshift but effective traction device to align Ring's broken bones.

August 17, 1943: His injured knee mending, Richard Varney left the hospital and rejoined the crew.

September 1, 1943: Ring seemed to be recovering steadily and satisfactorily from his crash injuries, according to reports from Pottenger, who visited Ring regularly. Suddenly a blood clot induced a fatal stroke. Hanner reported that "the doctor was extremely upset, like the rest of us." In a postwar statement, James Dixon said that Ring's body was buried in a lot near the hospital. No Americans were present at the burial.

Dimel's recovery from surgery at first was complicated by infection in some of his stitches. The Soviets appeared to be delaying the crew's departure from Petropavlovsk until Ring and Dimel were able to travel. With Ring's unexpected death and Dimel's satisfactory recovery from surgical infection, the way was now cleared for the Soviets to do whatever they were planning for the internees' future.

September 3, 1943: From the beginning the men wondered whether they would be repatriated quickly. Richard Filler (copilot) deduced from his premission briefing that the crew, if forced to land at Petropavlovsk, might be evacuated by American submarine. Hanner likewise thought that there was a "slim chance" of being sent to Alaska. "We understood that there were American consulates at both Khabarovsk and Vladivostok," Hanner stated. "We hoped that we could be released at either place."

When a four-engined Soviet flying boat arrived to take them from Petropavlovsk, many of the men immediately assumed that the flying boat would be the means of returning them to American control. They boarded the flying boat in early morning but were not told that their destination was Khabarovsk.

The long one-day trip ended when they landed on the Amur River and taxied to a seaplane ramp. They were then loaded immediately into blacked-out automobiles and driven to a barracks area surrounded by high walls.

September 5, 1943: After two nights and a day inside the walled installation, the men were returned to the flying boat and were aloft again to an unannounced new destination. They flew generally in a southerly direction. When they landed in the harbor, they were at Vladivostok. As in Khabarovsk, the internees were whisked in blacked-out automobiles to another restricted area for the night.

September 6, 1943: Awakened at dawn, the men again were put aboard the flying boat to be flown all the way to Magadan on the north coast of the Sea of Okhotsk. Here they were restricted to the second floor of a building near the docks.

The Soviets never explained why the men were taken more than a thousand miles on a vast zigzag course up and down the Soviet Far East to reach Magadan. If it were essential that the men should be routed to Magadan, they could have been flown directly from Petropavlovsk in a single day. Nor did the Soviets discuss the reason for transporting the men secretly between flying boat and restricted quarters in Khabarovsk, Vladivostok, and Magadan. The Soviets, however, seemed to assume the presence of Japanese agents in the Soviet cities, and the unusual routings and actions may have been the NKVD's plan to confuse the agents or to deny them any knowledge of the location or movements of American airmen interned in the Soviet Union.

Although they were not allowed to leave the second floor of the building where they were confined in Magadan, the airmen for the first time since leaving Petropavlovsk were able to observe outside activities through the windows. They could see cargo ships discharging Lend-Lease vehicles so new that the American Army white-star symbols had not yet been eliminated. In the opposite direction they could see a stockade whose watchtowers contained guards, searchlights, and machine guns. Daily they viewed groups of shackled prisoners who were marched from the stockade in the mornings and back in the evenings.

September 10, 1943: Taken directly to an air base, the internees boarded a waiting DC-3 type airplane for a nonstop flight eastward to Yakutsk. They still did not have any clue regarding their ultimate destination, but it was obvious now that they were starting across Siberia.

September 12, 1943: After flying to and overnighting at Irkutsk, the airmen resumed their daylight trip. The airplane made a refueling stop at Krasnoyarsk. The local Soviet commander and members of his staff invited the airmen to lunch. The Americans were ill at ease because they were wearing the same flying suits in which they arrived from the Aleutians a month earlier. By contrast, the Soviet hosts were dressed in fresh uniforms.

When they arrived at Novosibirsk's air base, the internees watched the landing of Lend-Lease P-39 fighters from Alaska via the ALSIB route. Later, although they were provided with a good meal and were introduced to the Soviet toasting ritual at the air-base Officers' Mess, they were again restricted to quarters for the night.

September 14, 1943: After leaving Novosibirsk, their airplane followed a route south and west to Alma Ata, where the airmen spent the night and then continued to Tashkent. The men were met by Soviet officials at the Tashkent air base and promptly driven through the city and beyond for 20 miles to the southwest. Here, near the edge of the town of Yangiyul, they were delivered to a large one-floor house that would be their temporary home.

Now they could move freely in and out of the house. Compared with the confinement that they had experienced since their arrival on Kamchatka, this latest facility, located in an apple orchard, offered a welcome change. "The time spent here," Hanner recalled, "was the closest to internee status that we had experienced."

At the house they were met by their cook, Reuben, and by their interpreter, Nona Fedorovna Solodovinova. Various members of the housekeep-ing staff were replaced often during the internment camp's operation for the remainder of the war, but Nona's presence was more enduring and well remembered, usually affectionately, by 200 of the various internees.

To some Americans, Nona seemed to have authority beyond that of an ordinary interpreter, and they were suspicious of Nona's possible connec-tion with the NKVD. To most of the internees, however, Nona's personal interest in some of the men's problems invited the men to confide in her. This unusual relationship between interpreter and internee encouraged many of the men to call her "mama," a name that she obviously relished. Her ability to perform her duties as a representative of the Soviet Union while demonstrating sympathetic attitudes of a caring person was similar to that of the York crew's Zietseva.

Nona was an attractive woman in her early forties. By all accounts she was a widow. She and her architect husband were said to have been from Leningrad. Before the war they were relocated to Tashkent, where her hus-band died. Her current means of livelihood and where she learned her fluent English were never explained. She was, by Soviet standards, very well dressed. Her wardrobe included an ample supply of silk hose, dresses, for-mal gowns, and an attractive fur coat. Many of the internees recalled her having large, expressive blue eyes.

September 14, 1943: A barber began coming daily to shave the men. Not having any shaving lotion, he doused a large piece of rock salt in water, rubbed it over the shaven areas, and then rinsed off the salt with cold water. The men's memories of their early days in internment camp faded, but they never forgot the rock-salt treatment.

September 19, 1943: Two springs flowed into a stream behind the house. These springs were their sources of drinking water. The internees were dis-mayed to see some neighbor women taking their baths in the smaller spring. Nona escorted the men into the town so that they could bathe in the com-munity bath facility.

September 2, 1943: A Red Army captain, temporarily assigned to over-see the internees, came from Tashkent to make one of his semiweekly in-spections. He spent the night at the house, as was his customary practice.

September 29, 1943: The internees were beginning to feel the stress and frustration of having nothing to do. They could hear the croaking of frogs in the stream behind the house. On impulse they went to the stream in a group, undressed, and wading into the stream and using pointed sticks, gigged enough frogs for a frog-leg meal. Reuben refused to cook the men's catch until Nona telephoned her superiors in Tashkent with a request that Reuben be ordered to cooperate. After this escapade, somebody (probably Reuben) told people in Yangiyul to avoid "the wild men from Borneo."

October 8, 1943: This was moving day. The internees with Reuben and

Nona Solodovinova, chief interpreter at the internment camp near Tashkent between September, 1943, and February, 1945. Photograph courtesy Richard D. Salter

Nona suddenly were relocated to the village of Vrevskaya. Here, 15 miles beyond Yangiyul, was the former school facility that would become the Soviets' permanent camp for American internees. The main building in the new camp was many times larger than the house in which the ten men had been living. Unlike the Yangiyul quarters, the building was not wired for electricity, so the men were furnished kerosene lamps for night lighting.

October 9, 1943: Additional Soviet camp personnel arrived. It was obvious, judging from the bustle of new activity, that additional internees were expected at the camp. During their journey across Siberia, Pottenger and Filler had made periodic inquiries concerning the whereabouts of York and his companions from the Doolittle Tokyo raid. They were told that they "were chasing York and his men and would probably catch them soon." The thought that the York crew might still be interned in the Soviet Union, 18 months after the Tokyo raid, was sobering.

Nona, however, put an end to speculation about the use of the enlarged internment facility. Seven additional American bomber crews, she said, had landed in the Soviet Union and were en route to the camp. Were the crews from the Aleutians? If not, who were they?

July 28, 1943: Meanwhile in the Aleutians, the Japanese successfully and secretly evacuated their Kiska garrison.

August 15, 1943: Unaware that the Japanese had eluded the American blockade of the island, a joint Canadian-American amphibious task force stormed the silent and vacant beaches of Kiska. So ended the Aleutian campaign. The redeployment of American bombardment aircraft, begun after the capture of Attu, continued.

September 10, 1943: The Eleventh Air Force mustered 19 bombers for another strike against Paramushiro, whose Japanese military installations were being steadily reinforced.[10] The briefing for the mission was held in the chapel on Attu. Seven B-24s should arrive at the target area first and drop their bombs from high altitude. Twelve B-25s would follow and attack the shipping targets and naval craft at deck level. The first-priority targets were cargo vessels, then seaplane tenders, and finally destroyers and cruisers.

Vladimir Sabich, copilot of Wayne Marrier's B-25, recalled that the crews were told that "in the event of serious battle damage, we were to try to make it to Russian territory." During the briefing there was also a hint suggesting that diplomatic arrangements might be made for any crewman landing in Siberia to be repatriated promptly to Alaska. This faint hope was offered, despite an August 30 announcement on Moscow radio that an unidentified bomber crew had been interned after landing in Kamchatka on August 12.[11] The hint of instant repatriation of Aleutian-based airmen therefore appeared to be only a psychological ploy to ease premission apprehensions. Sabich made a record of his premonition: "Have a hunch that all is not going to be well on this deal. In fact, most of us feel that at least half of our flight will be lost. . . . Wrote a long letter to Fran [his wife] trying to let her know how I feel without worrying her too much."

September 11, 1943: After a restless night, Sabich was out of bed at 5:30. He put on clean clothes "from head to foot so that I wouldn't operate in Russia in dirty clothes in case that we have to land there."

The B-24 bombers were delayed in take-off, which in turn postponed

10. Cloe, *Top Cover,* 125.
11. The landing of Pottenger's crew was reported in U.S. Consul Vladivostok message 32 to State Department, August 20, 1943, State Department General Files, Record Group 59, file 811.2361, National Archives (hereafter cited as State Department General Files). Five days later, the Soviets voluntarily released the news of the latest American bomber crew to be interned. Details, however, were lacking.

the departure of the B-25s. Some of the crews considered the tardy start of the mission an ill omen.

September 12, 1943: After crossing the international date line, the bombers approached their targets, and most of them executed their strikes on the Paramushiro installations and shipping as planned. Japanese antiaircraft installations and fighters were waiting, however, and reacted fiercely. Sabich had a vivid memory of the battle scene. "Every time I looked at the water, I swallowed to keep my heart down. The water was just whipped to a froth by machine gun bullets, shell fragments, 20-mm slugs, and big stuff that was throwing up geysers. . . . The tracers were so thick that they looked like Roman candles, and I can't figure out how anybody could have gotten through the barrage."

One B-24 and two B-25s were shot down. Two other B-24s and five B-25s, including the one piloted by the 77th Squadron commander, Richard Salter, were crippled but later landed intact at Petropavlovsk.

Roger Putnam's B-24 developed an engine problem. The windmilling propeller could not be feathered, and the resulting vibration steadily worsened. Realizing that he could not return to Attu, Putnam turned toward Kamchatka. He sighted a landing area near Petropavlovsk, but it was too small for the heavy bomber. Closer to Petropavlovsk was another landing field with a long concrete runway. Here Putnam was able to land without further mishap.

One by one, the pilots of six other battle-damaged bombers also tried to keep their planes in the air long enough to reach any landing area near Petropavlovsk, while Japanese fighters trailed and attacked them. The fighters' dwindling fuel finally forced them to break off the pursuit and allow the battered raiders to survive.

Norman Savignac's crippled B-25 arrived at the same landing field at Petropavlovsk a few minutes after Putnam. Savignac was followed by John Rodger's riddled B-25, which touched down but was unable to taxi after landing because of damaged landing gear.

Richard Salter's B-25 had been raked by gunfire during his bomb run. He evaded the enemy fighters, but when his left engine began to sputter, landing in neutral country was the only alternative to ditching. "We approached Petropavlovsk across Avacha Bay from the southeast," Salter said. "We were greeted by machine gun fire with tracers plainly visible. Tracers from below could also give the appearance of coming from my plane, and I thought that one of my gunners was shooting. Because I did not believe that the Soviets really tried to hit us, I yelled, 'Don't fire! Don't fire!'"

Salter's bomber was met outside the harbor by two Soviet fighters in formation. The fighters did not fire or make any hostile moves. "Instead," Salter reported, "the pilot of the lead plane dipped his wing to indicate the direction we should fly." The direction led to the landing field.

After narrowly escaping a direct hit by an exploding shell, Wayne Marrier discovered that the bomb-bay doors on his B-25 were still open. The hydraulic mechanism was wrecked, and the doors would not budge. Their bomber's speed slowed by the drag of the open doors, the crew realized that it was impossible to return to Attu on the fuel that remained in the tanks. They managed to repel the fighter onslaught, but another B-25 directly ahead of them did not. Sabich watched smoke streaming from the stricken bomber as it turned in the direction of Kamchatka.

"We could see the flames starting up," Sabich recalled. "Shortly thereafter [the pilot] landed in the water. He made a swell landing. The flames on his left wing were really going then. It sure was a helpless feeling to see those boys hit the water and not be able to help them in any way."

Marrier flew along the Kamchatka coast. About 20 miles south of Avacha Bay, Marrier and Russell Hurst, pilot of the remaining disabled B-25, sighted one another and then stayed together. When they neared Petropavlovsk, the two pilots started to fly their bombers over the harbor. They drew heavy antiaircraft fire from Soviet naval vessels even after Hurst lowered his landing gear to signal his intention to land. "We got the hell out of there," Sabich said. "We thought that the Soviets probably shelled us because our bomb-bay doors were open as though we were going to make a run on the ships in the harbor."

Hurst and Marrier retreated to a position about five miles offshore. They began flying in a wide circle while deciding what to do. Hurst finally told Marrier by radio that he was going to try an approach along the south edge of the bay. Hurst's B-25 disappeared in that direction. James O'Dair (Hurst's navigator) remembered that "when we flew over their submarine base, they fired on us and sent fighters after us. The fighter pilots motioned to us where to land."

While waiting for developments, Marrier's crew saw a B-24 bomber approaching the Petropavlovsk harbor area from the southeast. The bomber flew unswervingly above the harbor through an intense antiaircraft barrage. Carl ("Whitey") Wagner was the pilot. The B-24 miraculously was not hit. Joseph Kerns (Wagner's crew) later reported that the bomber drew the fire of five Soviet warships in the harbor. Wagner's brash course brought his aircraft to a point where the landing field could be seen.

Earlier, in the running battle with Japanese fighters near Shumushu, Wagner's B-24 had lost two engines. Wagner, at the controls of the crippled bomber, angled toward Kamchatka while trying to stay aloft. Surviving bombers bound for Attu listened while Wagner filled the air with radio instructions about writing to his wife. Weeks later, a note was smuggled from Siberia to the Alaska Defense Command headquarters. The note was written by a pilot who had landed in Kamchatka. "Inform my wife and the War Department," the note read, "that I and my crew are safe but interned." One of Wagner's fellow internees, when told 40 years later about the mysterious note, concluded: "That had to be from 'Whitey' Wagner! I know that he sent it, but I don't know how."

In the meantime, Marrier's crew monitored the radio for word from Hurst but heard nothing. Marrier could not wait any longer and decided to follow the route over which Hurst had disappeared. Marrier's B-25 did not draw any fire when it passed over the submarine base, but two fighters suddenly appeared, one on each side. The fighters held their fire while Marrier wagged his bomber's wings as a signal of peaceful intention.

The damaged bomber flew over the smaller landing field that Putnam's crew had seen. "Then we spotted a white concrete runway ahead," Sabich said. "As we flew over it, we could see four B-25s and two B-24s already parked on the edge of the field." The bomber turned and approached the runway. Like six other pilots before him, Marrier had arrived in neutral country. Not a man aboard the seven aircraft had been injured.

On Attu during the debriefing of the surviving bomber crews after their return from the Kuriles, Richard Salter's B-25 was erroneously identified as being the stricken plane that ditched off the coast of Kamchatka.[12] Actually, the bomber was piloted by Albert Berecz. Soviet observers near Cape Lopatka watched the running battle between bomber and fighters and the ditching of Berecz's craft. When the bomber crew members attempted to launch a life raft, the Soviets reported that the fighters machine-gunned them.

After Marrier's B-25 landed at Petropavlovsk, the Soviets posted a woman military guard at each of the American bombers. A Soviet officer, using hand signals, motioned Marrier and his crew to leave their bomber and walk to a camouflaged revetment where they joined the crewmen of the other bombers.

Several revetments lined the landing field. Most of them sheltered fighters. Each fighter, with its pilot already seated in the cockpit, appeared to be alerted for emergency takeoff.

A. T. ("Red") Miller (Putnam's copilot) later analyzed the tense scene. "Here the Soviets were confronted with a situation where they had seven U.S. bombers on their hands at a small base not too far from the Japanese target which the Americans had just attacked. It was apparent that the Japanese knew where the bombers had landed, and the Soviets must have been in sheer panic over what to do about it."

Sabich also observed, "I figure they were afraid that the Japs were coming in after after us." It seemed obvious that the Japanese fighter pilots, after pursuing the bombers along the southeastern coast of Kamchatka,

12. Intelligence Summary No. 2, 77th Bombardment Squadron, September 11, 1943, U.S. Air Force Historical Research Center.

were fully aware that the disabled planes had not been able to return to the Aleutians.

Everybody waited. One hour passed. Nothing happened.

Then an English-speaking Red Army officer appeared and told each crew in turn to go to their bomber and retrieve their belongings. Guns were immediately confiscated. Next, the airmen were loaded on an ancient bus and taken to a mess hall where they were served their first meal in the Soviet Union: raw (smoked) fish, soup, and Russian coffee. From there they went to a military recreation hall to wait. Despite the language barrier, Soviet airmen gamely tried to entertain them. Fatigue and tension began to overwhelm the Americans. Their day had already been 20 hours long. Gerald Green (Rodger's turret gunner) confessed that he could not recall exactly what happened after his bomber landed. "I only remember," he said, "that I was so weary that I slept on the floor [of the recreation building]." So did many of his fellow Americans.

At midnight they were informed that they would be moved to a hotel. Three Model-A Ford type trucks hauled them over a rutted, rough road to the northwestern edge of Petropavlovsk. "The hotel," Richard Salter said, "turned out to be the local Palace of Culture—a large square structure built of concrete blocks." On the lower level were a community theater and a floor for dancing. The walls were hung with the mandatory Soviet banners, war posters, and portraits of Marx, Lenin, and Stalin.

The Soviets had hastily converted rooms on the second floor into dormitories filled with undersized springless cots and mattress covers filled with straw. The exhausted men were anxious to use the uncomfortable beds, but first the Soviets insisted that they eat another meal similar to their earlier one at the air base. The 51 men were too tired to protest. For them, however, the longest day of their lives was finally ending.

September 13, 1943: The groggy Americans were aroused from bed at midmorning. The Soviets had dug a hole behind the building to be used as an outhouse. Red Army soldiers waited nearby with kettles of cold water so that the men could wash their hands and faces as a part of their morning toilet.

In daylight, they could see that their "hotel" was located on the side of a hill. The valley below led to Avacha Bay, where anchored ships were visible in the distance. In the opposite direction up the valley was a hospital where their meals were prepared. Two miles to the west of the hospital was a lake where small military seaplanes were based.

After breakfast, individual interrogation of the Americans began. The results were predictable. The Soviets persisted in their quest for information about the American bombing mission, and the American answers were evasive. The question-and-answer sessions were conducted through interpreters.

One of the most unforgettable interpreters was Lt. Pavel ("Paul") Stepanovich Trukhachev, whose English was limited but understandable. Paul was a small man with a round face and balding head, but his most memorable feature was his perpetual smile. It was he who later revealed to the internees that the Pottenger B-24 bomber had crashed north of Petropavlovsk in August and that one of the crew had died of crash injuries. He also reported that the ten survivors had already departed, but he did not provide any details. This news cheered the men, especially when Paul in his fractured English assured them that they would follow the Pottenger crew shortly.

On Kamchatka, there was a shortage of Russian-English language interpreters. At Tashkent, however, the Soviets managed to assemble a well-qualified group of linguists, all women. Fortunately, among the Americans were men of Slavic family backgrounds. They spoke some of the Slavic tongues such as Polish or Serbian. The similarities of these languages with Russian provided a basis for acquiring a degree of fluency in Russian later at Tashkent. In addition, Yiddish was soon discovered as a language that several knew and was used in private conversations between American Jews and Russian Jews as well as Jewish displaced persons. Because the Soviets also encouraged the teaching of Russian and the internees welcomed language lessons as a means of filling idle time, many of the American internees learned a certain amount of conversational Russian. While communication between Soviet and American was stilted and time consuming in the beginning, some airmen soon were able to express basic needs, ask questions, and make responses in Russian.

The Russian language learning process was a continuing one for the Americans. At the same time, the interpreters were learning, too. "It was lots of fun," A. T. Miller remembered, "to corrupt the interpreters' beautiful King's English with American slang. They became very good at using it!"

September 14, 1943: The impatient Soviets finally ended their fruitless interrogation of the men. Although they should have anticipated the Soviet announcement, the men were unprepared to hear that they were being interned until the war's end. James O'Dair wrote, "I had personally believed that some prearrangement had been made between the United States and Russia. I naively believed that we would not be interned." Like members of the Pottenger crew, O'Dair and others assumed that they would be returned to the Aleutians.

September 15, 1943: A daily routine for the men began to develop. They were served three meals, but the unfamiliar food was unappetizing because it tasted as though it had been cooked in fish oil. They were also given two ounces of spirits as an automatic ration. Card games were played endlessly during the day. In the evening the men usually watched a Soviet "blood-and-thunder" motion picture or an American one dubbed in Russian.

September 20, 1943: There were whispers among the men of a plot to escape, but the plotters failed to generate any enthusiasm, and the notion fizzled.

September 21, 1943: The Soviets found and delivered a volleyball, so the internees added the outdoor game to their daily ritual. Red Army soldiers from nearby military installations were eager to compete with the Americans. According to Joseph Dunwoody (Marrier's tail gunner), "The Russians had a whole new set of volleyball rules that most of us California beachboys never heard of!"

September 22, 1943: The internees were trucked to the Petropavlovsk community bathing facility and introduced for the first time to an invigorating Russian-style steam bath.

September 25, 1943: Moscow radio announced that seven American planes made forced landings on Kamchatka on September 12 and their crews were interned. Names or numbers of interned crewmen were not mentioned. [13]

September 29, 1943: A. T. Miller was both amused and provoked when he would daily question Paul the interpreter, "What's the poop, Paul?" — meaning, of course, "When are we leaving?" And Paul's response, in his own version of English, was unchanging. "In some days," he would say, "you will flow away from here."

September 30, 1943: A four-engined flying boat, probably the same one in which the Pottenger crew was evacuated from Petropavlovsk, landed in the harbor. The internees were told to be ready, as Paul had promised, "to flow away."

The men heard rumors that they were being sent westward, probably to Khabarovsk. However, Richard Salter said that nobody knew the internees' destination with certainty. "I do recall," he said, "that we had given up hope that we would be returned to Alaska."

October 3, 1943: The men fretted anxiously for two days when a weather front with snow moved across the Sea of Okhotsk and canceled plans for departure. On the third morning, the 51 internees, accompanied by an interpreter with a broad British accent, boarded the flying boat shortly before noon. Hours later the aircraft landed at Okha on the northern end of Sakhalin Island.

The men were escorted to a dining area where, some of them said, they ate their best meal since internment. Then they went to a nearby building

13. The U.S. Embassy in Moscow had not yet been officially informed of the landings and internments.

whose large rooms, separated by a hallway, had been equipped with cots, cotton mattresses, sheets, and blankets. "Great!" exclaimed Gerald Green. "We hadn't seen anything except sleeping bags [and, more recently, straw-filled mattress covers] for a year. We crawled in the beds and somebody turned off the electric lights." In a few minutes, however, pandemonium broke out. The women attendants, aroused by the men's yelling and cursing, turned on the lights.

Bedbugs were everywhere: on the walls, on the bed covers, on the men. Even the interpreter was distressed and called them, in his very proper English, "bloodthirsty little bastards." The women calmly set about crushing the visible bugs on the walls with their thumbs. Vladimir Sabich admitted that "many of us spent the rest of the night standing in the hall." Others tried to resume sleeping but insisted that the electric lights *not* be extinguished.

October 4, 1943: The flying boat laden with internees landed on the Amur River at Khabarovsk. During the five-hour flight, Sabich and others, noting that there was a minimum-sized Soviet crew and escort aboard the aircraft, amused themselves by wondering how difficult it would be to hijack the plane. (Months later, when they mentioned their notion to an American Embassy representative, they were told that such an attempt, successful or not, could have heightened Soviet-Japanese tensions and would have been diplomatically disastrous to Soviet-American relations.)

October 5, 1943: Richard Salter, the senior officer among the internees, assumed command of the group. He retained this responsibility until the group, which later included the Pottenger crew, was repatriated in 1944.

Although the Soviets had announced to the world what the Japanese had always known — that seven American disabled bombers had landed in Kamchatka — the whereabouts of the American crewmen themselves had not been disclosed. During the flight from Petropavlovsk to Khabarovsk, some of the internees noted that the Soviets aboard the flying boat appeared to be nervous. On arrival at Khabarovsk, the Americans were quickly moved to a Red Army officers' rest camp located within sight of the Amur River. Here they were fed and comfortably bedded. Soviet combat pilots from the German war front were also at the rest camp, and Americans and Soviets cordially intermixed because of a common interest in aviation. A. T. Miller recalled that they managed to do some relaxed "hangar-flying" in spite of the language barrier.

Outside the rest camp, however, the atmosphere differed because the nervous Soviets seemed to suspect the Japanese of having a continuing interest in what the Soviet Union intended to do with the internees. Joseph Dunwoody reported that when he tried to walk from his barracks to the edge of the river, he was promptly challenged. "A Russian officer came to me," he related, "and told me that I should not be there because the Japanese were always spying on everything along the river." Dunwoody returned to the barracks.

October 6, 1943: In preparation for continuing their odyssey across the Soviet Union, the 51 men were divided into three traveling units of about 17 airmen each. Each unit was assigned to a separate Soviet DC-3 type airplane with its Soviet flight crew, usually three airmen and an English-speaking escort. The first unit departed from Khabarovsk promptly, and the other two on successive days.

The men still did not know their destination, but they learned that their journey should be completed in three days. Unfavorable weather, mechanical problems, and scarce fuel supplies all contributed to make the three flights of varying duration. The transit time for the first unit was fastest — five days. The second unit required eight days, and the final one, nearly two weeks.

The Soviet pilots avoided night flying. Overnight stopovers were made at air bases where the internees were used by the Soviet local officials as excuses for serving a banquet. Daylight flights allowed the pilots to use the railroad tracks as visual navigational devices for the route generally via Irkutsk, Krasnoyarsk, Novosibirsk, Omsk, and Alma Ata and thence to Tashkent. The separate aircraft made intermediate stops for various reasons.

Vladimir Sabich learned that his DC-3 had formerly been used as a night bomber. He saw a metal patch in the top of the cabin covering a hole where a gun turret had once been mounted. The Soviet pilot occasionally broke the monotony of the long trip by allowing Sabich to take the controls of the aircraft. While in the cockpit Sabich noticed the blackout curtains that had been used to protect a former pilot's eyes from the blinding beams of enemy searchlights.

The Soviet DC-3 engines did not have starters. At one refueling stop, the internees observed ground crewmen using a Model-A Ford type truck with a power takeoff attachment to turn each propeller until the engine fired.

The simple task of refueling often was a time-consuming task. One unit was delayed for three days at one air base where the DC-3 made an unexpected landing for fuel because the air-base gasoline supply was exhausted. Normally, however, slow hand-pumps were used to transfer gasoline from storage drums to wing tanks. At one refueling stop, Joseph Dunwoody watched with fascination the series of actions. "After the plane had been gassed, two men poured the contents of two jugs of ethyl additive in the tanks. Next, three men climbed on each wing and rocked the plane until the additive and the gasoline had been mixed."

For the internees, speculation regarding their route and destination helped to break the monotony of the flight across Asia. For the Soviet crews, however, each long daylight flight often was a wearisome time, the relief from which, some of the Americans suspected, was the vodka that the Soviet airmen had in the cockpits. At some of the air bases, such as Krasnoyarsk and Novosibirsk, where the DC-3 planes landed for overnight rest or fuel, the internees reported seeing rows of Lend-Lease military planes, especially B-25 bombers and P-39 fighters.

During one overnight stop at Omsk, James O'Dair narrowly escaped the fatherly clutches of the Soviet air-base commander. At the evening banquet and vodka party, the commander was attracted to the fresh-faced youthful officer. O'Dair noted in his diary, "I was nearly adopted by the commander; he wanted to marry me off to his daughter. I pulled a fast fade-out."

October 8, 1943: Although the Foreign Office notified the American Embassy on October 1 that the internees on Kamchatka were "alive and well,"[14] seven days elapsed before the Foreign Office produced a list of the crew members.[15] Many of the names, however, were garbled, and additional communication and time were needed before accurate identifications were made available to Washington.

October 10, 1943: The first unit, headed by Richard Salter, landed at Tashkent air base and was immediately driven 35 miles to the village of Vrevskaya and then to the internment camp. Salter remembered that "Pottenger and his crew greeted us very excitedly and warmly. For some hours and maybe days we questioned and talked about Pottenger's crash and death of a crew member. We related our stories to them."

October 11, 1943: Additional Soviet personnel began appearing daily at the camp. Five Red Army battle veterans were the nucleus of the military unit. Two of the soldiers, familiarly known as Joseph and Peter, were assigned as guards. Soon two younger women, Olga and Sylva, joined Nona as interpreters. At the same time, the housekeeping staff, including Reuben the cook, was slowly expanded by several waitresses, laundresses, and charwomen. Most of the housekeeping staff lived in the village, but the interpreters occupied rooms located in one wing of the camp's main building.

October 13, 1943: As more of the internees arrived from Khabarovsk and as the camp started to assume the appearance of a more permanent establishment, the men began to fear that the Soviets could be serious about their obligation to intern them indefinitely. Whispers about escape again surfaced. Unlike the bleak and isolated Kamchatka, Uzbekistan was warmer and crossed by railroads that led southwest toward Iran and east to China.

14. U.S. Embassy Moscow message 1509 to State Department, October 1, 1943, State Department General Files.

15. U.S. Embassy Moscow message 1567 to State Department, October 8, 1943, State Department General Files.

Both routes would later be considered in unrealistic and ill-prepared plans of Americans who were determined to flee the internment camp.

October 15, 1943: The internees had been well fed during their trans-Asian odyssey to Tashkent. They literally had feasted, Russian-style, each time after their air transport had landed. Now, having been delivered to the internment camp, the men were abruptly faced with one of the stark realities of life in wartime Soviet Union — bureaucratic fumbling with food distribution. As in the case of the York crew a year earlier, the promised flow of Red Army rations for the Americans was slow in being established and maintained. Whatever food was available lacked variety, and individual portions served at mealtime were small. Unimpressed by frequent Soviet assurances of better and larger meals to come, the internees became more restless day by day.

A shortage of American cigarettes in the camp was partly relieved by a frequent ration of Soviet-made ones. The cigarettes were Tashkent products containing locally grown harsh tobacco. Only a few dedicated smokers could tolerate them, so most of the internees used their cigarette ration for gifts to local people or for barter.

October 16, 1943: When Pottenger's crew arrived at Yangiyul in September, Nona learned that James Dixon was a professional pianist. Nona may have reported this information to her superiors in Tashkent, or the Soviets may already have planned to provide a piano when the permanent camp was established at Vrevskaya. Whatever the reason, a piano that was somewhat out of tune was delivered and placed in the room marked "recreation." Undeterred by the piano's shortcomings, Dixon demonstrated his talent daily by playing the music to familiar hymns and popular songs entirely by ear. In mid-November, a Soviet piano tuner improved the sound of the instrument.

October 17, 1943: Although not the serious problem that the men had encountered at Okha on Sakhalin, the bedbugs that they found in the camp were irksome. The men obtained empty food cans from the kitchen and poured water and a skim of lamp kerosene in them. They then placed the legs of the cots in the cans. Although the Soviet staff ridiculed the practice, this control measure seemed to help in reducing the problem.

Bedbugs, however, were never completely eliminated. Charles Hanner remembered being bitten frequently. "One morning I woke up with my leg swollen from ankle to thigh," he said. "I was sure that I had elephantiasis, but they gave me some black medicine for five days, and the swelling went down." Hanner did not learn whether bedbug bite infection may have been the cause.

October 18, 1943: Maj. Gen. John R. Deane arrived in Moscow to organize the new U.S. Military Mission, which would coordinate the American military activities and interests in the Soviet Union.[16] The mission, which officially would become operational on November 1, absorbed the personnel and functions of the military and naval attachés. Among General Deane's responsibilities, with Soviet cooperation, was monitoring the welfare of American airmen who were now interned or would be in the future.

October 26, 1943: The Foreign Office revealed to the American Embassy that the 51 members of the American bomber crews in Kamchatka had been sent to Vrevskaya station (near Yangiyul and Tashkent), "where they would be permanently quartered." The embassy, informing Washington of the transfer, announced that arrangements for sending a representative to visit the men would be made with Soviet authorities.[17]

At the same time in the United States, the internees' next-of-kin, a few at a time, were receiving confidential notification of the missing men's safety "in a neutral country." The internees, however, were not aware of the notifications. Their concern over the mental anguish of their families was unrelieved.

October 27, 1943: Because the internees were being openly marched to the Vrevskaya community bathhouse, the local Uzbeks, displaced persons, and others living in the village quickly adjusted to the sight of the Americans in their midst. Consequently, when some of the men began to visit the village railroad station to watch the passing trains, there was no commotion.

Another place of internee interest was the village bazaar. This marketplace offered Uzbek goods, especially scarce food items, at black-market prices. The bazaar also provided an opportunity for some of the internees to meet friendly local residents.

October 28, 1943: The whereabouts of the five York airmen remained a mystery. Efforts to obtain any new information through the interpreters were unproductive, so the subject was reluctantly dropped. Instead, the men used every opportunity to inquire about their own situation.

"When are we going home?" they asked. Like the American soldiers in Siberia during 1918–20, they learned to say, "*Ya khochu domoi* (I want to go home). *Kogda* (when)?"

And the Soviet response, sometimes with a faint scowl, sometimes with a sigh of exasperation, became a monotonous one: "*Skoro* (soon)."

The men adopted two mongrel pups at the camp. One of the pups they named "Skoro."

16. John R. Deane, *The Strange Alliance* (New York: Viking Press, 1946), 3.
17. U.S. Embassy Moscow message 1731 to State Department, October 26, 1943, State Department General Files.

October 30, 1943: A tailor arrived at the camp and measured each American for a two-piece uniform. The men watched the tailor at work with
mixed feelings. They welcomed the thought of getting some alternate clothing because winter was near. They wondered, however, as did the York crew
a year earlier, whether the clothing provided further evidence that they
were not going to be released.

November 1, 1943: Kerosene lamps no longer were used in the camp.
A work crew installed wiring and overhead electrical sockets for bare-bulb
illumination — but no switches. In lieu of switches, a wartime rarity, the
flow of electrical current to the bulbs was controlled crudely but effectively
by hooking and unhooking the bare ends of two wires.

Electricity to the Americans meant better lighting. Electricity to the Soviets meant the means of receiving news and propaganda via radio and
relaying the broadcasts throughout the camp by a loudspeaker system. At
first the din aggravated the airmen, but they soon learned to accept it and
even to ignore it.

November 4, 1943: Major Urov, a Red Army combat veteran from the
German front, arrived to take command of the camp. Richard Salter, Major Urov's point of contact with the internees, remembered Urov as being
a stocky, stoic Russian approaching middle age. Nona told Salter that Urov
was in constant pain from a stomach wound that he had received in a tank
battle. He spoke no English and, without a means of casual communication with the Americans, seemed aloof and authoritative.

On two occasions Urov made efforts to be sociable. Once, he invited
Salter and "Whitey" Wagner, the other senior American officer, to go with
him on a boar hunt. Only Urov was armed. No game was found. Later,
he invited Salter and Wagner (with Nona for interpretation) to a supper
served in an unused room of the main camp building.

November 5, 1943: The fence and wall surrounding the camp were in-
effective barriers. The more daring internees, responding to invitations,
filtered from the camp at night for clandestine visits in the homes of their
new friends or at some prearranged rendezvous.

During some of these noctural contacts the men learned how severe the
food shortage was for people not directly involved in war-related produc-
tivity. The people in this ignored category were literally nonpersons. Some
of the night-roaming internees related eyewitness stories of suffering by
such persons almost within sight of the camp. During some visits the men
frequently smuggled edible remnants from their own portions of the camp's
evening meal. Compassion of this sort was not limited to the Americans.
One of the Soviet camp housekeepers gave pieces of bread to a hungry
itinerant woodcutter at the camp. Instead of eating the bread, the woodcutter tried to sell it at the village bazaar. When he was reported and questioned, he revealed the source of the bread. Major Urov, the new com-

mandant, promptly dismissed the housekeeper. The Americans never saw her again.

November 6, 1943: Donald Dimel's ruptured spleen had been surgically removed at Petropavlovsk on August 14. He recovered from the stitch abscesses following the surgery and was able to travel with Pottenger's crew to the camp at Vrevskaya. Suddenly he developed recurring attacks of sharp abdominal pain. Appendicitis was suspected, and a Soviet doctor was called from Tashkent. Because Dimel was still convalescing from his earlier surgery, the doctor decided not to operate.

November 7, 1943: Pottenger, Salter, and others were acutely concerned about the ultimate outcome of Dimel's relapse. Salter, using a lead pencil on a sheet of rough paper, wrote a short letter to the American Embassy, appealing for help. "I stressed that I believed that Dimel would die if he were not moved to a place where he could get competent medical attention," Salter recalled. "I gave the letter to Urov. How the letter was transmitted to Moscow, I do not know."

Meanwhile, the Soviets asked the Americans to join them in celebrating the anniversary of the Red Revolution. The Soviets provided the inevitable vodka. There were patriotic toasts to Roosevelt, Churchill, and Stalin to be drunk, and patriotic songs to be sung until late at night. The celebration became boisterous. Most Russians had good voices, but the music was most strange, A. T. Miller reported.

November 8, 1943: The internees wryly referred to themselves as "the Air Corps grounded in deepest Asia." Grounded for how long? Not much longer, some of them vowed. They seriously began to seek information, primarily from displaced persons in the village, for making escape maps.

During recent weeks, as Joseph Dunwoody watched the trains pass through Vrevskaya, "the seed of the idea of escaping started to germinate." He sold his fountain pen for rubles to finance his idea. He bought a supply of apples and bread from the black market for the trip. Three elderly men in the village, he said, advised him to go generally east through the mountains into China.

At the same time, Irwin Lans (Salter's crew) also was making his own preparations for departure. Lans said that he managed to trace the pertinent details from an area wall map in Major Urov's office. Then, he said, he transferred the tracing to a handkerchief on which, using a needle and yarn borrowed from the intepreter Olga, he embroidered a map replica with key towns and railroad routes. (Lans has reported that both the map tracing and the embroidered handkerchief are framed and hanging on the walls of his home.) Onions and potatoes stolen from the camp's food tunnel provided his initial food supply. His planned destination, he recalled, was southwest to Ashkhabad, thence through the mountains into Iran.

November 9, 1943: Their mutual determination to leave the camp automatically drew Lans and Dunwoody together. Tense and impulsive, they were ready to go.

Undetected by the guard, the two men left the camp and headed directly for the railroad tracks. (The details of what happened after they reached the tracks over 40 years ago are in dispute still. However, there is no disputing the fact that their escape plans collapsed the next day.) In the early morning Lans and Dunwoody approached a long, high trestle spanning a river. After some hesitation in the predawn darkness, they cautiously started to walk toward the other end. "We were half-way across the trestle when two shots rang out," Dunwoody remembered. "Apparently we had awakened the sentry. . . . The shots aroused the whole military post as daylight arrived."

At first the suspicious Soviets believed that the two men were escaped German prisoners. After interrogation, however, they were identified as Americans and later returned to the camp.

Salter promptly ordered the men to the former horse stable for three days of solitary confinement. Dunwoody said that his isolation drew sympathetic reaction from Nona. She brought him a book of Shakespeare's plays, and he passed his confinement time by reading *Hamlet* and *King Lear.*

After reflecting on their thwarted adventure, both Dunwoody and Lans came to realize how impractical were their plans to penetrate the lofty, frigid mountains guarding the passage either to China or to Iran. At that time of year, the mountains, if not the inhospitable tribesmen, would have been deadly obstacles.

November 11, 1943: The amount and variety of food for the camp were still below the authorized level. To supplement the meager rations, some foodstuffs were found and obtained at the village bazaar or elsewhere by purchase, barter, or other means. Chickens were favorite procurement targets, especially those at a nearby state farm. John Taylor and Edward Taylor (unrelated) earned a reputation for being the most astute procurers of chickens in the camp. (John Taylor, however, now says that such a reputation was undeserved because, according to his memory, he acquired only one such fowl.)

November 13, 1943: Dysentery, one of the area's prevalent and uncomfortable endemic ailments, raced helter-skelter through the camp, and the most severely stricken of the men were hospitalized in Tashkent. One patient reported that his medication consisted of "something like berry wine and some pills that looked like sulfa." Athlete's foot infection also began to spread from the internees' use of the village bathing facilities.

The American Embassy estimated that 95 percent of the men developed dysentery at various times during their internment. Until the Soviet authorities were asked to enforce public sanitation measures in the bathhouse, the athlete's foot infection also took its toll among the internees.

November 15, 1943: A major in the Red Army Medical Corps arrived to be the resident doctor at the camp. A room in the main building was set aside for his office and dispensary. Called simply "Doc," the camp physician had few facilities, drugs, or supplies with which to try to maintain a minimum standard of medical care.

Before Doc was assigned to the camp, a doctor from Tashkent had to be requested on a case-by-case basis to administer medical advice and treatment. Because of the bureaucratic channels for obtaining the services of a doctor and his travel distance, emergency medical attention was never possible.

Fortunately, even after Doc's arrival, the physical health of the men — despite dysentery, foot infection, some malaria, and colds — rarely deteriorated into a medical crisis. Any internee whose condition required further diagnosis and treatment was sent to the military hospital in Tashkent.

November 19, 1943: Most of the men now had been interned for two months, and the remainder for three. Did the American Embassy know that they were alive? Had they been abandoned? James O'Dair made a plaintive notation in his diary that expressed the general feeling in the camp: "We've been here quite some time now, and we don't know yet what's going on. There is no indication that our Government and parents have been notified about us. I sure wish that something would break soon because the suspense is getting to me."

November 20, 1943: Depressed, O'Dair continued to reflect his anxiety in writing. "If only an American representative would come from Moscow and let us know the poop," he wrote.

"Our hopes are still high about being returned home," he said, "but we are not counting on it too highly. As violators of international law, we must take what we deserve."

November 22, 1943: Frantic because of a family crisis that had developed at the time of his last combat mission, Thomas Corbett (Wagner's crew) had convinced himself that he could escape via the railroad to the vicinity of the Iranian border near Ashkhabad. He said that he was desperate and he wanted to try. He discussed his situation and plan with Wagner, who listened compassionately. In turn, Wagner asked for Salter's blessing. Wagner and Salter agreed to "look the other way," and they organized an escape kit containing food and rubles from the black market.

Corbett's disappearance from the camp was not immediately noticed. Unchallenged, he struggled aboard a jammed train bound for Ashkhabad.

November 23, 1943: In Moscow, Maj. John F. Waldron, an Army Medical Corps officer attached to the U.S. Military Mission, was assigned to go to Tashkent in order to verify and report the internees' state of health and conditions under which they were living. Through the Red Army's Foreign Liaison Office, or OVS, Waldron obtained Soviet permission to make the 2,000-mile railroad journey.[18] He waited impatiently for transportation to be arranged.

November 24, 1943: For two days Corbett kept to himself on the train in order not to attract attention. Then, because the food in his escape kit was low, he decided to buy some bread or fruit when the train reached its next stop. That decision was his undoing. His inability to speak Russian immediately aroused suspicion. Alert Soviet security officials detained him, and he was obliged to identify himself.

Although he had nearly reached his first objective (Ashkhabad), Corbett, like Dunwoody and Lans before him, had learned that any successful escape would require planning in far more detail than he or any of his fellow internees had dreamed.

November 25, 1943: As Thanksgiving Day approached, the airmen resolved to celebrate the special day as festively as their situation would permit. Through contacts in the village, they located two geese priced at $60 each. Harry Koepp (Salter's navigator) had carried nearly $200 in his pocket since he was interned, and he volunteered to finance the purchase of the geese, which became the main Thanksgiving entrée. Loyal Fry (Rodger's copilot) and O'Dair "had a big time hunting . . . chickens, and we finally succeeded in buying two for a nominal fee." The Soviets, always welcoming the prospect of a party of any sort, also agreed to provide other festive dinner items such as extra fowl, vegetables and pastries, together with wine, vodka, and spirits.

The geese and chickens were roasted over outdoor fires for the dinner, which was served at 11:00 A.M. "By the time the meal was finished," O'Dair said, "everybody was so happy that they didn't care whether the sun rose or set. I figure we all had a good time, and it is indeed one Thanksgiving that we shall not forget in the years to come." (Ironically, 45 years later, few of the internees who were present at the impromptu dinner can recall it.)

November 26, 1943: Thomas Corbett, whose attempt to escape was interrupted short of Ashkhabad, was returned to the camp. Although he had advance knowledge of Corbett's venture, Salter said that he had no choice but to mete out punishment (for failure, it seemed) similar to that imposed on Dunwoody and Lans: solitary confinement in the horse stable for three days.

November 27, 1943: Typhus fever, another disease endemic to the Tashkent area, reached epidemic proportions, and all the communities between Tashkent and Vrevskaya were quarantined. Even though the camp kitchen personnel and charwomen who lived in Vrevskaya were permitted to go

18. U.S. Embassy Moscow message 2021 to State Department, November 23, 1943, State Department General Files.

to their village homes each evening, the Americans were confined to the camp. Perhaps the internees did not understand the reason for their confinement. Perhaps they assumed that the confinement was the Soviet reaction to the attempted escapes. In any event, some of the men continued to evade the camp guards at night in order to make their visits beyond the camp borders.

November 28, 1943: There still was no word of any kind from the American Embassy. A Red Army colonel from the Tashkent Soviet Command visited the camp and complained to Salter about the lack of military courtesy. Salter, reflecting the internees' frustration, gave the colonel what amounted to an ultimatum: "I told him," Salter said, "if we did not get word to prove that our people in Moscow knew where we were, I would march our men out of the camp at the end of ten days!"

November 29, 1943: Although the men protested that their individual portions of food were still insufficient, they seemed to feel that their meals had improved since Major Urov's arrival. They could not understand, however, why they were not provided more fresh vegetables and fruit, some of which were grown locally. *Nyet,* Urov said, because the local farm produce was not for their use. Instead, it was harvested and sent to the fighting Red Army. Besides, Urov insisted, the Americans were better fed than the Red Army troops.

December 1, 1943: Some of the men had been working to convert parts of the outdoor grounds into playing fields for various sports. At last, the first game of the "baseball season" was ready to be played.

The game equipment was improvised. A bat was carved from a willow tree trunk, and a softball was made from unraveled woolen stocking yarn wrapped around a wine-bottle cork and covered with boot-top leather. The new softball diamond had a backstop of woven reeds and bases marked by hand-sewn bags filled with sand.

December 2, 1943: Transportation arrangements for Major Waldron's travel from Moscow to Tashkent were now approved, allowing him to board a train that would start him on what would be a three-week journey to his destination. Accompanying Waldron was Capt. Victor Ogorodnik, a staff officer from the OVS. The purpose of Ogorodnik's trip to Tashkent, he said, was to investigate the living conditions of the internees. By coincidence, his planned visit had a schedule identical to Waldron's, and he rarely allowed Waldron to be alone.

December 5, 1943: Major Urov delivered a telegram from the American Embassy to Salter. The text was garbled, but the sense of it read: "Maj. John Waldron and representatives of the U.S. Diplomatic Corps are coming soon to see you. Members of the U.S. Embassy and Military Mission greet you and send their best wishes. (Signed) Maj. Gen. Sidney P. Spalding."

The news of the telegram's arrival flashed through the camp, and the internees greeted it with elation. They were not lost! they whooped. The embassy knew where they were!

The air was filled with questions. Why had the embassy waited so long to contact them? Waldron "and representatives" were coming soon — how soon was "soon"? (Waldron would be the sole American visitor.) Who was General Spalding? (He was chief of the U.S. Military Mission's Lend-Lease Division. During General Deane's temporary absences from Moscow, Spalding was the acting mission chief.)

December 7, 1943: The Tashkent Soviet Command was also informed about the forthcoming visit. Following a trip to the Soviet military headquarters in Tashkent, Doc informed Vladimir Sabich that "the attaché may be coming by train." (The U.S. Military Attaché's Office had been abolished a month earlier, but the Soviets were not yet acquainted with the new U.S. Military Mission terminology and titles.)

December 9, 1943: The camp was restless yet unusually quiet, as though the men were listening for approaching footsteps. The only visitor, however, was a Red Army colonel from Tashkent. He conferred with Urov, after which the charwomen began vigorously scrubbing the floors and tidying the building.

December 11, 1943: Floyd Amundson and Robert Dyxin (Putnam's crew) ignored the quarantine and slipped into the village, where they were seen and reported to Salter. As their penalty, they were assigned to duty as Officers of the Day (OD) for an extended length of time. OD was a confining but not a difficult function to perform; it was coming to be recognized as a punishment detail at the camp.

December 12, 1943: Perhaps because morale had been lifted by the news of the approaching Moscow visitor, the internees' improvised and simple Catholic and Protestant church services were attended better than usual.

December 14, 1943: After several days of suspenseful silence, the Red Army colonel from Tashkent returned to the camp and predicted to Urov that the representative from the American Embassy would arrive about December 18. Many of the men, not trusting Soviet wartime train schedules, were skeptical. Wagner, however, was not. He issued a challenge by wagering two-to-one that Waldron would arrive at the camp, if not by December 18, then certainly not later than December 21.

Salter and Wagner saw the promised visit as an opportunity for them to write and deliver eyewitness reports of both B-25 and B-24 bombing missions over Paramushiro and Shumushu on September 11–12. Other internees, anticipating that Waldron could act as a mail courier, wrote letters, which now would have a better chance of being sent to their families.

December 19, 1943: The day on which the Red Army colonel had predicted that Waldron would appear came and went. Urov returned from a conference in Tashkent and announced that Waldron would be at the camp "any day now."

December 21, 1943: Waldron arrived in Tashkent in late afternoon. For whatever reason, he was further delayed in the city for another two days, a delay that cost Wagner $180 in lost wagers.

Meanwhile, Salter received a second telegram from General Spalding. The telegram reported the receipt of Salter's November 7 letter asking help for Dimel. Spalding said that the letter was received December 19, which meant that it had taken six weeks to reach Moscow.

December 22, 1943: There was a flurry of renewed cleaning activity at the camp, and tempers were short among the Soviet staff. Nona was certain that "the man" would come to the camp today. He did not.

December 23, 1943: Waldron, accompanied by Ogorodnik and an official escort from the Tashkent Soviet Command, was delivered by automobile to the camp in early afternoon. After the formalities of greeting the senior American officers and Urov, Waldron requested a general meeting with all internees present. Waldron had hoped to have a private meeting with the Americans, but that seemed impossible because Ogorodnik and Urov became his shadows. He told the internees that their Paramushiro raid had been widely reported in the United States, and he read a letter from General Deane congratulating the crews.

He quietly renewed the hope of release from the Soviet Union. He pointed out that the Soviets had no choice when the Americans flew their disabled planes into neutral country; the Americans were legally interned. He assured the internees, however, that the American Embassy was not pessimistic about their future.

Urov and Ogorodnik watched helplessly while individual internees thrust into Waldron's pockets an assortment of scribbled notes, the bombing mission reports, three cameras (which had been concealed since the time of the crash landings on September 12), two exposed rolls of film, and personal letters for safe delivery to Moscow in Waldron's diplomatic lock pouch. Salter recalled that Wagner also handed a flashlight to Waldron, but he never learned what was concealed in the barrel of the flashlight.

At one point, Waldron and Wagner frustrated the Soviet monitors by speaking pig-Latin, which even the astute Nona was unable to understand. Anthony Homitz (Pottenger's crew) and Vladimir Sabich engaged Ogorodnik and Urov in a spirited conversation to divert their attention, giving Salter an opportunity for a private discussion with Waldron. As a result, Waldron revealed that York was no longer in the Soviet Union because "he and his crew went over the hill, but they did so with Soviet help." Waldron said that he tried to obtain permission to go to Ashkhabad to see the York crew in April, but "the Soviets stalled while York was leaving the Soviet Union. So, when the Soviets began stalling my visit to Tashkent, I thought that you also were being helped into Iran."

December 24, 1943: Waldron made a cursory medical examination of each internee and concluded, as expressed in his official report, that the "general health of the interned men is good."[19] The only exception was Donald Dimel, for whom Waldron recommended further observation and treatment at the earliest opportunity in an American hospital in Tehran or the United States. He added that local Soviet medical authorities concurred in the recommendation because "Dimel is no longer a combatant and there is no need for internment, and Soviet physicians are unable to treat him further."

When Waldron departed Moscow three weeks earlier, he had put two vials of typhus vaccine in his baggage. One vial froze and broke during the long winter journey. Using the vaccine in the remaining vial, he was able to give each internee only a booster inoculation that, he said, should provide enough protection until additional vaccine could be obtained.

Waldron also brought with him a box containing books, magazines, athletic equipment, cigarettes, and toilet articles such as soap, razors, and dental supplies. He promised to try to arrange for additional items — clothing, medical supplies, and tinned food — to be shipped from Tehran.

He wanted to delay his departure from the camp, but the Soviet officials from Tashkent insisted on leaving in midafternoon. Sabich wrote that "Waldron will try to come again tomorrow and take a photograph of us that he will send home, but I don't think we will ever see him again." Sabich's prophecy was correct.

During his visit, Waldron urged that there be no further attempts to escape because those actions could upset any negotiation that the embassy might undertake to obtain an early release of the men. On his departure, he again assured the men that there was hope — but he made no specific promises.

Even as Waldron's vehicle disappeared up the road, the men tried to develop some sort of Christmas spirit by singing Christmas carols. James Dixon wrote out the words for four carols from memory: "Holy God," "Adeste Fidelis," "Silent Night," and "O Little Town of Bethlehem." He encouraged the early carol singing by playing the music on the piano. The singing continued intermittently during the remainder of the day, but according to Sabich, "all they succeeded in doing was to make everybody all the sadder." Sabich later wrote, "All in all it was the poorest Christmas Eve I have ever spent."

19. John F. Waldron, undated official report, "Trip to Tashkent, December 2–30, 1943," "Internees" files.

December 25, 1943: When Waldron arrived, he had brought excitement to the isolated men. His departure had the opposite effect: gloom settled over the camp.

The Christmas dinner menu was not a lavish one. It included, however, some chicken and the first polished rice that the men had seen in the Soviet Union. And, of course, vodka and a bottle of wine for each four-man table. A. T. Miller wrote that he did not remember too much about Christmas dinner except the bourbon whiskey that Waldron had brought to the camp. Miller said he thought that "we got lit up." Gerald Green reported, "It seemed like we had a small Christmas tree, but I don't remember where it came from."

After dinner, Salter called a general meeting of the men and distributed the toilet articles that Waldron had delivered. The magazines and books were made available for reading. So ended Christmas Day at Vrevskaya.

Not many internees were able to recall Christmas 1943. Sabich, however, made a record of his feelings. "This is sure a hell of a place to spend Christmas, and what a dull, dismal Christmas it is!"

December 26, 1943: The after-Christmas atmosphere in the camp continued to be somber. Many of the men, because the weather was turning colder, remained indoors and read.

Remembering Waldron's departure plea for the men to forgo any further attempts to escape, Sabich became agitated when he discovered that a map that he had drawn of an escape route to Tehran was missing. "There is sure going to be hell to pay if the Russians find the damn thing," he wrote. He searched frantically but found no trace.

The men had complained to Waldron that the Soviet security officials were searching the internees' rooms when the internees were absent at meals or the bathhouse. Sabich recalled that he had spent hours dismantling and modifying a small table beside his cot so that a hidden nail would lock the table's drawer. He doubted that the searchers ever learned the secret of the lock. The escape map, however, had not been hidden in the drawer. Sabich finally found the map eight days later on January 3, but he could not recall how or where the map reappeared.

January 1, 1944: Although the airmen were not in a festive state of mind, Urov urged the internees to join him and the Soviet staff in celebrating New Year's. Before midnight a cold meal was served, and beer and wine helped the internees to adopt some of the party mood displayed by the Soviets. In the aftermath of the midnight levity, the camp became quiet and remained so until after dinner when a Soviet music-and-dance troupe arrived to provide New Year's entertainment.

January 4, 1944: The combination of unpleasant weather and enforced inactivity produced a tense atmosphere in the camp. The airmen continued to brood about their predicament. Quarreling erupted. Some of the men aimlessly played poker for cigarettes, others slept or read, and still others continued to defy the quarantine by making evening trips into the village.

Early January, 1944: After Major Waldron completed his railroad return trip to Moscow on December 30, he prepared his detailed report. Since several of Waldron's recommendations required immediate attention, General Deane called them to the attention of Ambassador Harriman. In turn, Harriman made arrangements to discuss them with Foreign Minister Molotov.

When advised of Donald Dimel's condition, Molotov agreed that Dimel should be evacuated from Tashkent to Tehran by Soviet plane.[20] At the same time, Harriman told Molotov that the American commander in Tehran would be requested to assemble essential supplies for shipment to the internees, and he asked for a Soviet airplane to transport the supplies to Tashkent. Again, Molotov agreed. The ambassador explained that he had asked for only one planeload of supplies because he did not expect that the internees would have a lengthy confinement in the Soviet Union. The internees, he related, regarded the Soviet Union as an ally, and therefore it was difficult for them to understand the reason for an indefinite detention. Molotov said that he could appreciate that point of view and that he too did not expect their presence in Soviet Union to be prolonged.[21]

January 13, 1944: Dimel's abdominal pains became more acute, and he was transferred to the Tashkent military hospital.

Late January, 1944: The typhus fever epidemic worsened, according to reports from the Soviets. The quarantine was still in effect but was difficult to enforce. In addition, even before the quarantine was ordered, Salter had established a midnight curfew for the men to be in their rooms, but the curfew was not always observed. On one occasion, Urov sent one of his lieutenants into the village after midnight to return Thomas Corbett to the camp. In exchange for Corbett's promise not to repeat his breaking quarantine and curfew, Urov said that he would not report Corbett's violation to Salter. Urov kept his word and remained silent. Nona, however, later informed Salter.

January 31, 1944: The Soviet-made shirts and trousers for which the men were measured three months earlier, began arriving, with the first sets being delivered to Salter and Wagner. A. T. Miller said that the garments "were made of a heavy khaki woolen material. The shirt was always on the baggy side." Sabich said that "they looked pretty good. It was British material and resembled RAF stuff."

February 1, 1944: In Moscow, the Soviets were obviously satisfied that

20. Deane, *Strange Alliance,* 60.
21. Richard C. Lukas, "Escape," *Aerospace Historian,* Spring, 1969, 15.

the security involving the York crew's departure from the Soviet Union had not been breached, for there had been no revelation in the American news media or Japanese reaction in diplomatic channels. An intricate plan devised by the NKVD had been approved for the escape of the internees held at the Tashkent camp.[22] The plan was now ready for execution.

February 2, 1944: Urov was notified by telegram from Moscow that Dimel would be sent home immediately.

In Moscow, General Deane outlined the NKVD escape plan to Lt. Col. Robert McCabe and instructed him to contact General Ivanov of the NKVD to make the final arrangements. McCabe, as an assistant military attaché, visited the York crew at Okhansk in October, 1942. Now a member of the U.S. Military Mission staff, McCabe was the designated American escort officer who would lead the 60 internees from the Soviet Union in accordance with the unfolding NKVD plan.

In his official report, McCabe explained that later in the day he met with General Ivanov and Colonel Myakhotnik of the NKVD and General Evstigneev and Captain Kozlovski of the OVS. McCabe wrote:

> General Ivanov went over the plan carefully with me. He explained that Colonel Myakhotnik and Captain Kozlovski would accompany me. Both officers were well acquainted with the plan and would make necessary contacts along the way.
>
> I explained that I would take all the necessary precautions for security as far as the American personnel were concerned. I also described the purpose of the letter of instructions General Deane had given me to give to Major Salter, directing him and his men to proceed to the Caucasus for the purpose of ferrying Lend-Lease planes to destinations in Russia. This letter of instructions would make the order to move appear more authentic and the subsequent escape more real.[23]

February 3, 1944: At the camp, charwomen scrubbed and cleaned through the night of February 2–3 because an American doctor, they said, was coming from Iran. In the afternoon, Captain Haynes, a Medical Corps officer, arrived at the Tashkent air base in a Soviet airplane carrying two truckloads of supplies from the Persian Gulf Command's Camp Amirabad. He delivered the supplies to the internment camp after dinner. Among the contents of the boxes was clothing that had been ordered when Major Waldron had visited the camp on Christmas Eve. Other boxes contained medical supplies, fruit juices, and whiskey.

In Moscow, Colonel McCabe, Colonel Myakhotnik, and Captain Kozlovski boarded a train for a six-day trip to Tashkent.[24]

22. Deane, *Strange Alliance,* 60. NKVD's General P. D. Ivanov had responsibility for devising the elaborate escape plan.

23. Robert E. McCabe, undated official summary, "Report of Escape of American Internees (February 2–20, 1944)," "Internees" files, 1.

24. Ibid.

February 4, 1944: Captain Haynes announced that he was taking Donald Dimel aboard the Soviet plane with him to Tehran. Before departing, the doctor reinoculated each internee with typhus fever vaccine.

In Moscow, General Deane dispatched a top-secret message to the Persian Gulf Command marked "for General Connolly's Eyes Only." The message stated that 59 internees now at Tashkent would arrive at Tehran on or about February 20 under command of Colonel McCabe.

> The details of their departure from Russia are of utmost secrecy. I have instructed McCabe to take them directly to Amirabad, and it would be well if you could keep them separated from other officers and enlisted men to prevent leakage. . . . I will send you by air their names, grades, and serial numbers in order that you may issue orders sending them from Tehran to Algiers. Because of the possibility of leakage through Axis agents in Tehran, it would be advisable to send them to Algiers as soon as possible after their arrival in Tehran. . . . One of the internees, Sgt Dimel, is seriously ill. He will arrive in Tehran separately by air. . . . He should be instructed to preserve the utmost secrecy regarding the whole project.[25]

Actually, there were 60, not 59, internees being escorted by McCabe. Somehow, the name of Hutchen Hammond (Putnam's crew) apparently was never reported by the Soviets to the U.S. Military Mission. The omission was possibly due to the confusion encountered by the Soviets when they tried to identify the crews of seven American bombers arriving simultaneously at Petropavlovsk in September.

February 7, 1944: Because of chronic chest colds and fever, Vladimir Sabich and Arnold Saugestad (Wagner's crew) entered the Tashkent military hospital.

February 8, 1944: Richard Filler (Pottenger's copilot) was also hospitalized. "The camp food was not substantial," he explained. "I complained of a stomach pain because I thought that the hospital food would be better. When I entered the hospital, the first thing that the doctor did was to pump my stomach! When I was allowed to eat, the hospital food was the same as the camp's."

February 9, 1944: McCabe and the two Soviet officers from Moscow arrived at Tashkent after dark and went to a hotel. Myakhotnik and Kozlovski immediately began making arrangements for railway cars, food, and other items for the projected movement of the internees.

February 10, 1944: The two Soviet officers had additional conversations with local NKVD and Red Army officers regarding the final arrangements for the trip. Then, with McCabe, they were driven to the internment camp at Vrevskaya. McCabe wrote:

25. U.S. Embassy Moscow, unnumbered message to Tehran, February 4, 1944, "Internees" files.

Arriving at the camp late in the afternoon, I was introduced to Major Urov and Major Salter. . . . I explained to Major Salter the purpose of my visit and handed him the false order from General Deane for the movement to the Caucasus. Colonel Myakhotnik and Major Urov were both present at the time.

I then told Major Salter that I wanted him to announce the trip to all the men at a meeting before supper that night, following which I would give him certain instructions for the trip.

When Major Salter read General Deane's orders to the internees, there was loud and prolonged cheering. I explained that permission to utilize their services in the Caucasus had been obtained after prolonged discussions and negotiations with the Soviets and that it was of primary importance that nothing happen on the trip that might embarrass further negotiations. This meant first of all that no attempt would be made to escape, since the previous attempts had caused considerable embarrassment.[26]

February 11, 1944: McCabe's official report continued:

I discussed with Colonel Myakhotnik our impressions of what had occurred the night before. Both of us agreed that no one in the camp had any apparent suspicion as to what was being planned. Colonel Myakhotnik informed me that neither the local Soviet officials, those in the camp or on the railroads knew what was to happen. They had merely been told what they were to do as far as was necessary to perform their job. It was apparent that the Soviet security plans were thorough.[27]

Most of the excited internees did not question the truth of Deane's letter. Urov and Nona somehow learned what was the real plan. Nona told Salter, "You are not going to the Caucasus. You are going home!" If any others suspected what Salter knew, they kept their thoughts to themselves.

The three men in the hospital (Sabich, Filler, and Saugestad) were visited by Myakhotnik and Kozlovski, who informed them of the planned movement to the Caucasus. The news was a miracle cure. Within the hour the three men were dismissed from the hospital and were en route to the Vrevskaya camp. They found the camp noisy and rowdy.

The men were told to pack their clothing in preparation for moving. As one internee later complained, "We were not allowed to take a single thing that could be identified as Russian. Not even a cigarette!" The reason for this prohibition was not explained, nor did the exuberant men question it. At the request of the internees as well as the Soviet officials, a farewell banquet was served, after which the festivities with wine and vodka continued into the night.

February 12, 1944: The departure, originally scheduled for February 13, was postponed until the following day.

26. McCabe, "Report of Escape of American Internees," 2.
27. Ibid., 4.

February 13, 1944: Two railroad cars were placed on a sidetrack at the Vrevskaya village station. "We returned from Tashkent to check the two railroad coaches and other final preparations," McCabe wrote. "I inspected the food, clothing, and cars and found everything satisfactory. The food was divided up into individual rations for each man for a five-day trip, supposedly from the camp to Tiflis in the Caucasus."

Sabich made a record of the rations. Each man was given "1½ loaves of bread, ½ kilo butter, ½ kilo sugar, 16 hard-boiled eggs, 4 sticks of sausage, 1 can of sardines, 4 cans of beef, 2 small packages of cocoa, and knife, fork, spoon, and glass. We also got a gallon jug of preserved apples for each two men. Each man packed his grub in a pillow case."

February 14, 1944: In the early morning all 60 internees entrained. One of the railroad cars was a second-class coach (soft class) for the officers, and the other one a third-class coach (hard class) for the other internees. The conductor was dressed as a railroad man but actually was a member of the NKVD with a key role to play in the execution of the escape plan.

Several of the camp staff came to the station to watch the men board the cars. Kozlovski was not scheduled to go farther, but he, Urov, and Nona walked through the coaches to bid good-bye.

At the last minute, Myakhotnik and McCabe decided that the men could not take their puppy mascot Skoro with them. One of the men wanted to hide the puppy in the railroad car but was persuaded to put it off the train.

The coaches were coupled to the regular train bound for Ashkhabad. The final leg of the internees' odyssey through neutral country had begun.

February 15, 1944: As programmed in the plan's scenario, McCabe found an occasion during the afternoon to alert Salter that the conductor had reported "there was something wrong with the car Salter was traveling in, but the conductor did not appear to be concerned about it."

At 10:30 P.M. the conductor told Myakhotnik and McCabe that they were approaching the station where, according to the plan, the internees' coaches would be uncoupled. McCabe informed Salter that one of the cars was probably not in condition to proceed farther, so it might be necessary to cut off both of the cars in order to keep the group together. From this point on, McCabe wrote, the conductor did some excellent acting. He pulled the emergency cord to stop the train, and he and the engineer met outside the coaches. "There was considerable talking and pounding on the questionable car," McCabe said, "and also lanterns flashing around on the outside. Although some of the internees were asleep, most of them heard and saw what was going on."

One hour later when the train stopped again, the conductor told McCabe that the two cars would be detached at the next stop because of one car's dangerous condition. After pretending to discuss the matter with

Myakhotnik, McCabe told Salter that the cars would be cut off at a siding about 11 miles east of Ashkhabad.

"I told him that I was to go on to Ashkhabad on the train with Colonel Myakhotnik and make arrangements for them to proceed by truck into Ashkhabad. . . . I told him I would be gone probably three hours and wanted the men packed and ready to move as soon as I returned. There was to be no movement off the cars while I was gone," McCabe ordered.[28]

At midnight, the two coaches were shunted to the isolated siding as planned. The train, carrying Myakhotnik and McCabe, continued to Ashkhabad.

February 16, 1944: A short time later the train arrived at Ashkhabad, where Myakhotnik and McCabe were met by another NKVD colonel. In a hotel room the NKVD colonel outlined the arrangements that had been made.

1. The NKVD had selected a route through precipitous mountains and desert country from Ashkhabad across the Iranian border to Quchan, thence near Sabzevar and Semnan to Tehran.

2. A convoy would be formed of five Lend-Lease trucks, four to carry the men and one to haul gasoline and oil. The vehicles would appear to be tarpaulin-covered cargo trucks that would not attract any unusual attention, since all trucks crossing the border traveled under similar cover. The internees were to remain hidden until the trucks had safely entered Iran.

3. Myakhotnik would not accompany the convoy. Instead, he and the local NKVD colonel and the commander of the border station all would be at the border crossing point to make certain that the convoy entered the Soviet occupation zone of Iran without any delay or incidents.

Following the hotel conference, McCabe was taken to the truck park, where he met the convoy commander, Lieutenant Nikitin, and the five truck drivers, each of whom was attired in nondescript Central Asian dress. All of them were NKVD personnel.

At four o'clock in the morning, McCabe with the five trucks arrived at the railroad siding where the anxious internees waited in the two coaches. McCabe called the officers together and explained that he had obtained the trucks and local drivers to take them to Tehran.

"No one said a word when this was announced," Sabich recalled, "because he told us that we would have to be quiet. We were not to talk or smoke when the trucks were stopped, and no one was to peep out of the curtains."

McCabe directed Salter to divide the men among four trucks, with at

28. Ibid., 3.

least one officer in each truck. To both officers and enlisted men McCabe reiterated the necessity for absolute secrecy concerning their escape.[29]

Within 20 minutes the trucks were silently loaded. The convoy bypassed Ashkhabad on the southeast side and joined the main highway running south toward the border. Then the convoy commander stopped the trucks briefly. He asked McCabe, who was riding in the cab of the first truck, to get behind the tarpaulin curtains with the internees. At 5:30 the convoy arrived at the border, halted for a short time while the drivers' documents were inspected, and then continued into Iran.

In reminiscences about the escape, McCabe wrote, "I remained in the back of the truck for about an hour when the convoy again stopped. I was asked to get back into the cab with the driver and Lieutenant Nikitin. I understood that the reason for my being hidden was that the Soviets did not want the Iranian border police to see an American when we entered Iran."

The NKVD scenario estimated that the convoy would require 48 hours to complete the journey. The estimate proved to be a very good one: Harry Koepp clocked the elapsed time as being 52 hours. McCabe said, "I think . . . the Soviets tried to keep away from well-traveled roads to avoid any possible detection." For the first 12 hours the route took the convoy through towering mountains where the road curves were so sharp that the trucks had to back up in order to maneuver around them. The men huddled under the tarpaulin cover to share body heat against the biting cold. In the mountains the road was muddy, but the route across the flatlands was dry, and the crowded men choked on dust. Short rest stops were made every two to three hours. One longer rest stop of nearly four hours was used to allow the drivers to nap.

February 18, 1944: Shortly after four A.M. the convoy approached Tehran from the southeast. The trucks followed one another closely as McCabe guided the column through the silent city toward Camp Amirabad. To the casual observer, the column of trucks was simply another Lend-Lease or Soviet military convoy.

By seven A.M. Tehran time, the men had been unloaded at the door of a camp hospital wing, and the exhausted former internees had bathed, eaten, and gone to bed. They would be confined in the hospital wing during their short time in Iran.

When they awakened, the men were again told to surrender any item that might be a clue to the fact that they had been in or had come from the Soviet Union. The surrendered items were impounded, and some of them were released after the end of the war.

McCabe's official report noted, "I again explained to the entire group

29. Ibid., 4.

the secrecy of their movement from Russia, the necessity for the secrecy, and the security measures that must be taken. They also all signed a pledge of secrecy for the duration of the war, all copies of which were later burned without their knowledge."[30]

"I had been to Tehran before and knew many of the officers of the Persian Gulf Command," McCabe's report continued. "During my stay there, I met and talked with many of them, but none were conscious of the presence of the former internees in the camp as far as I could determine. The officers or men who, of necessity, knew of the presence of the internees never discussed it or asked questions."

In his concluding comments, McCabe said:

> The arrangements made by the NKVD and Red Army and General Connolly's Command were excellent. It is doubtful if the plans for security could have been made more airtight. However, the crews themselves were probably doubtful as to whether the escape was real or planned by the Soviets. Events moved so rapidly that the internees were too confused and tired to note everything that occurred. However, the manner in which one event fitted into the next so smoothly must have left some doubt in their minds about the escape.[31]

February 20, 1944: After two days of being paid, doctored, gorged, cleansed, and clothed, the 60 airmen, who now were identified as members of War Department Special Detachment No. 1, inconspicuously boarded trucks at the Camp Amirabad hospital. Three U.S. C-54 aircraft and security escorts waited for them at the Tehran airport. Before noon the former internees were airborne and bound for Cairo. In late afternoon after a nonstop flight, they landed at Payne Field, where they were isolated in barracks at the airbase.

February 21, 1944: While behind-the-scenes alternatives were being debated about where to move the "escapees," local authorities planned a tour of the pyramids for the men. According to Salter, the sudden appearance of a dust storm forced cancellation of the trip. Instead, the men remained on the base. Some of the men were allowed to visit the base Post Exchange after again being warned to observe the imposed rules of secrecy.

"All I remember about our stop-over at Cairo," A. T. Miller said, "was a continuous poker game played with the U.S. dollar partial payments which had been made to the men at Camp Amirabad." Vladimir Sabich, he recalled, "was in his element!"

February 22, 1944: They again boarded aircraft and began another flight westward. James O'Dair reported that the sun was shining and the visibility was perfect, so they were able to glimpse the Sphinx and some

30. Ibid., 5.
31. Ibid.

of the pyramids. For most of the men, this sight was their only vivid memory of their 40-hour delay in Cairo. Their transports landed at Benghazi for refueling, then continued to Tunis.

February 23, 1944: The former internees remained in the vicinity of Tunis for over a month. The officers were sent to a villa at Sidi-bou-Zid, and the enlisted men were given comfortable billeting in the nearby village of La Marsa.

Washington was still pondering the problem of how to ensure that the secret of the escape could be kept. Within a few days, Salter said, "I was ordered to report to General McNarney, who commanded the Fifteenth Air Force, at Caserta, Italy. He told me that they did not know what to do with us. He mentioned that serious thought had been given to putting us on an island somewhere in the Mediterranean."

As A. T. Miller later interpreted the situation, a decision was made for them to "spend more than 30 days in Tunis so it would seem that we had been stationed as a unit there." Then it could be made to appear that War Department Special Detachment No. 1 was being rotated back to the United States from normal duty abroad.

The officers were well situated in the villa owned and occupied by the Baroness d'Erlanger. "Some of us played bridge almost daily with the old lady and her friends," Miller said.

The airmen were given freedom of movement for the first time. Some of the officers took advantage of this new policy by making short sightseeing trips to Italy and Algiers. The relaxation of the earlier restrictions also allowed the enlisted men to visit Tunis.

During this time, Irwin Lans was still suffering from chronic diarrhea. Because of the secrecy, Lans wrote that when he went to a Tunis air-base doctor for relief, "I was unable to explain why I suffering. I could not explain where I had been or what I had eaten." Without these essential medical clues, Lans said, "the doctor did the best he could to alleviate the problem."

March 27, 1944: The 60 escapees, it had been decided in Washington, would be returned to the United States as soon as possible. They were promptly flown to Casablanca to await a ship.

April 7, 1944: The ship was the *Gen. Billy Mitchell,* a new troop transport that was completing its second round-trip Atlantic crossing. The ten-day voyage passed uneventfully. The indoctrinated men instinctively kept to themselves and were contented with the notion that they were finally on the way home.

April 17, 1944: After they disembarked from the *Mitchell* at Newport News, Virginia, the men were immediately requested to sign new certificates that rigidly and officially bound them to pledges of silence. This time the pledges, unlike those made to McCabe in Tehran, were not destroyed.

Some members of the second group of escaped internees marking time in comfort near Tunis in March, 1944. *Front row:* Norman Savignac, Winfred Vandiver, Richard Filler, James Pottenger, Vladimir Sabich, Wayne Marrier, and Floyd Amundson. *Back row:* Richard Salter, Norman Eastmoore, John Keithley, Robert Wiles, Harold Hodges, Carl ("Whitey") Wagner, (Colonel Irwin [OIC]), Russell Hurst, Benson Black, John Taylor, and Edward Taylor. Photograph courtesy Vladimir Sabich

May 5, 1944: To expand on the scope of the pledges of silence signed on April 17, the War Department's Military Intelligence Division issued a letter to each of the repatriates. Pertinent extracts of the letter included the following:

You are further advised that regardless of any mention you may observe in the press or hear on the radio concerning American airmen and their activities in the country from which you were recently repatriated, you are cautioned that at no time will you give any information whatsoever to anyone — family, friends or military personnel of whatever rank — concerning repatriation from or presence in the country of repatriation.

Details concerning your presence in that country, journey to that country and subsequent repatriation therefrom are matters of vital military security. The mere mention of your name or circumstances of your service in the press or on the radio will jeopardize the security and repatriation of your fellow airmen. . . .

You will acknowledge receipt by signing one copy on the line indicated below and returning it in the inclosed, addressed, double envelopes. . . . The other copy may be retained by you and shown *only* to officers of the United States Army, if necessary.[32]

August 4, 1944: Eventually, after two weeks of interrogation and several weeks of home leaves were completed, the former internees were briefly reassembled at the Army Air Forces Tactical Center at Orlando, Florida. Still concerned that information about the escape from the Soviet Union might leak, the commanding general of the center was directed to sign and issue a special memorandum for each man to carry on his person. The memorandum was meant not so much as a directive to inquisitive individuals but as a constant reminder to each former internee of his secrecy pledge.

"TO WHOM IT MAY CONCERN," the memorandum read. "The nature of [identification by grade and name] last overseas assignment and record is highly secret. He will not be subjected to interrogation by military personnel, nor will he be interviewed by the public press or radio regarding his service or experiences, nor will he be reassigned outside the continental limits of the United States."

In most cases, the military records of each man contained a three-word notation to cover the months of service that he spent in "neutral country." The notation was simply "missing in action." For the public record, none of the 61 men had ever been in the Soviet Union. Therefore, they could not have escaped from the Soviet Union.

32. Letter, War Department Military Intelligence Division G-2, Washington, D.C., May 5, 1944, subj.: "Military Security."

5

Navy Flyers Interned
1944

> *We had been saved from the sea. Somebody had put a run-*
> *way under our damaged plane. We had been fed and*
> *given a place to sleep. . . . After all these years, I remem-*
> *ber the friendliness of the Russian soldiers and people.*
> — John P. Vivian, July, 1987

Vice President Henry Wallace flew from Alaska across Siberia and thence to Tashkent before continuing his 1944 journey to Chungking, China. On June 14, Ambassador Harriman met Wallace in Tashkent, where together they visited agricultural experiment stations and observed the work of Soviet scientists who were developing improved cotton, potatoes, and melons.[1] Neither Harriman nor Wallace was aware that the nearby internment camp, now empty, would soon be occupied again, this time by U.S. Navy flyers with clipped wings.

In the same 1944 summertime period, Eric Johnston, president of the United States Chamber of Commerce, was on an official tour of the Soviet Union. He entered the Soviet Union via Alaska and across Siberia on the ALSIB route. During his visit to Tashkent, a well-dressed, English-speaking woman acted as a Soviet hostess. Her name was Nona.

Before the Johnston party's short visit was over, Nona revealed that a group of Aleutian-based American airmen recently had been interned and confined under guard near Tashkent. Nona had been assigned to be their "mama." When the men departed, she said, several of them wanted her to give them her address so that they could write to her when the war was ended.[2]

---

1. W. Averell Harriman and Elie Abel, *Special Envoy to Churchill and Stalin, 1941–1946* (New York: Random House, 1975), 331.
2. W. L. White, *Report on the Russians* (New York: Harcourt Brace, 1945), 282–83, 295–96.

Nona's casual disclosure that interned American airmen had come to and later had gone from Tashkent on the surface appeared to be an indiscretion of which the NKVD was not immediately aware. However, given the Soviet obsession for hiding the movements of the American internees, this kind of indiscretion may have surfaced and contributed to her abrupt disappearance eight months later.

The Eleventh Air Force temporarily suspended further bombing missions against Kurile Island targets following the army's major losses in September, 1943. Bombardment squadrons of the Navy's Fleet Air Wing Four, however, were based in the outer Aleutian Islands to keep the enemy under pressure.

Casco Field, constructed on Attu, became the navy's principal base of air operations against Paramushiro and Shumushu for the remainder of the war. Four squadrons — VPB-131, VB-135, VB-136, and VB-139 — were rotated at Casco Field so that two squadrons were available for operations.[3] Crews from these units manned two-engined warplanes, the PV-1 *Ventura* and, later, the PV-2 *Harpoon*. Both possessed the speed and maneuverability that put them in the fighter-bomber category.

November 16, 1943: A bomber from VB-136, airborne for nearly ten hours, flew from Attu to the vicinity of Paramushiro and returned. For the first time, the navy had demonstrated that the PV-1 bomber was capable of reaching and hounding the Kurile military bases.[4]

December 20, 1943: In order to meet requirements for obtaining photographs of Kurile installations, Fleet Air Wing Four ordered a night photo-reconnaissance probe by a slow PBY aircraft. Soon, however, all future photo-reconnaissance missions were assigned to the speedier, nimbler PV-1. The flights were hazardous but became relatively routine.

May 5, 1944: VB-135, having recently arrived on Attu to replace VB-139, was ordered to fly its first Kurile Islands mission — the usual night armed photo-reconnaissance.[5]

Nine bombers were assigned to strike Shumushu. One of the crews belonged to John Vivian. "We flew on course for four and a half hours until the clock said we should be over the target," Vivian wrote. "The radar, however, showed no indications of land. . . . I opened the bomb-bay doors and jettisoned the bomb load. Then we came to a heading that would take us home." The return flight was one of high tension through continuous rain.

Another crew belonged to Howard Schuette. Byron Morgan (navigator) later reported, "We penetrated two cold fronts between Attu and Shu-

3. Charles L. Scrivner, *The Empire Express* (Terre Haute, Ind.: Historical Aviation Album, 1976), 7.
4. Ibid.
5. Ibid., 15.

mushu. The island was 100 percent cloud covered. We released our bombs on a radar run and turned for home." By Morgan's calculations, the PV-1 had gone beyond the point of no return. In order to lighten the plane's load, "We stripped the aircraft of everything we could shove overboard . . . and we landed at Attu with bare minutes of fuel remaining." One of the mission's bombers, however, vanished.

June 10, 1944: Since May 5, VB-135's missions continued every night when the gambling odds on the weather were not too great. The missions were not without cost. Two additional bombers and their crews were lost. More recently, VB-135 was vainly trying to locate and photograph a suspected air base on the north end of Shumushu.

June 11, 1944: The weather over the Aleutians could change rapidly, and the weather over the northern Kuriles was equally unstable. In an effort to obtain a current report of weather conditions in the Shumushu area for the VB-135 mission that night, John Vivian's aircraft approached Shumushu during daylight.

"The further we flew from Attu, the better the weather became," Vivian recalled. "About 200 miles from Shumushu I kept asking myself, 'Why not dash in and get a picture of that new airfield?'" His crew was willing, and he asked Attu for permission to make the navy's first daylight reconnaissance of the enemy base. While waiting for the approval, the bomber reached Shumushu and located the air base on the southern part of the island.

"Look at that concrete runway!" somebody said over the interphone. Casco Field on Attu had only steel-mat runways.

The photographic run completed, Vivian turned for home. After the fact, Attu approved of Vivian's action but warned him of bad weather at the base. "As we approached Attu we were just over the water and under the ceiling," Vivian said. "We managed to sneak in by following the shore line around the field." The developed film revealed that there were 29 bombers parked on the Shumushu field.

June 12, 1944: Volunteer crews manned the six bombers on the first daylight bombing strike against the Japanese strongholds since the Eleventh Air Force's September 11 disaster. Because of clouds and fog over Shumushu, radar was used to pinpoint the bombing of the air base. Damage could not be assessed visually.

Some of the bombers swung south and found Paramushiro clear of overcast. They discovered and photographed another new air base under construction.[6] The strike was considered to have been successful and marked an end to restrictions against daylight raids.

June 14, 1944: Six loaded bombers flew to Shumushu to strike again

6. Ibid., 16.

at the enemy planes on the airfield and to divert the attention of the Japanese from an approaching U.S. Navy surface fleet en route to bombard the Kuriles.[7] "This time we didn't catch them napping," John Vivian wrote. "The bombers were not on the field, but the air was filled with fighters."

It was a fierce encounter between bombers and fighters, and navy aircraft carried marks of the fight back to Attu. Vivian had talked via radio with Howard Schuette and knew that Schuette was taking his damaged bomber to Kamchatka. When Vivian reached Attu, he discovered that Russell Bone and his crew were also missing. "None of us," Vivian said, "remembered seeing Bone [in the Shumushu area]."

Bone later claimed that when it was apparent that he would have to divert his bomber to Kamchatka, he sent a message to Attu. The message was never received, and VB-135 feared that Bone was lost at sea.

June 15, 1944 (Kamchatka time): Separated from the other bombers in his flight, Russell Bone's aircraft lost an engine to gunfire during the strike and was forced to make a decision. As a result, he and his crew became the first navy airmen to crash-land in "neutral country" and to be interned by the Soviet Union.

Aboard Schuette's bomber, Byron Morgan remembered that "we made a high speed bombing run . . . over the airfield at Shumushu. The fighters picked us up after we left the target. . . . One fighter chased and fired at us for 150 miles before turning back." None of the crew had been scratched during the fight. One of the main fuel tanks, however, had been punctured, and Schuette knew that it was impossible to reach Attu on the remaining gasoline. "The decision was easy," Morgan said. "We turned and headed for Petropavlovsk."

Schuette made landfall about 50 miles south of Petropavlovsk and began looking for an airfield southwest of the town. "We saw a grassy field with a long east-west concrete runway," Morgan said. "A stubby Soviet fighter climbed to look us over as we headed for an emergency landing. The Soviet pilot rocked his wings, and we put down our landing gear [indicating a wish to land]."

Led by the Soviet fighter to the field, both the American bomber and the Soviet escort landed. An armed Red Army soldier waved the Americans from the bomber. Not far away they could see the weathered remains of two Army B-24 bombers (undoubtedly those that had landed last September 12). In the distance was a parked Navy PV-1 *Ventura*. Near the Navy plane was seated the crew, which the newcomers recognized as being Bone's.

Lt. Mikhail ("Mike") Dondekin, the same frail, trembling interpreter whose awkward use of English had been the internees' conduit to Soviet

7. Ibid., 16–18.

officialdom when Pottenger's crew came to Petropavlovsk, arrived and took charge. (Some of the airmen later looked upon Mike with disdain, while others felt sympathy for him.) Mike brought the two crews together, asked them to surrender their side arms, and then recorded their names. Presumably the name list would be sent to Moscow, where the American Embassy would be advised of the airmen's safety. Unfortunately, months would pass before the embassy could confirm the men's presence in the Soviet Union.

Next, Mike ordered the men aboard two Model-A Ford type trucks. They bounced over a rough dirt road to the Petropavlovsk naval base, where they were lodged in a two-story wooden building that served as an officers' club. On the upper floor were rooms in which cots had been placed for the 14 men, and on the ground floor was a dining room where food was soon to be served. This "welcome to the Soviet Union" meal for the exhausted, emotionally drained men included vodka, raw (smoked) salmon, cabbage soup, tea, and compote.

June 16, 1944: One by one the airmen, beginning with Bone and Schuette, were interrogated by a Red Army colonel assisted by a middle-aged woman interpreter. Before leaving Attu, the navy crews had been briefed about seeking haven in Kamchatka, if necessary, as an alternative to ditching at sea. However, they were given no specific instructions about what to tell the Soviets. Among themselves, Morgan said, "we all agreed that we would not reveal any military information about our Attu base or about our operations." So, claiming that they were on training missions, the Americans succeeded only in irritating their questioner.

June 17, 1944: The secluded officers' club building that temporarily housed the men was on a hillside overlooking the harbor. Standing or sitting outside the building, they had an overview of the picturesque deep-water port. They were warned, however, not to wander from the front of the building. They were also warned not to do anything that would attract attention to themselves. Their presence in Petropavlovsk, Mike told them, was a secret.

If the men were curious about earlier internees who might have passed through Petropavlovsk, they apparently decided not to inquire about them. Mike was their only source of information, but his disability and obvious penchant for secrecy discouraged questions.

Nevertheless, they could not resist asking Mike what was going to happen to them. Mike's answer, they learned, was the standard one: "Soon you will go home." When? "Moscow will say."

June 18, 1944 (Attu time): VB-135 had lost over one-third of its crews since reporting for operational duty in the Aleutians. Replacement crews were beginning to arrive at Casco Field. Fate did not spare the newcomers. Vivan noted in his diary, "We lost our first replacement crew to Russia."

A bomber with George Mahrt and his crew, together with four other warplanes, was airborne from Attu at sundown. Hours later, while near Paramushiro, Mahrt discovered that about 500 gallons of fuel had been accidentally siphoned from one of his main tanks, making it impossible for him to return to Attu. He sent a message that he would attempt to reach Petropavlovsk.

June 20, 1944 (Kamchatka time): It was not yet daylight after one of the shortest nights of the year when Mahrt approached Petropavlovsk. The area was fogbound. Using radar, Mahrt avoided the mountains behind Petropavlovsk while waiting for first light. Then, finding a hole in the fog, Mahrt slipped his bomber through it and, too late to do anything, plowed into trees. The bomber's tail snagged, one wing crumbled, and the nose ripped off forward of the cockpit instrument panel. There was no fire. Dazed, the crew escaped injury.

When this latest group of internees from VB-135 was delivered to the naval base, the seven men joined the Bone and Schuette crews as strangers. Even though the first two crews had been in the Soviet Union for only five days, Mahrt and his crew had been assigned to VB-135 parent squadron an even shorter time.

June 20, 1944 (Attu time): Jackson Clark and his crew returned from a raid on Paramushiro to find the Attu area obliterated by low clouds and fog. "We attempted three different range approaches," wrote John ("Butter-fly") Mathers (navigator). "On one approach we nearly had a mid-air collision with another aircraft also trying to find Casco Field. Finally, we decided to try to reach Amchitka."

The decision was too late. The fuel gauges had reached the zero mark.

Clark related how he ditched the bomber a few miles off Attu near the island of Agattu. Because the ditching was tracked on radar, a crash boat was immediately dispatched to the scene. The bomber sank within a minute of ditching, and the seven-man crew barely had time to inflate a life raft. About one hour later the crash boat located the raft. Cold and wet, the entire crew survived.

June 23, 1944: At Petropavlovsk, the three interned American crews moved from the naval base up the valley northwest of the port city to a remote Soviet naval air station on the shores of a lake. The airmen were quartered in a three-room rustic building that also served as the station dispensary. Apparently the internees' transfer to a "holding camp" was ordered so that the Americans could be isolated from prying eyes in Petropavlovsk.

The Red Navy kept several old pusher-type seaplanes at the lake. The seaplanes took off and landed, as if in practice, at infrequent intervals. From a nearby unpaved airstrip a few ancient navy biplanes were sent aloft, usually on Sundays, to allow members of a volunteer parachute group to jump. The excited parachutists sometimes landed in the lake — perhaps deliberately, because they made no effort to avoid the water. In their new location, the American airmen were permitted greater freedom of movement, such as walking around the lake's shoreline, and even swimming and fishing.

July 23, 1944: A month later, dawn was breaking and visibility was poor when Jackson Clark began his bomb run on the Shumushu airfield. After the bombs were released, four persistent Japanese fighters found and then attacked Clark's bomber "until we were about 100 miles from the target." Fortunately, none of the crew was hit.

Battle damage to the bomber, however, was extensive. Clark did not know how long he could keep the riddled craft in the air. The right engine was steadily losing oil, and there was not enough fuel to return to Attu. For the second time in five weeks, he was facing the prospect of a ditching. This time, he realized, he might not be lucky. Therefore, "I thought I had to go to Petropavlovsk," he later wrote. He reported his decision by radio to Attu.

When the Soviet landing field came in view, Clark circled widely before making an approach. The crew could see several Soviet fighters on the field as well as two PV-1 *Ventura* bombers at the field's edge. One of the fighters took off and intercepted the bomber. "The pilot wagged his fighter's wings and gave hand signals to follow him, which we did," Clark said. After landing, Clark reported, "Several armed soldiers surrounded the bomber and motioned us to get out and follow them."

Clark recalled, "A truck took me to the Petropavlovsk military headquarters and the rest of the crew to camp. I was held for about five hours. Most of the time was spent waiting for an interpreter. I hoped," Clark said, "the Soviets would not intern us if we could make them believe we were on a 'navigation' flight [the interrogators ignored that story]. . . . I then told them I didn't know anything. After they questioned me for about one hour, they finally got tired and took me to camp, too."

July 23 was Red Navy Day, so the Clark crew joined the other 21 Americans at the naval air station in time to be included in the celebration being held in the station's recreation building. Morgan remembered the vodka toasts and the patriotic speeches in Russian, which none of the Americans could understand. One of John Mathers's most vivid memories of his first day in "neutral country" was watching the dancing: men danced with men, and women with women, with only a scattering of mixed couples.

July 24, 1944: At the same time as 27 Americans rested following the Red Navy Day celebration, another VB-135 crew was on the verge of joining them.

For some time the Japanese had been using early-warning picketboats, similar to those that had been astride the ocean approaches to Tokyo in

1942, about 100 miles east of Paramushiro and Shumushu. On this day John Vivian found an armed 60-foot picketboat. Vivian dived and sank the boat with a direct bomb strike, but not before the enemy's 40-mm guns raked one engine of the bomber.[8]

Oil pressure immediately began to drop. "I nursed the engine along as we set course for home," he said, "but it just wasn't going to run." The Pacific Ocean was fog covered. Vivian could not see whether the water was smooth enough for a successful ditching. "On the other hand," he recalled, "Kamchatka stood out in clear weather with not a cloud around it." Thomas Edwards (navigator) gave Vivian a new course heading for Petropavlovsk.

"As we crossed the shoreline just north of Petropavlovsk, the Soviet coast batteries opened up on us," Vivian wrote. "The bursts were behind us but correct on altitude. We could see an airport . . . [which looked like] a sod field with a concrete strip in the center."

The crew watched fighters taking off. The fighters "made no effort to turn into us but disappeared aft," Vivian said. "We later learned that the shooting was a display of neutrality and the fighters had been alerted to drive off any Japanese fighters that might have followed us."

Vivian remembered that he made a "stinky" landing that overshot the concrete strip onto the sod. Looking across the field, he could see three other navy bombers — the disabled aircraft of the Bone, Schuette, and Clark crews.

July 25, 1944: There were now five interned crews from VB-135 at the camp. The Clark and Vivian crews had arrived within a day of one another. They brought the distressing and frustrating news that the other three crews, after nearly six weeks of internment, were still listed as missing in action. VB-135 on Attu knew that Schuette and Mahrt had announced their intention of trying to reach Kamchatka, but Bone was still totally unaccounted for. Moscow thus had not yet been able to advise Washington that the crews were "safe but interned in a neutral country."

As the ranking officer, John Vivian automatically became the commanding officer of the internees, a responsibility that he retained until late November. With the presence of the two latest crews, the internees now numbered 34 men — far too many to be housed in the dispensary building. Tents were pitched, and the overflow internees were moved under the square shelters. Three or four men shared each tent.

John Mathers was one of the tent occupants. Both he and Byron Morgan retained pleasant memories of a Soviet sailor, Alexander Rusky, who was their cook. One of Rusky's other duties was to awaken the airmen each morning. This he did very well by carrying a mechanical portable

8. Ibid., 18.

record player while he walked among the tents and in the dispensary. The scratchy record player blared a popular Russian song.

Rusky was also particularly adept in teaching the airmen the correct way to drink vodka in the Soviet style. Byron Morgan recalled that Rusky made certain that each man was given a full tumbler of vodka two times each week.

August 12, 1944 (Attu time): VB-135's sister squadron operating from Attu was VB-136. Six bombers from the latter unit departed for Paramushiro with an airfield and canneries as their designated targets.[9] For Carl Lindell and his crew, it was their thirteenth mission. It proved to be an unlucky one.

High winds and navigational difficulties threw the raiders off course, and they made landfall over 100 miles south of Paramushiro. The bombers returned to the target area but, faced with the prospect of a fuel shortage, jettisoned their bombs and set a return course for Attu.[10] Five bombers reached the base. Carl Lindell's did not.

Lindell encountered enemy antiaircraft fire and was attacked by two fighters. According to Russell Manthie (Lindell's gunner), "The bomber received several hits, and the starboard engine was running rough." The propeller was feathered.

C. J. ("Pat") Brown (Lindell's radioman) recalled that the crew had been briefed on what to do if a crash landing on Kamchatka became necessary. Brown, on Lindell's order, radioed a terse message to Attu: "Starboard engine trouble, 500 gallons of gas, proceeding to Petro." Using his emergency checklist, Brown then switched to the Petropavlovsk tower frequency and notified the Soviets by a prearranged code-wave signal, "American bomber forced down."

August 13, 1944 (Kamchatka time): "As we approached Soviet air space, antiaircraft fire erupted, and several Soviet fighters aimed shots in our direction," Brown said. "The pilots then warned us by rocking their fighters' wings. Those actions were orders, we thought, that we should land. Fearing that the Soviets had not heard our first transmission, I got on the radio and repeated the message to Petropavlovsk tower."

"We had been briefed," Carl Lindell said, "to lower our landing gear and circle the Petropavlovsk airfield three times. I tried to comply, but the antiaircarft fire boxed us in, and I landed as fast as possible." The bomber touched down and went off the end of the field and into the trees. After the aircraft came to rest and the crew spilled out, some of the men could see several other damaged navy bombers parked at the edge of the field.

---

9. War Diary, "Bombing Squadron One Hundred Thirty-Six," August 1–31, 1944, U.S. Naval Historical Center, 3.

10. Ibid., 3–4.

"A squad of soldiers escorted us to an underground building," Brown said. "There we met a nervous lieutenant [Mike], who 'greeted' us in broken English and began to question us individually." As already agreed among themselves, the men stymied Mike's probing with the standard recitation of name, rank, and serial number.

Lindell and his crew were later delivered to the crowded navy camp. Lindell said that he and his two officers — James Head (copilot) and Murlin Richardson (navigator) — shared a tent.

August 20, 1944 (Kamchatka time): Jack Cowles and his crew manned one of the six navy aircraft sent to bomb and strafe two Paramushiro airfields. Cowles reported that his bombs had not released on his first run. His wingman observed Cowles's returning to the target area.[11]

Finding a number of enemy vessels in the Paramushiro Strait, Cowles attacked, but in the hail of antiaircraft fire he lost one engine and his hydraulic system. The crew of the crippled plane repelled repeated onslaughts by Japanese fighters. Cowles tried to contact Attu by radio, but his signal was too weak to be heard. He managed to keep the riddled bomber in the air long enough to reach Cape Lopatka, where he belly-landed it on the tundra and skidded into a ravine. The fuselage was split, allowing the crew to escape before the plane exploded seconds later. Leonardo Panella (copilot) was badly burned on the right hand and arm and less so on the face. Cowles's arrival in neutral country brought VB-136's second crew to internment.

August 23, 1944: Finally, after over two months of marking time, most of the navy internees were leaving Kamchatka. A Soviet four-engined flying boat (probably the same one that had evacuated army internees in 1943) was in the Petropavlovsk harbor waiting for them to board. However, the Soviets limited the number of men to less than a full load. Although in 1943 the same or similar flying boat carried 51 Americans, the seaplane's age was the reason for the current restriction, they claimed. Whatever the true reason, the 34 men of the first five navy crews were earmarked to go.

Watching them leave were Lindell and his men. Although they had not yet been informed, the remaining crew would be joined soon by the Cowles crew that was en route from the remote crash site in the Cape Lopatka area.

Following the 1943 established route, the flying boat carried the five VB-135 crews routinely to Okha on Sakhalin island. The men gorged themselves on fresh vegetables and fresh meat — "a wonderful meal," John Vivian recalled, "made more so by the menu at Petropavlovsk."

And again the men were escorted to a building containing clean beds (and bedbugs). Unlike the situation in 1943, the men did not turn off the

11. Ibid., 5.

overhead electric lights—they could not. The switches had been removed, and the ends of the electric wires had been soldered. Even with the lights continuously burning throughout the night, however, the men were still lightly bitten by bedbugs and were exhausted from lack of sleep when they boarded the seaplane the next morning.

August 24, 1944: After their flying boat landed on the Amur River at Khabarovsk, the men were delivered to a military hospital where they were comfortably quartered and given freedom to walk on the hospital grounds. Most of them, however, developed dysentery and confined their walking, for the most part, to the toilets.

Mike, the interpreter at Petropavlovsk, had made an empty promise when he assured the internees, "Soon you will be home." Immediately after they arrived in Khabarovsk, they received the stunning news from their Soviet escorts: the airmen were *not* on their way home. They were, instead, en route to a city in south central Asia (Tashkent) where they would be interned for the duration of the war. The 34 men were divided into two groups for the westward movement, and then they waited for the scheduled trips in two DC-3 type aircraft to be arranged.

August 27, 1944: The first group departed. John Vivian, the senior officer, was originally scheduled to travel with these men, but severe dysentery forced him to postpone his trip and travel with the men of the second group, most of whom were also ill.

August 29, 1944: The remaining group followed. The aircraft bearing both groups oriented their flight route to that of the trans-Siberian railroad. Fortunately, the weather was clear and the rails plainly visible to the pilots, so the flights were uneventful. The three-day trips were interrupted by overnight stops at Irkutsk and Novosibirsk, scenes of banqueting and toasting to the point of excess. Unable to refuse the hospitality of their Soviet hosts, many of the dysentery-stricken Americans were also nauseated by too much vodka.

August 31, 1944: Fatigued and ill, the men in the second plane landed at the Tashkent air base, where they were met by Captain Kozlovski from the Red Army OVS in Moscow. Kozlovski had been in Tashkent for some time to complete the arrangements for reopening the internment camp, which, John Vivian believed, would be the airmen's home until the end of the war. The arriving men were trucked through Tashkent and Vrevskaya to the camp, where they joined their fellow navy flyers who had been the vanguard from Khabarovsk.

As the internee commander, John Vivian was conducted on an introductory tour of the camp. He quickly concluded that, although the wartime living conditions were crude, the camp in every respect was a major improvement over the primitive situation that the airmen had left behind them in Kamchatka. The camp's main building contained cots with cotton

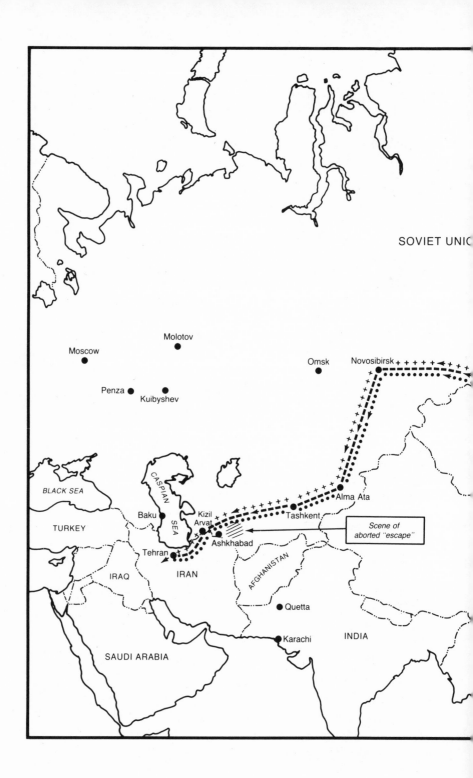

SOVIET UNION

Moscow

Molotov

Penza

Kuibyshev

Omsk

Novosibirsk

BLACK SEA

CASPIAN SEA

Baku

Kizil
Arvat

Tashkent

Alma Ata

TURKEY

Ashkhabad

Scene of
aborted "escape"

Tehran

IRAN

AFGHANISTAN

IRAQ

Quetta

Karachi

INDIA

SAUDI ARABIA

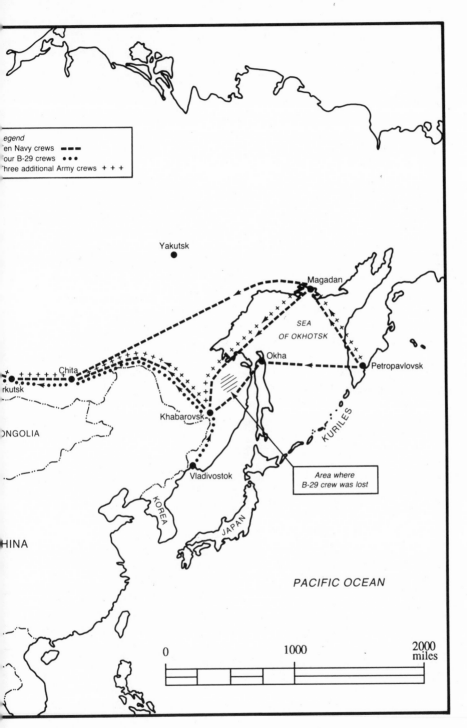

Yakutsk

Magadan

SEA
OF OKHOTSK

Okha

Petropavlovsk

Chita

Irkutsk

KURILES

Khabarovsk

MONGOLIA

Area where
B-29 crew was lost

Vladivostok

KOREA

JAPAN

CHINA

PACIFIC OCEAN

0   1000   2000
miles

MAP 3. Route of internee group 3

mattresses, sheets, blankets, and pillows. By comparison, the quality (if not the quantity) of the food was an improvement. And the Soviet military and civilian staff that had been assembled appeared to be adequate to administer the camp in an orderly manner.

One of the first persons whom Vivian encountered was Nona. Of the entire camp staff, Nona was the only member who was a "carryover" from the time when the camp ceased to operate in early 1944. At the beginning, Vivian wondered about Nona's true role in addition to her function as a skilled interpreter, but he later came to realize that she was the best Soviet friend that the men had in the camp.

The new camp cook was Toica, a large woman much younger than Nona. (Some of the men remember the cook's name as being Natasha or Tasha rather than Toica.) Like most of the Soviet staff, Toica spoke no English, but some of the Americans, including Vivian, found it convenient to practice their smattering of Russian with Toica as she bustled around the cooking pots in the kitchen.

Alexandra, middle-aged, was the chief housekeeper. She supervised the many women who performed various chores, including laundry of bed linens and underclothing.

Red Army major Putakana was the camp commandant. He has been remembered as an intense, taciturn man who spoke only in loud imperative tones. A stocky middle-aged man with thin black hair, Putakana apparently was assigned to the camp duty while recovering from a lung ailment and ulcers. The Red Army guard detachment was composed of wounded soldiers on recuperative duty.

The new guards, incidentally, were more diligent and alert. A few of the internees managed occasionally to elude the guards in order to visit Vrevskaya or Tashkent, but the camp's perimeter in general was now considered to be secure.

August 28, 1944 (Kamchatka time): VB-136 sent six bombers to attack shipping and shore installations on Onekotan, the island south of Paramushiro. John Dingle attacked a picketboat and in turn became the target for three Japanese fighters. Dingle was later seen to veer northward in the direction of Kamchatka. He reported by radio that his bomber was heavily damaged and that he and his crew were proceeding to Petropavlovsk.[12] Upon his arrival at the Petropavlovsk field, what was planned to be a safe landing developed into a crash landing because his brakes locked. The six-man crew, some members of which had cuts and bruises, was questioned and interned and then joined the Lindell and Cowles crews.

12. Ibid., 7–8.

September 10, 1944 (Kamchatka time): William Head and his crew in a crippled army B-25 bomber landed and were interned at Petropavlovsk (see chapter 7).

September 11, 1944 (Kamchatka time): Two navy bombers from VB-135 were sent for a routine sweep against shipping in the northern Kurile Islands waters. Darryl McDonald in one of the bombers attacked a beached ship suspected of being an observation post and radar station. Following the attack, McDonald climbed through a thin cloud layer and found five Japanese fighters waiting to pounce. McDonald tried to outrun them until enemy bullets sprayed the bomber and found the right engine. Barely remaining aloft on the one remaining engine and pursued by the persistent fighters, McDonald's bomber approached Petropavlovsk. After the Japanese fighters finally ended their chase, McDonald managed to fly his mangled airplane to the landing field through a ring of Soviet antiaircraft fire.

McDonald said that he lowered his wheels to indicate his intention to land, but when he touched down, the bomber's right landing gear collapsed and the bomber ground-looped. The six-man crew was shaken. John Rosa (plane captain) injured his shoulder but not seriously.

After the initial internment processing, which included preliminary interrogation, the men were delivered to a former schoolhouse located adjacent to an antique radio station seven miles northwest of Petropavlovsk. Both radio station and schoolhouse were situated near a knoll from which the town could be glimpsed.

Here McDonald's navy crew joined Head's army B-25 crew. Captain Petrov, crippled by war injuries, was in charge of the Soviet radio station as well as the internees' well-being. His Red Army radio station detachment provided guards and a cook.

The rustic schoolhouse, made of logs and rock, had been converted to a military barracks. At one end of the building were a kitchen and dining room, and at the other end was the large dormitory equipped with wooden cots and bunks. Since Head's army crew and McDonald's navy crew together numbered only 12, the men were uncrowded (but not for long). Outside the barracks were a Russian-style steam bathhouse made of rock and a primitive outhouse for the men's use.

Unknown to McDonald and his crew, the three Navy VB-136 crews at the naval air station a few miles away were being prepared to leave Kamchatka.

September 12, 1944: The 17 airmen in the Lindell, Cowles, and Dingle crews were put aboard a DC-3 type transport and flown directly from Petropavlovsk to Magadan. On arrival they apparently were put in the same building where Pottenger's army crew had been confined in 1943. Through the windows they too could see armies of prisoners, shoulder to shoulder and row on row, being marched to work. The internees' interpreter described the mass of guarded prisoners as "enemies of the State."

September 14, 1944: From Magadan the men were flown to Chita, then to Irkutsk and Novosibirsk before starting their final flight to Tashkent. Because of periods of bad weather, there were long layovers, sometimes as much as two days, at each of the scheduled overnight stops. The layovers were filled with the usual dining and toasting rituals hosted by local units of the Red Air Force.

September 2, 1944: At Tashkent, Howard Jarrell and his army B-29 crew out of China arrived at the internment camp (see chapter 6). Jarrell found the 34 navy flyers depressed by dysentery and anxiety.

Because of the chronic illness among many of the men, the camp's outhouse had continuous occupancy. One internee recalled that men stood in line to use the crude facility, and when one of those with a severe case obtained temporary relief, he often came back to the line and awaited his turn again.

Did anybody outside the Soviet bureaucracy know that the navy men were alive? Jarrell and his ten men were uniquely fortunate. After he landed at Vladivostok, Jarrell was able to contact the American consul, who promptly reported Jarrell's situation to the American Embassy in Moscow. The American consul, however, had no means of knowing about the navy airmen's internment in Kamchatka. So now the navy men daily waited anxiously for some sort of signal that would indicate that they had not vanished into a wartime bureaucratic void. By this time in mid-September, it had been three months since some of the men had been reported as missing in action.[13]

One means of fighting boredom was by card playing with worn decks that some men usually carried in their flying suits. Another was watching Soviet movies and old American movies with Russian dubbing, which were sometimes available. John Vivian said, "When we saw a Russian film, Nona would tell us about the development of the plot while the operator was changing the reel." Officers and men alike also agreed to perform some sort of light kitchen duty, such as potato peeling, as another means of filling time.

David Wilson (Vivian's copilot) originated the idea of publishing a newspaper "to have something to do" as well as to inform and entertain the brooding men. Frank C. Ogden (Jarrell's navigator) prepared the format

13. Byron Morgan related how his father became frustrated by the official navy silence and wrote a series of inquiries to Washington. Not until October 18, 1944, however, was the elder Morgan notified of Byron's safety "in a neutral country," four months after his landing at Petropavlovsk.

and solicited volunteers to write the content, which ranged from news to satire and even poetry.

Provocatively named *Nyet Pravda,* the publication first appeared on September 18. It was hand-printed on a sheet of green paper and then posted on a wall where it could be seen and read. Its wry comment about camp conditions, the "major" (the camp commandant), and the "dysenteric crisis" as well as the connotation of *Nyet Pravda* (no truth) caught Nona's attention. She was upset because she believed that the men were ridiculing the Soviets. "It's the wrong thing to do," she said, and she removed *Nyet Pravda* from the wall.

The newspaper died after a few issues. Shortage of paper, Soviet displeasure, and according to B. J. Miller (Clark's copilot), loss of internee interest killed it.

In one of its last issues, *Nyet Pravda* announced the arrival of the Lindell, Cowles, and Dingle crews at the internment camp. The 17 new men now brought the total number of Americans in the camp to a record 62. The growing camp population was beginning to aggravate the problem of how to keep the men mentally and physically occupied.

September 23, 1944: One of the newcomers, C. J. Brown (Lindell's crew) remembered being with a group whose restless energy turned to finding means of recreation. Without athletic equipment, the men decided to fabricate a softball and bat to use. Not aware that the 1943 internees had fabricated similar equipment, they made a softball by winding yarn from worn-out stockings around the rubber heels from Brown's flight boots. A goatskin, hanging in an outbuilding, was stolen and used to cover the ball. When the goatskin was reported missing, Major Putakana was furious. He lined up the internees and demanded, through Nona, that the thief step forward. When nobody responded, the major shouted in vain.

Next a bat was needed. In 1943, the commandant, Major Urov, ignored the fact that somebody cut down a tree in order to make a bat. When the present internees did the same thing, Major Putakana assembled the men once more and denounced the culprit who destroyed the tree. Again, when nobody confessed, the commandant was enraged but helpless.

October 3, 1944: From Washington, the Navy Department began the process of notification to next of kin that some of the airmen missing since midsummer were known to be in a neutral country. No other details were available. The relatives of most of the navy men assembled in the internment camp, however, did not receive the welcome notification until the latter part of October.

October 5, 1944: A three-man American team from the U.S. Military Mission in Moscow suddenly appeared at the Vrevskaya camp. In the visiting team were navy captain (later admiral) Harry D. Felt, an Army Medical Corps lieutenant colonel, and army major Paul Hall, who was the team interpreter. Major Hall later played a crucial role in the escapes not only of this group of internees but of the following group as well (see chapters 8 and 9).

General Deane in Moscow had been informed through American consular channels that the Jarrell B-29 crew had been interned at Vladivostok. Deane's Military Mission staff later learned from the Soviets that some navy crews had likewise arrived in Kamchatka. The names of navy personnel had been delayed in reaching Moscow, and the identifications had been vague and incomplete. After Deane was told that internees again were being concentrated at Tashkent, his staff sought and obtained permission to visit the internment camp.[14]

"The real purpose of the visit," Vivian was told, "was to find out who was in the camp and to get correct spelling of names and correct serial numbers so that the next of kin could be advised of our safety." The internees were disappointed that the team had not brought any mail. And there would be no mail until the team returned to Moscow and furnished Washington with an accurate personnel list.

The question of release was raised repeatedly. The visitors, however, were unable to make a definite answer. Release depended, according to Captain Felt and Major Hall, on the outcome of continuing diplomatic pressures and negotiations in Moscow. Frank C. Ogden remembered that, on the third evening of the visit, Captain Felt said that "we were to be released . . . to work in a Soviet aircraft factory in Tbilisi in the Caucasus." Then Felt winked, "and we knew that it was a big fake."

After a five-day visit to the camp, the U.S. Military Mission team returned to Moscow. During the visit, however, the team doctor examined each man and gave typhus and typhoid fever booster inoculations. In addition, the team delivered boxes of supplies: a six-band radio set capable of receiving international (BBC) broadcasts, softball and other athletic equipment, an army paperback book library, clothing, playing cards, candy, and even American tobacco.

October 24, 1944: Following the visitors' departure, camp morale soared for a short time. The internees now had athletic items to use and books to read, and the dysentery cases seemed neither so many nor so severe. However, as the days shortened and cooled, the continued lack of variety and substance in their diet became a constant complaint, and the lack of fuel for the wall heating stoves caused concern.

Uppermost in the airmen's minds were unspoken questions. What about their future in the camp? Was Captain Felt's wink sufficient reason to hope for transfer? If they were not going to Tbilisi, then where—and when?

November 7, 1944: The camp staff used the occasion of the anniversary

14. Richard C. Lukas, "Escape," *Aerospace Historian,* Spring, 1969, 16.

of the Red Revolution as an excuse for a Russian-style celebration in which the American internees were invited to join. Rations of vodka, wine, and beer were available in generous amounts. Amid the dancing and singing the Americans became exuberant. Recent chronic dysentery had drained most of the aggression from the internees. Now, in the party atmosphere, the men became newly energized and quickly shed their inhibitions. Despite the presence of the Tashkent military commanding general at the celebration, high-spirited Americans smashed several doors and windows.

Some of the internees recalled the event as a near-riot. For others, the details of what may have happened faded from memory. Still others were unable to remember the celebration at all.

Major Putakana, with Nona as interpreter, later angrily lectured the listless internees.

September 17, 1944 (Kamchatka time): In August, as commander of Navy Squadron VB-136, Charles Wayne promptly wrote letters to the next of kin of three VB-136 crews (Lindell, Cowles, and Dingle). The letters contained announcements that the airmen were missing in action. Now, Wayne himself was missing.[15]

While over Japanese targets on Paramushiro, Wayne's bomber was attacked by fighters, which caused the loss of an engine and other damage. Wayne wanted to gamble on being able to fly his aircraft to its Attu base. John Murphy (copilot), after assessing the condition of the crippled bomber, persuaded Wayne that such a flight was not feasible. Even surviving the shorter flight to Petropavlovsk seemed questionable until the estuary swamps near the town were sighted. Here Wayne crash-landed his bomber, fortunately without injury to the crew.

Since the departure of the Lindell, Cowles, and Dingle navy crews from Kamchatka on September 12, Mike the interpreter moved permanently to the schoolhouse barracks where Head (army) and McDonald (navy) crews were domiciled. On this day Donnie Broadwell (McDonald's navigator) recalled that the telephone rang, after which Mike went to Petropavlovsk, "so we knew that a plane had landed." Later, Wayne and his crew arrived at the barracks, followed by "a Russian woman interpreter and much gold braid to question the new crew."

Wayne's crew was the fourth and the last one from the Navy's VB-136 Squadron to be interned. The five men brought the current number of American resident internees to 17.

September 19, 1944: William Head (B-25 pilot) reported that after a meal of buckwheat and soup, "one of my crew came to me and reported that Charles Wayne was sick. . . . When we found him, his lips were blue,

15. Scrivner, *Empire Express,* 26.

and he was having trouble with his breathing. We sat him on a log, exercised his arms, and gave him water. After belching he began to stir," Head said. "When we lifted him to walk, he vomited. Then he said he felt better."

A Red Army doctor was called to examine Wayne, and the doctor ordered him to the military hospital. Wayne remained there for two days. The word was passed, Head said, that Wayne was allergic to buckwheat.

September 25, 1944: In the barracks the telephone rang as explosions from antiaircraft shells were heard. "Mike departed for the landing field," Broadwell said, "and we could see a B-24 coming in."

The new arrival was John Ott and his army crew of 10 men, raising the total American internees at the Kamchatka collecting point to 28.

October 3, 1944: With the addition of the Ott crew at Petropavlovsk (see chapter 7), the rising number of Americans tried to relieve the monotony of internment by organizing volleyball and basketball games. The initial competitions were between American teams. Later, the games pitted American against Red Army teams.

October 9, 1944: A two-engined Soviet air transport arrived, and the men were advised that they would fly from Petropavlovsk "within the next three days." The internees heard and spread a rumor that their destination was Tashkent.

October 17, 1944: After many vague and unexplained delays, the Soviet transport plane was finally scheduled to fly from Petropavlovsk. For reasons that also were never made clear, the 28 internees were divided into two groups, with the first group of 15 leaving immediately and the second group of 13 being advised that they would remain for the time being.

In the first group were Head's six army B-25 airmen, who had been at Petropavlovsk for the longest time; Wayne's five airmen, who had been the latest navy flyers to arrive; Darryl McDonald and Kenneth Miles (copilot) of the earlier navy crew; and John Ott and Leonard Karkoszynski (tail gunner) of the army B-24 crew.

Remaining for delayed departure were four of McDonald's navy crew and nine of Ott's army crew. In retrospect, McDonald said that the decision for splitting his and Ott's crews was one that the Soviets arbitrarily made. Some of the army crewmen believed that Wayne, as the senior American officer, made such a decision so that he could move his own navy crew intact from Kamchatka without any further delay.

The mixed navy-army group was flown to Magadan. Although closely monitored by Soviet escorts, the men were comfortably billeted, then well fed and entertained. Their departure from Magadan was delayed for several days by weather conditions.

October 22, 1944: After a routine flight, the internees arrived at Khabarovsk, where they were taken directly to a Red Army rest camp north of the city and near the banks of the Amur River. This military facility to rehabilitate Red Army officers from the German front was probably the same rest camp through which American internees from the Aleutians were funneled in 1943.

October 28, 1944: At Khabarovsk, Richard McGlinn and his army B-29 crew out of China arrived from a hospital and joined the army and navy internees from the Aleutians at the rest camp (see chapter 6). In the meanwhile, Wayne was told at the rest camp that his Aleutian airmen would not be moved from Khabarovsk until the remainder of McDonald's and Ott's crews from Petropavlovsk rejoined them.

October 20, 1944: At Petropavlovsk, the 13 internee stragglers were scheduled to follow the earlier main body of airmen from Kamchatka on this date. In fact, however, their departure was delayed day by day because of weather, the nature of Soviet wartime bureaucracy, and the isolation of the Siberian Far East. The men vacillated from hope to hopelessness as time slowly passed and winter weather became more severe.

November 1, 1944: William McQuillin and his army B-25 crew landed at Petropavlovsk (see chapter 7). The seven men raised the internee population on Kamchatka to 20.

November 7, 1944: Finally, the four remaining navy airmen and the 16 fellow army internees were flown from Petropavlovsk to Magadan.

November 11, 1944: After a frigid winter flight from Magadan to Khabarovsk, the men overtook the other navy and army internees at the rest camp.

November 15, 1944: Thirty-nine Americans (all of the internees in Khabarovsk except for McQuillin's seven-man crew) boarded a trans-Siberian railroad train that carried them across Asia to Tashkent. It was a memorable and uncomfortable 11-day trip. During the Siberian crossing the temperature dropped to 40 degrees below zero. The hard-class coaches were virtually unheated. The lack of adequate blankets and the unrelenting attacks by bedbugs made the trip seem endless.

November 26, 1944: The new arrivals at the Vrevskaya camp brought the internee populations to a new high mark—101 men, of whom 62 were navy aviators. The navy airmen were not only thousands of miles from the sea, but, like their army companions, had no real hope of wartime flying again.

The new arrivals also carried seniority with them. Charles Wayne (navy) was now the ranking officer in the camp, so he automatically relieved John Vivian of his senior command function. Before the American flyers in the camp were later repatriated, an additional 29 army airmen joined the ranks (see chapter 7), but the navy contingent, having traveled thousands of miles from Kamchatka to Uzbekistan, was now complete.

6

Superfortresses in Siberia
1944

In a four-month period between late July and late November, 1944, four disabled B-29 superfortresses landed or crashed in the Soviet Far East. The losses occurred during the time when massive B-29 blows were being organized against Japan from distant bases in China. Each superfortress carried a crew of 11 men. All 44 men were interned and later moved to the camp near Tashkent, Uzbekistan.

The original B-29 bases in India were too far removed from the ultimate enemy targets located in the enemy's industrial heartland of Manchuria and Japan. A complex of four forward fields was constructed in south central China, after which, in the summer of 1944, superfortresses were ordered to cross the Himalayan hump and move to new takeoff points near Chengtu.

July 29, 1944: Seventy-one bombers began a 1,600-mile flight to An-shan, Manchuria.[1] Their target was the mighty Showa Steel Works. Howard Jarrell's B-29 was the last to go aloft because of nagging electrical problems. Jarrell reached the An-shan objective successfully and dropped most of his bomb load. One of his engines unexpectedly began running wild, and he was unable to control the propeller. The bomber's instability and fuel overusage made it impossible for him to reach unoccupied Chinese territory. Closer at hand was the Soviet Union's Vladivostok, and Jarrell pointed his B-29 across Korea in that direction.[2]

As he neared Vladivostok, "the sun was getting pretty low," Jarrell said. "I wanted to land before darkness set in." When the bomber flew over the

---

1. Keith Wheeler, *Bombers over Japan* (Alexandria, Va.: Time-Life Books, 1982), 59.
2. War Department General Staff G-2, March 8, 1945, "EX Report No. 553, Release from Internment from USSR, Jarrell, Howard R.," U.S. Theaters of War, WW II, ETO, Record Group 332, National Archives, 2–3 (hereafter cited as War Department, "EX Report No. _____, [name]").

Vladivostok harbor area, it drew antiaircraft fire. At the same time, several Soviet fighters rose to meet the unidentified aircraft.

"The fighters fired bursts at the bomber," Jarrell recalled. The gunners wanted to fire back, but he refused permission until the ship had been hit.

The Red Navy fighter of the squadron commander approached, and the pilot waved the other fighters away. Jarrell intended to land on the concrete strip nearest him, but the squadron commander led him to a smaller grassy field used by the fighters.

This landing field north of Vladivostok was a naval air base undoubtedly not far from or the same field where Edward York and crew had landed in 1942. Hungry and tired, the B-29 crew was taken to a mess hall and fed, and then to a barracks where interrogation through an interpreter was begun by high-ranking Soviet officers. The unproductive, off-and-on questioning would continue for several days.

The Americans were advised that they were now interned. "I never dreamed that would happen," said Frank C. Ogden (navigator). "I figured that we would get repaired and gassed up, and then fly home"—to Chengtu.

July 30, 1944: The Soviets had never seen a warplane like the B-29, so many of their questions were about it. Except for the malfunctioning engine, an unreliable electrical system, and a faulty radio set that would receive but not transmit, the interned bomber was intact. However, would the plane fly again? The fighter field on which the B-29 had been forced to land was too short for a takeoff.

What ultimately became of the bomber, Jarrell could only surmise. Having left the landing field the night before, the Jarrell crew had seen the bomber for the last time.

August 4, 1944: The interrogation had been monotonous but not stressful. Finally, the crew was loaded into old Ford buses and driven south to the outskirts of Vladivostok for billeting in a Red Army barracks area reserved for married couples.

August 7, 1944: From the time of their July 29 landing, the airmen had repeatedly requested that they be permitted to see the American consul in the city. (In 1942, when Edward York landed near Vladivostok, he too had asked—in vain—for contact with the local American official.) Suddenly, with only a 30-minute advance notice, Consul Angus Ward and Mrs. Ward arrived at the airmen's barracks.[3] From the consulate, the Wards brought whatever surplus items were available, such as cigarettes, toilet paper, magazines, and canned foods. Mrs. Ward carefully recorded the name, rank, and serial number of each man for forwarding to Moscow and Washington.

3. Ibid., 5.

Ward reiterated that the 11 men had been interned. Ward also advised that General Deane in Moscow had issued a blanket order: "No American internee will attempt to escape."[4] The unspoken purpose of the order was to prevent a repetition of earlier escape efforts, which, by some miracle, did not have tragic results. In addition, General Deane, having gained Soviet cooperation for the mass escape of 60 American airmen in February, did not want unauthorized American actions to jeopardize any NKVD plans for smuggling future internees from the Soviet Union.

Ward came to see the men again on August 27, but he brought no encouraging news. Ward himself was leaving his Vladivostok post. If he knew that the airmen also were on the eve of departure, he did not tell them.

August 29, 1944: Jarrell and his men were flown north to Khabarovsk.

August 30, 1944: After food, drink, and a short sleep, the men were roused and put aboard a westbound air transport destined for Tashkent. The flight followed what had become the standard air routing for most of the past American internees when they were moved to the south Asian camp. Overnight stops were made at Irkutsk, Novosibirsk, and Alma Ata.

September 2, 1944: At the internment camp Ogden reported, "We were greeted by 34 cheering Americans." Now the Jarrell army crew was outnumbered by navy crews. Even more navy crews would increase the camp's population before any additional army airmen from China and the Aleutians would make their appearance in late November.

June 15, 1944: The first B-29 strike at Japan proper from the Chengtu area bases was launched against "the Pittsburgh of Japan"—the Imperial Iron and Steel Works at Yawata. The target, located on the northern tip of Kyushu, escaped serious damage. The appearance of the superfortresses, however, served notice to the enemy: the B-29s would come again.[5]

August 20, 1944: Superfortresses for the second time struck at Yawata. Because the antiaircraft fire was intense and the fighter resistance stubborn, 14 of the raiders failed to return to their Chengtu bases. One of them was the B-29 piloted by Richard McGlinn.[6]

After he released his load of bombs, McGlinn was in the process of turning his B-29 to escape the heavy flak barrage when one of the engines was hit. McGlinn ordered the propeller to be feathered and started crossing the Yellow Sea toward China. He soon realized, after discussing the bomber's predicament with Lyle Turner (navigator), that the B-29 was too severely damaged to reach Chengtu. If the bomber continued on its

4. Ibid.
5. Wheeler, *Bombers over Japan,* 57–59.
6. Missing Air Crew Reports, no. 07523.

present course, it would be forced to crash-land somewhere in Japanese-occupied China.

The alternative was to fly to Soviet Siberia. Turner charted a course across central Korea toward Vladivostok. With the coming of darkness the weather turned turbulent, and neither Turner nor McGlinn could locate Vladivostok. There was always the possibility that the plane was too far to the west of Vladivostok and therefore over Japanese-occupied Manchuria, so McGlinn elected to continue flying until he and Turner were certain beyond doubt that they were deep inside Soviet territory.

Knowing that the B-29 could not stay aloft any longer, McGlinn prepared his crew to abandon the bomber by parachute. He made certain that the bomber was headed north to intersect a railroad that he believed ran from the Amur River valley eastward to the seacoast. He instructed his crewmen that when they landed they should go north and try to locate the wreckage. McGlinn cut the engine switches. "Good luck to all," he said. "See you below!" In 90 seconds the entire crew jumped from 11,000 feet into the darkness. McGlinn was the last man to leave the plane.[7]

The area into which the men jumped was a vast wilderness, much of it unexplored, northeast of Khabarovsk. Situated between the Amur River on the west and the Sea of Japan on the east, the wilderness was dominated by the north-south Sikhote-Alin range of mountains, whose backbone peaks were as high as 6,500 feet.

The airmen were ill prepared for leaping blindly into this trackless country. Originally, McGlinn's parent squadron had operated from Indian bases before advancing to the Chengtu bases, so the crew's emergency instructions had been oriented on how to survive in India or China, not Siberia. Fortunately for them, the airmen's ordeal in Siberia occurred during the late summer rather than winter. If the season had been advanced two months, how many could have survived?

For use in an emergency situation, the men stored a nominal amount of food rations in their parachute-seat kits, but only enough for days, not weeks. They carried side arms (one man had a carbine) and some ammunition as well as other survival items such as matches, signal whistles, signal mirrors, ponchos, compasses, knives, and even small American flags by which to identify themselves. Some possessed Chinese yuan or Indian rupees, but nobody had foreseen the need for Soviet rubles. Only Eugene Murphy (bombardier) had a small area map of Siberia on his person.

August 21, 1944: The 11 men landed in three widely separated groups.

McGlinn descended through rain. When he landed, his parachute canopy caught in a tree, and he was suspended in his harness. Unable to see

7. War Department, "EX Report No. 542, McGlinn, Richard M.," 2.

anything because of the darkness, he waited several hours for daylight. By the first glimmer of dawn he discovered that his parachute was in the crown of a giant tree.

Well soaked by rain, McGlinn found himself swaying 60 feet above the ground. From this height he could look in all directions. "As far as the eye could see, there was nothing but dense forests," he said.

It required all of his agility and patience — and another several hours — for him to work his way from his lofty pendulum to the ground. Among his precious possessions in his emergency vest was a signal whistle. Stiff and wet, he blew the whistle again and again. He listened. Was he alone? Finally he heard the faint note of an answering whistle.

The second whistle belonged to Charles Robson (tail gunner). The two men forced their way through the thick undergrowth toward one another until they met. Together they continued to blow their whistles. There was no response from any of the other nine men.

McGlinn and Robson were united to form the first group for the struggle to survive.[8]

John Beckley (right gunner) also crashed through the boughs of a large tree, but his parachute did not break his fall. His nose was split, and one of his ribs cracked. "I wrapped myself in my poncho and my parachute and went to sleep," he said.

In pain, Beckley could not sleep soundly. At daybreak the echo of far-away shots roused him. "I started to yell," he reported, "and then I heard a voice." Abandoning his parachute, he pushed his way through the brushy and hilly wilderness toward the voice. Within the hour he and Otis Childs (radar operator) made contact. Childs was unhurt, but he had a first-aid kit, and he used it to clean and dress Beckley's bloody nose.

"Then we fired a clip of pistol ammunition, and this time Louis Mannatt (left gunner) was attracted to where we were waiting," Beckley recalled. "Mannatt was carrying his parachute, and we used this to construct a shelter." They built a small fire to dry their wet clothing.

Not far away, Eugene Murphy (bombardier), Almon Conrath (engineer), Melvin Webb (radio operator), and William Stocks (chief gunner) had all landed near one another, so that they were able to assemble as soon as dawn broke. They spent the entire morning struggling toward the north as McGlinn had instructed them to do. Then they could go no farther because the perpendicular face of a huge mountain blocked their way. Before deciding which way to go, they fired pistol shots. Beckley, Childs, and Mannatt immediately responded, and soon the seven men were joined to form the second group from the B-29 crew.[9]

8. Ibid., 3.
9. War Department, "EX Report No. 544, Beckley, John G.," 7.

After resting and eating sparingly from their scant store of emergency rations, they discussed what they should do. "We found no trace of the other four members of the crew," Murphy reported. "We were of the opinion that they were on the other side of the huge mountain that blocked our way." Murphy's small map of Soviet Siberia contained so little detail that it did not help them in any way in determining where they were generally located. The map did show, however, a railroad that ran parallel to the Amur River from Khabarovsk north to Komsomolsk, and another one that ran from Komsomolsk in an easterly direction to the coast. Were the men lost in the area east and south of the railroads?

The men gambled that the answer was yes. They located a tiny stream about a foot wide. They started walking, picking their way through the forest along the bank of the trickling waterway that seemed to lead them generally toward the Amur River.

Lyle Turner (navigator) also landed in the deep forest. So did Ernest Caudle (copilot). After daybreak the two men began walking, fortunately, toward one another. Sound rather than sight brought them together. In the hope that they were traveling in the right direction, they also began to follow the flow of a small stream. Their pairing formed the third separate group of McGlinn's lost crew.[10]

September 2, 1944: Turner and Caudle made their way slowly day by day as their stream merged with other flowing water and became larger. Their rate of travel was slowed by the rough terrain, by their bulky parachutes, which they used as night shelters, and more important, by their search for food. Their emergency rations were eaten during the first few days. Thereafter, they hunted first for any squirrels and frogs that they could find. Finally, they had been reduced to eating moss, berries, leaves, and even snails when they could find them.

Unknown to any of the lost airmen, Turner and Caudle were near the larger group. By following the descending streams from the mountains, the two groups had arrived at the same waterway, which was now a river, the Monamo.[11]

In the meanwhile, the larger seven-man group moved downstream. The tired, discouraged airmen ate sparingly from their emergency rations and supplemented their diet with any game that could be shot. One member of the group had a survival pamphlet, and "we ate anything and everything the book named as edible, including angleworms."

"We finally decided to build a raft large enough to accommodate the seven men and float down the river," Beckley said. The exhausting effort required several days of construction time. "We used up much of our en-

10. War Department, "EX Report No. 543, Turner, Lyle C.," 5.
11. War Department, "EX Report No. 544," 8.

ergy building this raft. When it was finished we found that it would hold only three men without sinking."

Elsewhere, McGlinn and Robson remained lost and wandering in the wilderness. As McGlinn reported later, "Anything that we could catch, whether it crawled or flew, was food." They could not know, however, that their ordeal was only beginning.

September 3, 1944: The group of seven dispirited men did not have the strength to build a larger raft. Among them they agreed that the three strongest men — Beckley, Murphy, and Webb — would ride the raft down the river until help was found.

The three floated the raft to midstream and left their four companions standing on the riverbank. In late afternoon they entered a series of rapids that tossed the raft out of control. "The raft overturned and spilled what equipment we had, such as first-aid kits and ponchos, into the water," Beckley said. "We did not lose any food, mainly because we had none. We hoped to shoot game along the way."

By some miracle the men succeeded in recovering the raft and crawled aboard. Less than one hour later the raft was caught in a logjam near an island in the river. "We tried to free the raft," Beckley reported. "We couldn't. We were too weak." Instead, they conserved their strength so that they could swim to the island, where, wet and hungry, they passed the night.

September 4, 1944: On the island, Webb shot a squirrel and Beckley caught a frog, and these provided breakfast for the men. They tried again to free the raft from the logjam, but the effort was hopeless. After resting, they decided to swim to the riverbank and then walk downstream.[12]

September 5, 1944: Turner and Caudle, likewise walking along the riverbank many miles upstream, unexpectedly found the camp where Conrath, Stocks, Childs, and Mannatt were waiting for help to come. The new combination group of six men could now count nine positive survivors from the abandoned B-29. None of the men had seen any sign of habitation or other human activity for two weeks, so the relief of finding one another stimulated them to new action.

Why wait for help that might never come? They decided to break camp and resume walking downstream as resolutely as their weakened legs would allow.

September 9, 1944: After four days of walking with little progress, Turner reported, "We decided that we too would have to use rafts to take us down the river." The slow raft construction from fallen trees and other debris was begun.[13]

12. Ibid.
13. War Department, "EX Report No. 543," 6.

September 10, 1944: Since abandoning their own raft, Beckley, Murphy, and Webb had been walking for seven days. They had been subsisting on wild berries, moss, and what infrequent small game they could shoot. Their ammunition, they knew, was almost gone.

Suddenly, they saw the collapsed buildings of an abandoned village on the opposite side of the river. Overjoyed by the realization that they were approaching the outer fringe of the wilderness, the three men stopped to rest. Without warning, a small girl stepped from the tall grass between the village and the riverbank. The men reacted immediately, shouting and waving small American flags that they had carried in their pockets. The child, apparently frightened, turned and vanished behind the vegetation. Certain that the girl was not alone, the men waited. Nearly one hour later, although their optimism was beginning to fade, their patience was rewarded when the child appeared with a woman, presumably her mother.

The woman pointed downstream. A man and a boy paddling a dugout were approaching the bank to meet the airmen. Unable to speak a common tongue, both parties experimented with sign language. The man and boy coaxed the Americans into the dugout and ferried them across the river where the woman was waiting to feed them some raw vegetables.

By signs, the men learned that a village was located downstream. The men, led by the woman and girl, walked the two-mile distance to a cluster of log-and-bark dwellings. Here they were cordially greeted, fed again, and provided a covered floor area on which to sleep. Later, the Soviets officially documented the internment of the three men as the day when they walked into the village.

September 11, 1944: "We were able to make the villagers understand that there were more men upstream . . . many days upstream," Beckley later reported. A village search party was organized, but it apparently never went far enough upriver to contact the airmen.

While the search party was being assembled, however, the three men were put in a dugout and paddled to another village down the widening river. Here they met two Soviet officers. "They could not speak English, either," Beckley said, "but they treated us well. They fed us and found a place for us to sleep."

September 12, 1944: The town of Troitskoye on the Amur River was only two hours away by horseback. Here the Soviet officers delivered the dirty and exhausted men, lost for over three weeks, to the Border Patrol headquarters. One of the Border Patrol officers understood a limited amount of English. "The first thing we did," Beckley said, "was to tell him about the four men who were waiting for rescue." A number of Border Patrol aviators, curious about the appearance of the bedraggled Americans in their midst, had been drawn into the headquarters to listen to the

Americans. When the B-29 airmen reported the missing men, there was a flurry of activity as some of the aviators hurried from the building to start a search by airplane.

After the Border Patrol officials were satisfied with the men's explanation of what had happened, the three new American internees were taken to the Troitskoye hospital for recuperation. The hospital was a one-story wooden structure with primitive facilities. Beckley especially remembered that the hospital attendants "did everything in their power to take care of us." The men were made to lie in bed most of the time while a military doctor and another doctor, brought from Khabarovsk, treated them for malnutrition, exhaustion, cuts, and bruises.

September 16, 1944: As a result of rest and food at Troitskoye, the interned men were able to endure the 150-mile voyage by motor launch up the Amur River to Khabarovsk. Here they were again hospitalized by the Border Patrol for an extensive period of recuperation.[14]

At Khabarovsk, they were questioned immediately about the missing B-29 crewmen. The Soviets knew that two days earlier some of the men had been sighted far up one of the river valleys to the east of Troitskoye, These men, they believed, were the four Americans for whom the search had been initiated at Troitskoye.

And what about the others — McGlinn, Robson, Turner, and Caudle? The three American internees could not provide a clue. They had neither seen nor heard them since they leaped from the B-29 bomber four weeks earlier. The pilots of all Soviet aircraft flying over the wilderness area were ordered to watch for any sign of the lost men.

September 14, 1944: After five days of slow work, the six men on the banks of the upper Monamo River completed the building of two rafts for their float trip and were ready to launch them when they heard for the first time the alien sound of an airplane engine overhead. They frantically used their signal mirrors and managed to attract the attention of the Soviet pilot. The flashing mirrors brought an end to the aerial search that had been conducted from Troitskoye.

The pilot dipped the wings of his plane to indicate that he had sighted them, and then he returned to Troitskoye. The excited Americans remade their camp. Their confidence surged. "We were sure that we were about to be rescued," Turner said. After waiting for so long, the men forced themselves to relax and wait again.

September 15, 1944: Another Soviet airplane appeared overhead and dropped a supply of food and a note in English to the men. Be patient,

14. War Department, "EX Report No. 544," 8–9.

the note said. Help was on its way. The note also told the men that their three companions who had gone downstream were safe.

September 19, 1944: The men waited for four days. They had no way of knowing that the Soviet rescuers, coming upstream by boat, had to force their way past numerous snags and portage around rapids before they could reach the stranded men. After having arrived at the airmen's riverside camp, the rescuers were surprised to find not four but six of the missing crew. All of the B-29 crew were now accounted for except McGlinn and Robson.

September 23, 1944: The trip taking the six men from the wilderness likewise required four days to travel by boat and horseback. Rescued and rescuers followed a route generally the same as that earlier used to evacuate Beckley, Murphy, and Webb. At Troitskoye the Border Patrol officials formally interned the Americans and then sent them to the local hospital. While in the Troitskoye hospital, Turner was convinced that the Soviets "gave us everything they had, and even more — the nurses even brought us food from their own homes." Welcome news was also delivered to the rescued men: a Soviet pilot, flying over a remote portion of the wilderness, had sighted two men, who used smoke and mirrors to attract attention.

After nearly a week of treatment, the six men were escorted to Khabarovsk for further hospitalization.[15]

When the crew parachuted from the B-29, nine of the men apparently landed on the mountain range's western slope and slowly worked their way toward the Amur River valley. McGlinn and Robson, on the other hand, seemed to have landed on a mountainous highland. In accordance with his own injunction, McGlinn tried to continue leading Robson in a northerly direction that, unknown to either of them, took them deeper and deeper into the wilderness. In the beginning, because of the difficulty in penetrating the dense brush in the forests, they took advantage of the easier walking on the fringes of swamps and marshlands. "Although we traveled many hours every day, we were able to cover only short distances," McGlinn later reported. "If we walked as much as five miles in a day, we considered that to be excellent." They searched for trails, particularly along the banks of streams, but found none, not even animal trails. "We did find some animal tracks, most deer and bear, but not any wild beasts themselves," McGlinn said.

The two men never completely gave up hope. However, as day followed day and week followed week, an optimistic outlook was difficult to maintain. They fought tiny biting and stinging insects day and night, and their

15. War Department, "EX Report No. 543," 6.

constant search for food reflected their growing desperation. They had husbanded their emergency rations by carefully allotting themselves meager daily portions sufficient to maintain life but not strength. So they looked to the forest and the waterways for supplemental edibles of any type, repulsive and otherwise. Approaching the point of emotional as well as physical exhaustion, they sometimes wept from frustration if a tasty morsel escaped their frantic grasp. Each of them was losing about a full pound of weight every day.

September 22, 1944: A month had passed since the men had landed in Siberia. McGlinn and Robson were building a fire beside a small river, and smoke from the fire wafted upward. It had been six days since Soviet pilots had been notified to look for signs of the missing American airmen. At this time on this day the smoke, which was an unusual sight in the wilderness, caught the eye of a passing pilot, and he banked his airplane for a closer look. By this time the two eager men, thankful that a bright sun was shining, were flashing their signal mirrors. The men and the pilot instinctively knew that the lost were found.

September 23, 1944: An airplane returned, this time swooping over the riverbank site where the two Americans stood with their arms waving wildly. The pilot dropped a supply of food. He also dropped a note in English: "You are in Soviet territory, and Soviet pilots are at your service."

September 24, 1944: More food was dropped, together with maps of the area and instructions to proceed down the river to a village marked on the map as Tolomol. McGlinn and Robson attempted to comply with the instructions, but their progress along the riverbank was very slow. Not only were they exhausted, but McGlinn developed a severe case of dysentery. "When the first packet of food was dropped," he remembered, "I ate continuously for hours. I then went to sleep, and when I awoke the next morning I ate for four more hours. It was the wrong thing to do, but when a man goes without food for such a long period, he loses his better judgment." The dysentery persisted for two months.

September 26, 1944: A Soviet plane again located the pair and dropped more food and a note: "Stay where you are. A rescue party will arrive soon." In the meantime, a Soviet engineer, engaged in surveying for a railroad under construction from Komsomolsk, on the Amur River, eastward to the coast, was at his working post in the wilderness. He was instructed by radio to contact the lost men and bring them first to Tolomol village and then to Komsomolsk. The engineer immediately went to Tolomol, engaged two guides, and began the rescue mission.

September 27, 1944: The rescue party quickly found McGlinn and Robson, and without delay they were evacuated by dugout down the river to Tolomol. The village's inhabitants "were very friendly and generous with what they had," McGlinn said. "The treatment received at the hands of the natives and the Soviet engineer could be likened only to the loving care that any close relative would receive from one of their kin." When they departed, McGlinn and Robson gave the villagers their knives and their Indian rupees. The men in turn were each given a pair of moccasins, much like those that some early American Indians wore. McGlinn gave his pistol to the engineer who had led the rescue expedition.

September 29, 1944: The Soviet engineer with his party and the two American airmen traveled for two days, first by dugout through rapids and logjams and then by motor launch to Komsomolsk. The gaunt, hollow-eyed men were immediately taken to the hospital for medical care and re-cuperation.

Forty days after arriving in Siberia, McGlinn and Robson were the last members of McGlinn's crew to be interned. All 11 members of the B-29 crew had managed to survive. Whether the Soviets ever located the wreck-age of the B-29 in the unexplored wilderness at a later time was never reported.

October 4, 1944: After a week in the Komsomolsk hospital, the two men were considered well enough to undertake the tiring voyage up the Amur River past Troitskoye to Khabarovsk. The voyage was completed without any additional problems. They were delivered to the Border Patrol hospi-tal, where the other nine members of McGlinn's crew were waiting.[16]

The recuperation of the entire crew continued at the hospital for sev-eral weeks. "The medical treatment which we received was good," Beckley said, "but by this time most of us were in comparatively good health and needed little attention. A doctor examined my cracked rib and stated that it was all right." Since the men were not allowed to go outside the hospital grounds, they spent most of their time resting in bed and regaining their strength.

When the interned airmen entered the hospital, Border Patrol officials asked them to surrender any weapons and cameras in their possession. Those men who still carried their weapons complied with the request. No personal search was made, however, and when the men arrived at the Tash-kent camp in late November, seven cameras were still secretly in their pos-session. Officials also asked for and retrieved the maps that had been dropped to McGlinn prior to his rescue.

October 28, 1944: The B-29 crewmen at last were well enough to be transferred to the Khabarovsk Red Army rest camp where 15 other army and navy internees from the Aleutians were waiting. At the rest camp, Mc-Glinn said that, as was the case at the Border Patrol hospital, "we were asked not to go outside the limits of the fence surrounding it." McGlinn added that "this restriction was for our own protection and for the pro-

16. War Department, "EX Report No. 542," 3–5.

tection of the Soviets, who did not want too many people to know of the presence of the Americans, particularly in the areas close to Manchuria."[17]

McGlinn was convinced that "we were treated far better than the average Red Army officer. We were given many considerations as far as food was concerned, and we had only to look outside to see what the civilians were enduring to appreciate our own position." Part of the food to which McGlinn referred included Lend-Lease supplies.

The rest-camp beds were clean, and the sheets were changed once each week. To replace some of their tattered clothing, the men were issued two-piece underwear, trousers, and Lend-Lease army shoes. After so much rest and recuperation, the men were growing restless. Outside, ice was forming on the Amur River, and snow was now a foot deep. Despite the intense cold, some of the internees frolicked on skis in the rest-camp grounds. However, most of the fidgety internees passed the time indoors by reading outdated English-language magazines and playing cards. The card games led to gambling. Although the Soviets openly disapproved of the gambling activity, they did not demand that it be stopped. At night, Soviet propaganda films (and a few American ones dubbed in Russian) were shown in the dining hall.[18] Infrequently, women assigned to duty in the rest camp also came to the dining hall in the evening to dance with some of the Red Army officers and the American internees.

November 11, 1944: Remembering their own reunion at the Khabarovsk hospital, McGlinn's crewmen shared in the rejoicing and excitement when 20 army and navy internees from Kamchatka arrived at the rest camp. Among the new men were 13 who were rejoined with their divided crews, one army (Ott) and one navy (McDonald).

Now, the B-29 crew and most of the other army and navy internees at the rest camp sensed that they were ready to be sent elsewhere. To Tashkent? Soviet interpreters gave vague answers to that question.

November 11, 1944: At the same time that the reunion was occurring at Khabarovsk, Weston Price and his B-29 crew were approaching the Soviet Union. Starting from one of the airfields in the Chengtu complex, Price's B-29 and seven others formed to strike a Japanese aircraft factory at Omura on Kyushu. En route, however, the formation ran into violent weather and heavy clouds, so much so that Price lost all contact with the other bombers. Price made the decision to use the cloud cover and continue the mission individually. Problems with the radar equipment made target selection difficult, but the bombs were dropped, after which Price turned and headed through the clouds for China.

17. War Department, "EX Report No. 542 (Incidental Intelligence)," 4.
18. War Department, "EX Report No. 544 (Incidental Intelligence)," 3.

Two hours later the superfortress broke from the cloud cover. Instead of being over the coast of China, Price and Melvin Scherer (navigator) discovered that they were over the sea off the coast of Korea and flying into the teeth of a 100-mile-per-hour headwind. From that position and considering the headwind situation, Price and Scherer knew that their storm-battered bomber could never reach unoccupied China. Aware that he had to make a choice, Price veered the bomber and asked Scherer for a bearing to the nearest Soviet base—Vladivostok.

Price landed the B-29 at a naval air base north of Vladivostok. Apparently Price's approach to the air base, either by accident or design, was from a direction that did not excite the Soviet defenders because Price did not report any antiaircraft fire or fighter interception.

The superfortress did not appear to have suffered any damage as a result of the violent buffeting that it had endured in the storm. The uninjured crew was escorted from the bomber to an adjacent naval building where, after eating, the men were bedded for the night. As happened with other interned crews, they were not allowed to return to the bomber for any reason.[19]

November 12, 1944: During the morning hours, the interned crew was interrogated through interpreters by a group of senior naval officers. "We had been briefed to tell the Soviets that we were on a training flight if forced to land in the USSR," Price said later. "They laughed at this. . . . They used every argument and trick to get information, but were never pleasant about it."

They were transferred to the custody of the Border Patrol. After being moved to a rest camp near the city, the internees again were subjected to intensive interrogation. Price said that he found it very embarrassing to have to lie and would have preferred to have been able to tell the interrogators about his bombing mission to Japan.

The internees remained at the Border Patrol rest camp for nearly a week. They were temporarily protected from the severe winter weather as long as they remained indoors in the rest camp's housing. Their clothing, however, was insufficient and inadequate. They needed heavier, warmer garments, Price reported, especially gloves and undergarments.[20] As events later developed, Price and his crew eventually crossed Siberia at the winter's coldest time.

November 15, 1944: At Khabarovsk, the McGlinn B-29 crew together with two navy crews (Wayne and McDonald) and two army crews (Head and Ott) were outfitted with heavier clothing and prepared for moving to Tash-

19. War Department, "EX Report No. 554, Price, Weston H.," 6–7.
20. War Department, "EX Report No. 554 (Interrogation, Briefing, and Equipment)," 2.

kent. Instead of winter flying, they would be traveling by trans-Siberian railroad in temperatures that ranged to 40 degrees below zero.

An additional army crew (McQuillin) had arrived with the other internees from Kamchatka. The seven men were ordered to remain in the Khabarovsk rest camp and wait for another B-29 crew (Price) known to be at Vladivostok.

The senior internees (McGlinn for the army and Wayne for the navy) were concerned whether sufficient blankets would be available for the men to use during the long railroad trip. Even though the Soviets assured them that two blankets per man would be provided on the train, the American officers considered even two blankets would not be enough for minimum warmth. However, they had no recourse but to accept the Soviets' decision.

The 39 Americans boarded their railroad cars in the early afternoon. The only heat was from a small coal-burning stove at one end of each car. The men found this heating arrangement, McGlinn said, to be completely unsatisfactory because the fuel promised to be replenished along the route was not forthcoming.

To complicate the lack of heat, the internees discovered only one blanket on each bunk. Because of the American clamor, after two days into the trip the Soviets managed to collect and issue a second blanket for each man.

In addition, the cars were infested with bedbugs. McGlinn reported that Wayne was bitten even before the train departed from Khabarovsk. At one point during the trip across Siberia, McGlinn said, a doctor was put aboard the train to treat sore throats and issue aspirin tablets and bedbug powder.

November 26, 1944: After an 11-day train trip via Irkutsk and Novosibirsk, the 39 internees arrived at Tashkent and were greeted at the Vrevskaya camp by the 62 other Americans interned there. Two superfortress crews were now present in the camp. Two additional crews were yet to arrive.

November 17, 1944: Price and his B-29 crew were next transferred to Red Army jurisdiction at Vladivostok and immediately underwent yet a third interrogation, but not as intensive as the earlier ones. When the questioning was over, Price was told that he and his men were leaving Vladivostok.

November 18, 1944: The internees were moved north to Khabarovsk and into the Red Army rest camp. McQuillin and his army crew were expecting them.

November 21, 1944: William Mickish, from the same B-29 squadron as Price, was pilot of one of the bombers assigned to make an additional strike at Japan's Omura aircraft factory. Like Price, Mickish encountered heavy clouding en route to the target. After jettisoning his bombs and flying over the target, Mickish was attacked by enemy fighters. One engine was disabled by gunfire. Mickish was forced to feather the propeller but managed to escape further damage from the fighters. He relayed a radio message to his Chengtu base that he was "going to Russia, one feathered."

Mickish's predicament, like Price's, was further complicated by violent headwinds (over 120 miles per hour) encountered after leaving the Omura area.[21] When he approached Vladivostok, Mickish was harassed by intercepting Soviet fighters. He landed safely without further damage at Vladivostok, and the internment and interrogation of the B-29 crew promptly followed.

December 3, 1944: Mickish and his crew, having been transferred to the Red Army rest camp at Khabarovsk a few days earlier, were joined with Price's B-29 crew and with McQuillin's B-25 crew. The 29 men were put aboard a railroad car for a 13-day journey to Tashkent.

December 16, 1944: With the arrival of the last of the B-29 crews, the internment camp population at Vrevskaya was topped at 130, twice the size of any earlier or later collection of American internees there.

21. Missing Air Crew Reports, no. 09865.

7

Other Army Flyers Interned
1944

Now fare thee well, we here shake hands
And part, I hope, to meet no more.
I'd rather lie in happier lands than
Longer live upon your shore.
— "Ode to Leaving Kamchatka"

The Eleventh Air Force, stunned by the disaster on September 11, 1943, when it lost nearly half of its available bombers in a mission against the northern Kurile Islands enemy bases, slowly regained its composure through refittings, replacements, and retraining. It scheduled no combat missions for five months. When missions were resumed, the 77th Bombardment Squadron was restricted to using its B-25s for sea searches and attacks on enemy shipping at sea, leaving the 404th Bombardment Squadron's B-24s to probe Paramushiro and Shumushu when weather permitted.

Finally, after nearly a year of being denied access to enemy land targets in the Kuriles, the 77th Squadron on September 1, 1944, was ordered to send six B-25s to Paramushiro. Although only one bomber found a target and struck it successfully, the 77th was again in the business of harassing the enemy's bases.

Meanwhile, the Navy's Fleet Air Wing Four had been engaged in missions to the Kurile Islands for several months and had lost numerous bomber crews, some of whom were now interned in "neutral county." These interned navy crews would soon be joined by three army crews from the 77th and 404th squadrons.

September 9, 1944: Six B-25s were sent to attack shipping near Paramushiro. This time, however, two bombers failed to return to Attu. They were the 77th Squadron's first losses in a year.

The bombers located enemy vessels and started their strafing and bombing runs. The ships responded with a heavy curtain of antiaircraft fire. One surface-skimming B-25 struck a ship's mast and crashed, and another lost its left engine.

William Head and his crew manned the second bomber.[1] They were North Pacific flying veterans, having completed nine previous over-ocean missions. Today's tenth mission was the closest they had come to Paramushiro.

With oil streaming from a bullet hole in the damaged engine, Head feathered the propeller. "We all knew that we would have to go to Kamchatka," he said. In their premission briefing at Attu, "we were told that it was all right for us to land in the Soviet Union if necessary," John McIntosh (navigator) recalled. "Better that than being a prisoner in Japan."

"Petropavlovsk was supposed to have the nearest landing field," Ralph Hammond (copilot) reported. "In the event we could not reach Petropavlovsk, we should crash-land anywhere in Kamchatka and make our way to the nearest village and turn ourselves over to the Soviet authorities. We knew that we would be interned."

September 10, 1944 (Kamchatka time): Head's emergency instructions were to fly north of Avacha Bay and turn inland to approach the designated Petropavlovsk landing field. Head ignored the instructions and instead flew directly on an approach to the town "because we had only one engine and were low on fuel," Hammond said. "We were over the bay close to the harbor when the Soviets opened fire on us. We did an abrupt turn out of the bay and flew north!"

While Head was flying the bomber on its revised course, Hammond was reading the text of a prepared message into the radio microphone. In essence, the message in Russian advised the Petropavlovsk airfield that an American crew on a training mission was making an emergency landing.

As the bomber turned inland north of the town, a Soviet fighter approached. Its pilot signaled for Head to follow him to the landing field. On the ground, the crew was herded to an adjacent building. Head was interrogated first, then the other crew members. "Mike" Dondekin, mentioned as having been a principal Soviet interpreter during the early internment of the navy crews at Petropavlovsk, was also the interpreter for Head's crew. The Soviet interrogators, all senior Red Army officers, had heard the "training mission" alibi so often that they had become more amused than annoyed by the American lie. Head remembered the questioning as being polite.

The six men were moved to the schoolhouse that had been converted to a barracks northwest of Petropavlovsk. There they came under the con-

1. John H. Cloe, *Top Cover for America* (Missoula, Mont.: Pictorial Histories Publishing, 1984), 133.

William Head's crew shortly before its last mission. *Front row:* Ralph Hammond, William Head, and John McIntosh. *Back row:* William Crowell, John Carr, and Warren Lawton. Photograph courtesy J. E. Mills

trol of Captain Petrov and his Red Army detachment from the adjacent radio station.

Some of the navy airmen who arrived at a later time regarded Petrov as arrogant and arbitrary, but Head and his men had a more favorable reaction to Petrov's personality. Hammond especially remembered with pleasure one evening when Petrov and his wife entertained Head, McIntosh, and Hammond in their home. "It was a very pleasant time," Hammond said. "Petrov showed us books with pictures of Russia. His wife served tea with some Russian pastries."

On the day of arrival the Americans were provided a banquet with vodka. As the days passed, however, their meals consisted usually of tea, black bread (sometimes with Lend-Lease butter), soup, and perhaps fried grain, which Head believed to be buckwheat.

The Red Army unit from Captain Petrov's radio station was responsible for the internment camp's security. The Americans were allowed to use the grounds of the former school for exercise, but Mike reminded the airmen that they should not wander from the area. "You will be caught . . . and returned," he said. "Be patient," he advised.

The men found some basket hoops attached to trees. Lacking any kind of pneumatic ball, they fabricated a rag ball from old socks. "Ours was strictly a run-pass-shoot basketball game," Hammond said. "One afternoon we played some of the visiting Red Army artillerymen from an anti-aircraft battery that had fired on us over the bay. Needless to say, our game with them got a little rough."

Soldiers from the radio station detachment also were attracted to the Americans' makeshift games. These soldiers liked volleyball, and Red Army–American competition was organized and played on a crude court in front of the schoolhouse. The Soviets provided a conventional air-filled volleyball, and it later was used to replace the rag ball as a basketball.

September 18, 1944: During the week since the internment of Head's army crew, two navy crews (McDonald and Wayne) had arrived and raised the total number of Americans in the schoolhouse to 18. It was about this time that evening outdoor campfires were burned for entertainment, probably begun by Red Army soldiers from the radio station detachment. A fire pit was dug beyond the schoolhouse, and logs were dragged near the pit for seating. Some of the internees recalled that they "went to a campfire and listened to the Russians sing," and then they "were singing with the Russians." The airmen's evening campfire and commingling with the Soviets continued whenever the weather allowed.

September 24, 1944 (Aleutian time): Eight B-24s, including the one piloted by John Ott, were ordered from Shemya to strike targets on the southern tip of Paramushiro. At midpoint while maneuvering around a weather front, Ott reported to the flight leader that his No. 3 engine had developed oil-pressure problems. However, he continued to Paramushiro. Due to a mechanical delay in opening the bomb-bay doors, the bomb load missed the assigned target. The bomber was immediately attacked by fighters, but the B-24 escaped serious damage. With engine problems and harassment by a dozen fighters, Ott's straggling bomber fell behind the formation bound for Shemya. Lacking sufficient fuel to return to the base, Ott feathered one propeller and headed for Petropavlovsk.[2]

September 25, 1944 (Kamchatka time): Ott unfeathered the propeller as he passed north of Petropavlovsk and prepared to locate the landing field. "The Soviets shot at us from three or four batteries," Ott reported, "but the shots were low and behind and were evidently meant only as a warning. A fighter was sent up and buzzed the bomber a few times." Ott

2. War Department, "EX Report No. 551, Ott, John E.," 1–2.

landed the B-24 without any further problems. He and his crew were taken to a nearby building for questioning.[3]

"We believed that we probably would be interned," Gilbert Arnold (navigator) said, "but nobody knew for sure." In the event that an emergency landing was made at Petropavlovsk, "we were told to say that we were on a long-range navigational mission and became lost."

The B-24 was the first heavy bomber to arrive at Petropavlovsk in a year, and the Soviets were anxious to update their information. The interrogator was persistent, but "nobody was mistreated," Arnold said.

Next, they were driven in trucks to the schoolhouse where the other internees were being confined. After nine o'clock in the evening they were finally fed a ration of boiled wheat, black bread, and a fig. The exhausted men fell into barracks cots with boards instead of springs, straw-filled mattress bags, and a blanket. Arnold was one of the men who had his first experience with bedbugs.

September 26, 1944: Shortly after midnight, Ott was roused by two Soviet officers who took him into Petropavlovsk for further questioning.[4] Ott reported that he was "dined and wined" with salty fish and vodka. In Ott's opinion, "it was an extremely hard interrogation." Questions were interspersed with vodka toasts to Roosevelt, Churchill, and Stalin. Finally the interrogators gave up, and Ott was returned to the schoolhouse at 4:30 A.M. "The wooden sack was most welcome," he remembered.

But not for long. At 6:30 he was roused again, this time to accompany his crew on a tour of the immediate area. They were advised of the boundary limits beyond which they were not to go. They were reminded that at night the internment camp perimeter was guarded by a large roving dog that the airmen called "Douglas."

The Soviets lost no time in introducing the new crew to volleyball, the game at which the Soviets excelled and expected to win. "They were very good," Arnold admitted. Volleyball would be played until the last internee departed.

September 27, 1944: Ott encountered Mike the interpreter and evidently must have voiced a complaint about being interned. Ott did not make a record of what he told Mike, but he recalled vividly the interpreter's prompt response. "You no like it here?" Mike asked. "Better yes be food for fishes?"

September 28, 1944: Two Soviet flying officers with two guards requested Ott and Charlie Clark (engineer) to go with them to the airfield. Going directly to their B-24, Ott and Clark were told to start the engines and then were quizzed about the various instrument readings. The Soviet officers apparently expected Ott to fly the bomber for them so that they could

3. Ibid., 2.
4. Ibid., 3.

learn its operation. Ott, however, refused to discuss the instruments and, citing the damaged condition of the B-24, declined to pilot it.

Although the internees' diet had been modified by the arrival of a shipment of Lend-Lease Spam even before the Ott crew joined them, the meals were reverting to monotonous servings. Arnold and some of his fellow crewmen discovered that edible provisions—especially potatoes—were stored in a root tunnel that contained food for the radio station detachment. The men quickly found that it was not difficult to filch food from the tunnel. Potatoes were the easiest to take and conceal. They were later roasted in the hot ashes of an outdoor fire. As days went by, enough bricks were found to build a crude outdoor oven that, when heated from above, would bake not only potatoes but "liberated" fish as well.

September 29, 1944: Each of the Americans was issued, in addition to a toothbrush and tooth powder, a set of two-piece underwear and a quilted jacket. Because of the clothing issue, the men jumped to the conclusion that they were soon departing for an area with a colder climate.

After the evening meal, Captain Petrov and the dog Douglas caught Arnold and others in the act of roasting potatoes. "We had an interesting evening," Arnold remarked sardonically. Apparently Petrov never fully realized what the men were doing, because the root tunnel's supplies continued to be the future target of stealthy foragers.

September 30, 1944: A Red Army officer from Petropavlovsk came to the camp and told the men that they definitely would leave Kamchatka soon. While at the camp, the officer redefined the boundaries of the area in which the internees must remain until an airplane arrived to evacuate them. He made no threats, but the internees—especially those who had been testing the guards' vigilance and patience—knew that they would have to note the boundaries and not overstep them.

October 2, 1944: Bedbugs, always a prevalent nuisance at the camp, became more aggressive as winter approached. It was dysentery, however, that sent the first internee to the hospital—John McIntosh (Head's navigator).

October 6, 1944: Every morning when they awakened, the men's first thought was a common one: Is this the day when "the great speckled bird" would come to take them from Kamchatka? Arnold's second thought on this day must have been, What's wrong with my eyes? An army of bedbugs had attacked his face, and his eyes were badly swollen. Frank Perlich (Ott's copilot) was even more severely bitten, so much so that the Soviet authorities decided to hospitalize him for treatment.

October 8, 1944: The first freeze of the winter was not unexpected, but nonetheless the men complained bitterly about the cold barracks, for which there was inadequate heat. After over a week of waiting for the anticipated air transport to be announced, the airmen were becoming disgruntled; the frigid temperatures did not improve their morale.

October 9, 1944: A friendly new interpreter brought cheering news to the internees. A Soviet transport plane, earmarked for moving the men westward from Kamchatka, had landed at the airfield. A wave of excitement rippled through the camp. According to rumor, the internees were bound for Tashkent, but at this point the destination did not matter: anywhere, as long as it was not Kamchatka.

October 11, 1944: Although they had never been given a precise time of departure, the men showed their disappointment when overcast skies made flying improbable. Captain Petrov, however, helped to erase the shadows of gathering gloom in the camp by announcing that the plane would definitely fly tomorrow.

For the first time since their arrival at Petropavlovsk, the morale of the internees soared. At the finish of their evening meal of black bread and fried potatoes, the men burst into spontaneous singing, which continued into the night.

October 12, 1944: No departure. The pilot was reported to be ill. There was widespread disbelief among the airmen.

October 16, 1944: For the past four days the weather seemed perfect for flying, but the Soviet authorities never explained why they did not take advantage of it. Arnold felt a surge of anger, and the other 27 Americans must have reacted in generally the same way: "I'm tired of this barbed-wire-enclosed radio station!"

October 17, 1944: At 10:30 A.M. the plane was finally readied to fly. All 28 men had been led to believe that they would travel as a group. There was no general warning that the movement plan had been modified because, Ott said, "everything was hush-hush." When a Model-A Ford type truck arrived at the camp to take the men to the airfield, they were told that only 15 would go: Head and his army crew, Ott and his army tail gunner, Wayne and his navy crew, and McDonald and his navy copilot.

Nine army men and four navy men, who called themselves the unlucky thirteen, had no choice but to watch the truck drive away with "the lucky fifteen" and to wait their turn for air transportation. Their turn, they were told, was three days away.[5] In reality, it would be three *weeks* before they departed Kamchatka.

Gilbert Arnold and Thomas Shelton (Ott's waist gunner) were among those remaining in the camp. Disappointed and frustrated, the two men ignored the ground rules concerning the boundaries of the camp and walked into the adjacent village of dilapidated sod huts. "We were caught, and Captain Petrov was angry," Arnold noted in his diary, "but it didn't particularly bother me. . . . If the weather holds good, we should leave in a few days. I hope so; I'm not used to being cooped up."

5. Ibid.

The "lucky fifteen" were flown to Magadan. Aside from the impact of seeing prison camps and shackled prisoners, Ott said that the layover in Magadan was a time of pleasant living compared with the situation that they had left in Petropavlovsk. Their beds had mattresses and sheets. Fresh meat was served, and vodka and beer were available with every meal. Arrangements were made for the men to attend movies, opera, and folk-dance performances.

October 22, 1944: After being flown to Khabarovsk, the 15 internees were taken directly to the Red Army rest camp. As did their American predecessors, the new arrivals enjoyed considerable freedom of movement in the compound, where over 100 Red Army officers and a few women were also housed. The Americans frequently played volleyball with Red Army officer teams, watched movies shown in the dining hall, and attended dances where they were allowed to dance with some of the women.[6]

October 24, 1944: At the first dance, Ott met a young Red Army pharmacist whom Ott described as "my Russian goddess." Sasha was an attractive, rounded, dark-haired woman assigned to duty at the rest camp's dispensary. At that moment of meeting, Ott and Sasha seemed to be drawn to one another. Ott felt momentary regret that, according to rumor, the internees might be leaving Khabarovsk the next day.

October 25, 1944: The rumor of early departure was unfounded. Instead, the men were told that they would remain at the rest camp until the other members of the McDonald and Ott crews arrived from Kamchatka.

Ott arranged to see Sasha again. The language barrier itself did not present a serious obstacle to the attraction of one for the other, but Sasha's reluctance to become involved in friendship with a foreigner did present a problem until their association reached a comfortable stage. They continued to meet at evening dances, although there were other opportunities for rendezvous.

October 28, 1944: McGlinn and his B-29 crew were transferred from a Khabarovsk hospital to join the 15 army and navy internees at the rest camp.

November 8, 1944: Sasha had become less cautious. Although she and Ott had not met daily, they managed to see one another frequently. She came to the camp's celebration of the anniversary of the Red Revolution on November 7 to dance with Ott, and she returned the next day for two visits, one in the morning and one in the evening. Ott later believed that this was the time when their clandestine association came under the scrutiny of the NKVD.

November 9, 1944: Snow had been falling for hours. Ott used skis to go to Sasha's pharmacy in the dispensary building for a meeting with her.

---

6. War Department, "EX Report No. 551 (Living Conditions)," 2.

When he entered the dispensary, however, he found the camp commandant (a Red Army lieutenant colonel) and a major waiting for him. Sasha was standing near them. Ott looked at her. Sasha's eyes were wide and glistening. "Sasha was terrified," Ott remembered, "because the colonel was taking a dim view of the situation."

The colonel chided Ott. Then he poured wine for the customary toasts to Roosevelt, Churchill and Stalin, and Ott was free to go, leaving Sasha alone with the two officers.

October 18, 1944: On Kamchatka, the "unlucky thirteen" who remained in the camp have never forgotten how dejected they felt, because each additional day on Kamchatka seemed an eternity. Depending on the weather, the volleyball games resumed, with the Soviet teams continuing their string of victories over the Americans. As day followed day, the Americans analyzed the Soviets' playing technique and learned how to reposition the American tall and short players to the best advantage on the court. "It took us time to do so," Arnold reported, "but eventually we were able to draw even with them — and finally we beat them!"

When they played "basketball," the Americans made the rules for a game that was half-basketball and half-football. As a result, the internees were able to vent some of their frustrations on the Soviet teams. Physical contact during the rough games inevitably caused minor injuries such as abrasions and black eyes. Thomas Shelton, however, wrenched his knee and was hospitalized for treatment.

One of the more agile of the Soviet team players was Nick Gregory. Short and nimble, Nick gained the admiration of many of his American opponents, especially Gilbert Arnold. "After a time, we became friends," Arnold said. "He came to the schoolhouse where we traded language lessons and he taught me to play chess. He gave me his name and address. I never wrote to him because, after the start of the Cold War, I did not want to get Nick in trouble with his government."

October 24, 1944: Captain Petrov and Mike again promised the internees that they would leave "soon." The men no longer reacted to such promises. Their concern was that they would be forced to remain in Kamchatka all winter unless their air transport arrived promptly. Snow season, they knew, was fast approaching.

October 27, 1944: Rather than continue complaining to Petrov about the shortage of wood for heating fuel, the internees began cutting and splitting their own wood supply from dead timber on the camp grounds. In addition to warming the barracks, the wood also heated the steam bathhouse and water for washing clothes.

October 30, 1944: The first snow had fallen. Before noon some of the internees and their guards tentatively started to toss snowballs at one another. The playful exchange quickly changed into a more serious game as additional men joined each side. "We organized our side into a skirmish line and an artillery line," Arnold said "The Soviets could not stand against us for long." Other snow battles followed.

With the coming of darkness, the snow clouds cleared away, and a full moon rose. The internees impulsively decided to play volleyball in the snow by the light of the moon. The Soviets were flabbergasted by the noisy nocturnal horseplay. Were all Americans so crazy?

October 31, 1944: From Attu, the 77th Squadron assigned a mission of photographing the eastern shoreline of Shumushu and bombing a fish cannery on Paramushiro to two B-25s, one of which was piloted by William McQuillin.[7] Under a low ceiling, McQuillin completed his photographic run at Shumushu and then turned south to Paramushiro, where he slammed his bombs into the canning factory. The air around the B-25 was filled immediately by a swarm of fighters firing bursts of 20-mm shells. Nicholas Horin (tail gunner) was struck in the arm with a fragment. The bomber's right rudder control was badly damaged, but McQuillin was able to take the plane into the low clouds and escape the fighters. Because the B-25 commenced to vibrate due to damage, McQuillin ordered his crew to be ready to use their parachutes. Fortunately, he and Donald Ward (copilot) managed to bring the bomber temporarily to stable flight and turn it to a northerly course toward Kamchatka.[8]

November 1, 1944 (Kamchatka time): McQuillin had been told during his premission briefing at Attu how to approach the Petropavlovsk landing field and how to contact Petropavlovsk by radio. As McQuillin flew north of Avacha Bay, Joseph Brishaber (radio operator) issued the emergency radio call over the assigned frequency. No answer was heard, but soon two Soviet fighters appeared and escorted the bomber to the snowy landing field.

After McQuillin landed safely, Mike the interpreter arrived and took charge. While Mike was arranging for Horin, who was bleeding badly from his wound, to be rushed to the hospital, another officer took the weapons of the crewmen.

McQuillin was promptly interrogated. Because he had not been briefed about responding to Soviet questions, he told only that he had been on a photographic mission when he was attacked by Japanese fighters. He never mentioned that three cameras with the film exposed during the Shumushu reconnaissance were still in the bomber, and he never learned whether the Soviets discovered them. Refusing to say anything more, he

7. War Department, "EX Report No. 552, McQuillin, William L.," 4.
8. Ibid., 5.

and the six other members of his crew were driven to the schoolhouse, where they found the "unlucky thirteen." McQuillin had hardly been introduced to his fellow internees when Soviet officers took him aside and again thoroughly questioned him. He continued to be uncooperative.

McQuillin recalled that during his brief time at the landing field, he saw several American Navy bombers, a number of B-25s, and two B-24s. On all of the aircraft the Soviet red star insignia had been superimposed over the American white one.[9]

Although he was unaware of its presence among the clutter of parked aircraft, a Soviet air transport plane had landed a few hours ahead of McQuillin. This airplane was scheduled to remove the American internees from Kamchatka as soon as favorable flying weather developed.

November 7, 1944: After six days of overcast skies and intermittent snow, the weather cleared. For the Soviets, the date was cause for celebrating the anniversary of the Red Revolution, but for the internees the date was also cause for American celebrating—because they had been told to be ready to go to the airfield and depart! The date was also Arnold's birthday, and leaving Kamchatka was a "wonderful birthday present." Captain Petrov and Mike Dondekin gave Arnold a sports medal as a remembrance present, and Nick Gregory gave him a poignant birthday gift—an embroidered handkerchief made by Nick's mother.

All 20 men—the "unlucky thirteen" and McQuillin's seven—vacated the schoolhouse and boarded a Lend-Lease DC-3 at the airfield. The cabin was red-carpeted and stank of fish, but the Americans, anxious to leave Kamchatka behind them, hardly noticed the stench. The most direct route to Khabarovsk was via Okha on Sakhalin Island, and the pilot followed a bearing over the Sea of Okhotsk in that direction. The pilot was notified about one hour from Petropavlovsk that Okha was closed by weather, and he then turned to the right and headed for Magadan.

The Soviet bureaucracy at Magadan was not prepared for this emergency diversion of American internees, especially when everybody was celebrating the Red Revolution anniversary. The pilot made arrangements for the men to be billeted in the town. "We had more freedom of movement in Magadan than we did in any other place in the Soviet Union," Arnold said. "Nobody seemed to be responsible for us every second of the time."

November 8, 1944: The hard-drinking Soviet crew of the DC-3 ate each meal with the Americans. The pilot, copilot, engineer, and interpreter engaged in endless toasts, but few of the Americans could match the Soviets drink for drink.

9. War Department, "EX Report No. 552 (Interrogation and Briefing)," 2–3.

Internees and their Soviet escorts after arrival at Magadan. *From left:* Frank Perlich (Ott's army crew), Donnie Broadwell (McDonald's navy crew), the Soviet pilot, John Rosa (McDonald's navy crew), the Soviet copilot, and Gilbert Arnold (OH's army crew). Photograph courtesy Gilbert Arnold

November 9, 1944: During the morning the Soviet flyers entered the internees' room and looked around. By finger-pointing they selected two army and two navy airmen—Frank Perlich and Gilbert Arnold (Ott's crew) and Donnie Broadwell and John Rosa (McDonald's crew)—and beckoned them to follow. "We walked to a photographer's shop," Arnold recalled. "The pilot clapped his hands for service, and we posed for a group picture." The Soviet flyers wanted each man to have a copy. "I hid mine in the lining of my coat, which now contained my sports medal, the embroidered handkerchief, three carefully folded pages of maps from an old Russian atlas, and the early notes for my diary," Arnold said.

November 10, 1944: For many of the internees, the hours of relative freedom in Magadan were marred by the sight of the mass of political prisoners being marched down the streets of the town. "Those miserable wretches, as well as Japanese flak and fighter planes, are etched on my memory today as if I saw them yesterday," Arnold wrote, 44 years after the event.

November 11, 1944: After an all-day flight from Magadan, the internees arrived at Khabarovsk and joined the 26 other American airmen. The reunion in the comfortable rest camp atmosphere would be brief because now there was no longer an excuse to delay their movement westward and away from the suspected scrutiny of Japanese agents.

As a forewarning of the Siberian winter weather that was awaiting the Americans, the temperature remained bitterly cold. The Amur River was already frozen except for a small open channel near the middle of the broad waterway. Despite the harsh air, however, many of the idle internees continued to find skis with which to amuse themselves on the deepening snow.

November 12, 1944: A thoroughly frightened Sasha met Ott at the movie and dance in the evening. "Sasha had caught hell from the commandant," Ott said, "and she was going to be punished." He could not understand why this was happening to Sasha because of her association with him, but he sensed her fear.

November 14, 1944: During the long layover at the rest camp, Ott had formed a cordial relationship with an interpreter identified simply as "Steve." Unlike the men who acted as interpreters on Kamchatka, Steve spoke fluent English. Ott completed Steve's education in English by giving him lessons in American slang. On this date Steve informed Ott and the other pilots that all the men (except McQuillin's crew) would depart tomorrow by railroad. Steve himself, he said, would be their interpreter on the train.

November 15, 1944: The rest camp stirred with unusual activity as 39 internees prepared to leave Khabarovsk. Those men who did not have heavy clothing for the trans-Siberian railroad trip were each given extra stockings, a mackinaw-style coat, Lend-Lease army shoes, and a cap with earflaps.[10] The 28 army flyers (Head, Ott, and McGlinn crews) and 11 navy airmen (McDonald and Wayne crews) were loaded aboard a charcoal-burning bus and carried to the railroad station. Ott saw Sasha standing briefly on the station platform in a farewell gesture, and then she was gone. Steve knew Sasha's story. He told Ott that she could be sent to a Siberian camp "to be taught discipline."

Accompanied by Steve and an NKVD officer, the internees boarded the train and were assigned to two hard-class coaches, 32 to one car, and the remainder to the second. The train, pulled by a steam locomotive, had ten other coaches and a dining car. All of the wooden-benched coaches were loaded nearly to capacity with both adults and children. Toilet fa-

10. War Department, "EX Report No. 551 (Living Conditions)," 2.

cilities were present in each coach, but they were usually frozen and useless. The train was staffed and operated by an all-woman crew — car attendants, dining car personnel, and, presumably, the locomotive fireman and engineer.

Unlike the NKVD escort, Steve proved to be a more thoughtful traveling companion on the long trip across Asia. A specific time was set aside for the American internees to eat in the dining car. At mealtime they had to walk through other cars in order to reach the diner. "The living conditions in the coaches containing Soviet groups and families deteriorated rapidly," Ralph Hammond reported. "The stench was terrible . . . and by the time we reached the dining car our appetite was gone. We begged Steve to do something about it. He apparently did, because thereafter the train was stopped and we were allowed to walk along the track to the dining car. When our meal was over, the train was again stopped so that we could walk to our car."

In the dining car, the focal item of the internees' special rations was some form of potatoes. For breakfast, mashed potatoes and another item, perhaps a slice of Spam or dried fish. At noon, fried potatoes, borscht, and tea. At night, mashed potatoes and black bread.[11]

From Khabarovsk to Irkutsk the train passed through the Siberian countryside ranging from flatlands to rolling forest-covered hills. The subzero temperature permeated the railroad cars, whose coal-burning stoves, one per car, provided virtually no heat. At times the coach windows were covered by ice. The men bundled themselves in their clothing day and night. Trying to sleep on the wooden benched caused sore hips and aching backs. It was never too cold, however, for the bedbugs.

One night Hammond remembered waking up when the train stopped. "I saw the woman car attendant carry a white-hot metal grate in a bucket into the car," he said. "The grate had been heated in the locomotive firebox. She deposited the bucket with the grate in the middle of the car. The radiated warmth from this grate was the only heat I can recall."

At each scheduled train stop, the station usually had a public hot water spigot. The passengers would dash from the train with kettles in their hands, fill their kettles, and return to the train. In this way, they could brew their own tea. Black marketeers on station platforms offered supplemental food items for sale. At the request of some of the internees, a car attendant bought six apples at one of the stations for an equivalent cost of about $15.[12]

"The station platform was filled with people, many of whom were on crutches," McGlinn recalled. He saw others who had wrapped themselves

11. Ibid.
12. Ibid., 3.

in rags as the only protection from the Siberian cold. Less fortunate were the trainloads of people who were being moved in locked freight cars toward the Soviet Far East. [13]

November 19, 1944: After nearly 2,000 miles of travel since leaving Khabarovsk, the train skirted the lower end of Lake Baikal and made a major stop at Irkutsk, where some passengers departed while others boarded. One of the new passengers was a pretty young woman named Yekaterina who preferred to be called "Kati." A schoolteacher from Yakutsk, the gold- and diamond-mining capital northeast of Irkutsk, Kati was on vacation and traveling westward toward Moscow.

Kati was assigned to a first-level bench in an adjacent foul-smelling coach. "She instantly brightened the car," Arnold said, "and somehow the odor did not seem so bad." Among the school subjects that Kati taught was English. The Americans had been thrown into the company not only of a pretty woman with a shy but delightful personality but of one who could speak English as well.

November 20, 1944: The train rolled toward Krasnoyarsk through deepening snow and frigid temperatures. Putting discomfort temporarily aside, American airmen continued to vie with one another for opportunities to visit and talk with Kati.

November 21, 1944: The time for Kati's departure was nearing. In the early afternoon the train arrived at Novosibirsk, where one branch of the railroad would continue toward Moscow, and another toward Tashkent. Kati took a photograph of herself from her luggage and autographed it to give one of her persistent American admirers. It was her way of saying good-bye.

After six days of being cooped up on the train, the airmen were led into the huge Novosibirsk station building and were fed borscht, noodles, and goat meat. Then they were marched to a community bathhouse where they undressed for bathing and a change of underclothing. John Rosa (McDonald's crew) deposited his diary notes in his shoes. When he returned to dress, his diary was gone.

In the meanwhile, the internees' two coaches had been moved to the Novosibirsk railroad yards. Once aboard, the airmen prepared to spend a restless night in the icy railroad cars.

November 22, 1944: Their coaches were coupled to a southbound train, and the internees commenced the last leg of the trans-Asian trip to their permanent camp near Tashkent.

The new train lacked a dining car. Instead, food for the internees had been loaded at Novosibirsk, and meals were served by Steve and the coach attendants. The men recalled that the food, although monotonous, was an

13. War Department, "EX Report No. 542, McGlinn, Richard M. (Incidental Intelligence)," 2–3.

Yekaterina ("Kati"), the English-speaking schoolteacher who was a passenger on the same train as the internees between Irkutsk and Novosibirsk. Photograph courtesy Gilbert Arnold

improvement over what had been available in the earlier dining car. For one thing, there were no potatoes. The meals were selected from Spam, dry toast, cheese, smoked or dried fish, condensed milk with hot water, and tea.[14]

November 24, 1944: After traveling almost due south from Novosibirsk for two days, the internees' train approached Alma Ata, the capital of

14. War Department, "EX Report No. 551 (Living Conditions)," 3.

Kazakhstan. Although there were high mountains to be seen marking the border with China to the east, the train was now crossing flatlands and soon would pass below the snowline. Camels were becoming a common sight, as were herds of goats and sheep.

November 26, 1944: When the men detrained at Tashkent in Uzbekistan, trucks were waiting to take them to Vrevskaya and the internment camp. For the 39 men who had endured the hardships of Kamchatka and had survived in the wilderness of Khabarovsk Territory in the Soviet Far East, the living conditions in the Uzbekistan camp were a welcome change.

8

The Third Escape
January, 1945

In mid-October, after navy captain Harry Felt and army major Paul Hall visited the Tashkent camp, they returned to Moscow and confirmed to General Deane that 51 navy flyers and an 11-man army B-29 crew were in the camp. During his next visit with Foreign Minister Molotov, Ambassador Harriman mentioned that the 62 men at Tashkent "must be a nuisance." Was it time for them to leave?

Although he did not deny that the men would be allowed to escape soon, Molotov said that the airmen in the meanwhile needed rest and that the internment camp, located in south central Asia, was well situated for that purpose. As a result of the visit, Harriman concluded that while there was an oblique promise that the men would soon be released, the Soviets were not yet ready to act.[1]

October 20, 1944: The NKVD was fully aware of the presence of 28 army and navy airmen in various locations of the Soviet Far East (Petropavlovsk, Magadan, and Khabarovsk) in addition to 11 B-29 crewmen whom the Soviets considered to be too ill for travel. In a meeting between General Deane and NKVD general Ivanov, it was agreed that when the 28 American airmen reached Tashkent, an escape would be permitted. Lt. Col. Robert McCabe would again lead the escape. Other arrangements would be made for the B-29 crewmen likewise to escape when they had sufficiently recovered and were released from the hospital at Khabarovsk.[2]

November 27, 1944: General Kutuzov of OVS informed McCabe that 39 internees, including the B-29 crew that had previously been reported too ill to travel, were at Tashkent. With these newcomers, there were now 101 Americans at the camp. Agreement was quickly reached that the same Soviet-American team that had supervised the escape in February — Colonel

1. Richard C. Lukas, "Escape," *Aerospace Historian,* Spring, 1969, 16.
2. Ibid.

Myakhotnik of the NKVD, Captain Kozlovski of the OVS, and McCabe — would likewise oversee this evacuation.

The 39 new internees found the camp to be running smoothly under the leadership of John Vivian (navy). Both Charles Wayne (navy) and Richard McGlinn (army) however, were senior in grade to Vivian. Wayne promptly assumed the command responsibility, with McGlinn and Vivian becoming the respective links in the command structure with the army and navy crews. Wayne's style of command and personality were radically different from Vivian's, and Wayne at once became the center of controversy among the internees, navy and army alike.[3]

The camp's paperback book library and shortwave radio receiver helped to make the men's waking hours more pleasant. However, the winter nights were frigid, and the new arrivals quickly joined the others in complaining bitterly about the shortage of fuel for the wall heating stoves and for the shortage of blankets.

The camp commandant, Major Putakana, eventually allowed the use of two buckets of scarce coal per stove each day. Some men schemed to steal wood and coal from the camp's meager fuel stockpile. Others searched for scrap wood in the outbuildings.

At first, Putakana insisted that Red Army soldiers were issued one blanket and therefore one blanket should also be sufficient for the Americans. After the internees' protests became known to the Tashkent Soviet Command, he decided to authorize a second blanket.

With 101 restless and unpredictable men in the confined camp area, Putakana warned the internees, old and new, of the dangers that were associated with trying to escape. Not only had General Deane issued an order against such an action, but Putakana discouraged the men by relating that two attempts a year earlier "were almost fatal."

November 29, 1944: A flurry of activity by the Soviet staff helped to feed a rumor that the internees were leaving Tashkent soon, and American morale soared. Although the men did not know what exactly was happening, the Tashkent Soviet Command had been informed that the Soviet-American team of officers was en route to Tashkent with precise instructions.

November 30, 1944: The aircraft bearing McCabe, Myakhotnik, and Kozlovski landed at Tashkent during the morning. Leaving the Soviet officers in Tashkent to handle the logistic details of the forthcoming secret escape, McCabe came directly to the internment camp, where he deliv-

3. In part because of the isolation of American airmen in interior Asia, the senior officer of each group assembled at Tashkent faced a variety of complex command problems. In this particular group, the problems were further compounded by the large number and interservice mix of idle, worried men.

ered a bag of mail containing the first letters that the men had received since their families had been notified that they were "safe in a neutral country."

McCabe then assembled the internees and read a bogus secret order from General Deane. The order directed the movement of the men to Tbilisi in the Caucasus area as predicted by Captain Felt during his October visit to the camp. McCabe then announced that the transfer would commence on December 3, three days hence.

The NKVD plan that would permit the internees to escape to Tehran was identical to the earlier plan that was executed without a hitch in February. Only Nona the interpreter recognized the similarity of the plan as McCabe repeated the false information. She was the only member of the camp staff who was present when the February group departed.

Reaction to McCabe's announcement was mixed among the men. All of them were elated that they were leaving the camp's confinement and inactivity. Some of them were disappointed that they were not leaving the Soviet Union entirely, but others secretly suspected that the announcement was a prelude to what they dared to hope—that indeed they were going home.

In Washington, meanwhile, Drew Pearson had written his "Washington Merry-Go-Round" syndicated column for national release even as McCabe spoke in the Tashkent camp. Pearson never revealed the source of the story contained in the column, but it would have been interesting to know why the informant fed Pearson a tale of pure fiction.[4]

The story, in a nutshell, told about the 1942 landing of a "Doolittle Tokyo raid" bomber on Japanese-controlled Manchurian soil west of Vladivostok. The crew was rescued by a Red Army tank column whose commander refused a Japanese demand that the Soviets surrender the American crew. Shortly after being carried safely across the border into Soviet territory, the crew was turned over to Clyde Pangborn, who flew the bomber crew to Alaska.

The Japanese had reason to believe that the York crew was the only bomber crew from the Doolittle raid to have landed in the Soviet Union. Pearson's fictional story implied that the Soviet Union had defied the Japanese by secretly returning the interned York crew to American control in violation of the Soviet-Japanese neutrality pact. That implication was what the Soviet Union had been trying to avoid. It would be several days before the impact of the story was felt in Moscow.

December 2, 1944: At the internment camp, exhilaration was rampant among the men until McCabe announced that the departure from Tash-

---

4. Drew Pearson, "Washington Merry-Go-Round," November 30, 1944, Lyndon Baines Johnson Library archives, Austin, Texas.

kent had been delayed until December 5. The news dampened the men's spirits, but not for long. A surprise performance by a visiting Red Army dance ensemble and chorus helped to divert the internees' attention from the disappointing development. After all, the Americans reasoned, most of them had been waiting for months for a sign of hope. Why be impatient now? What could be the difference if they remained two additional days in the camp?

In Washington, Henry C. Cassidy of the Associated Press, perhaps reacting to the fairy tale that Drew Pearson had released two days earlier, filed a more realistic story about the internment and escape of the York crew.[5] According to Cassidy's story, the Doolittle raiders had lived in pampered captivity, had endured prolonged boredom, and finally had been given access to easy escape. Cassidy accurately charted the internees' wandering across Siberia, wintering in the Ural Mountains, and moving to Ashkhabad on the Soviet-Iranian border, where they drove a truck into Iran.

Whether the public readership believed the details in the Pearson column or those in the Associated Press story made little difference insofar as the ultimate conclusion that could be reached. In either case, the Soviets would seem to have arranged for or allowed the York crew to escape either to Alaska or through Ashkhabad. Ashkhabad was on the direct rail route from Tashkent to Tbilisi. For the waiting internees at Tashkent, the Cassidy story could not have appeared at a worse time. Moscow was not yet aware that the Soviet-American secret had been revealed, but it would know soon.

December 3, 1944: Among the men at the camp, individual preparation for departure continued at a slower pace. Many of the internees recalled that they could have been ready to leave "within a few minutes" after McCabe made his initial announcement. Unknown to the men, however, the various facets of the intricate NKVD escape plan were being knit into a clandestine operation that needed to mesh in every detail, which required much behind-the-scenes preparation time.

During the afternoon, members of the camp staff distributed a souvenir Uzbek cap to each internee. The embroidered headgear was close-fitting like a skullcap, black, green, and white in color and unique to the native dress in Uzbekistan.

Illness, especially dysentery, perpetually shadowed the camp, but the men were determined that nothing would keep them from leaving at the appointed time. During this day, however, Samuel Gelber (Bone's navy crew) had been suffering abdominal pain that became increasingly worse by the hour. By nightfall he was in agony, and the camp doctor confirmed

5. Henry C. Cassidy, "'Escape' of Tokyo Raid Crew from Russia Revealed," *St. Louis Post-Dispatch,* December 2, 1944, 1, 5.

a diagnosis that Gelber was suffering from acute appendicitis and required surgery.

A light snow was beginning to fall. "I was carried from the barracks on a stretcher by two Red Army soldiers," Gelber said. "I'll never forget how, once outside the building, they set the stretcher on the snow while they smoked a cigarette." Then Gelber was loaded into a truck and taken to the Tashkent military hospital. Fearing that the appendix had burst, doctors operated immediately. General anesthesia was not available, Gelber said, so a combination of local anesthesia and swallows of vodka was used while the emergency surgery was performed. "I passed out from the pain," he said.

Once the ordeal was over, Gelber was disconsolate. "I knew everybody in the camp was leaving," he said. "I knew that I was going to be left behind." He resigned himself to abandonment.

December 4, 1944: The Soviet camp staff, led by Nona, initiated the idea of a farewell dinner for the men and began collecting cold meats, pastries, and extra rations of vodka and beer. A special guest of honor was the general from the Tashkent Soviet Command. The noisy gathering of Soviet overseers and American internees proved to be an opportunity for reducing tensions, and the men welcomed the occasion of joint relaxation for the first time since the November 7 "riot." "The party was a huge success!" Gilbert Arnold noted.

December 5, 1944: One hundred army and navy airmen completed their preparations for departure. Each man was issued a musette-type bag into which they put sufficient food for their individual consumption until they reached their destination. Their rations included condensed milk, canned fish, black bread, cheese, boiled eggs, Lend-Lease Spam, butter, and sugar. In addition, "we were instructed to take with us a change of socks and underwear," John Mathers recalled. As a final gesture, the camp staff distributed an additional souvenir to each American: a small cigarette lighter whose circular metal case was only slightly more than one inch in diameter. The flint sparking device and the wick protruded from the rim like the fuse on an ancient bomb.

After nightfall a convoy of tarpaulin-canopied Lend-Lease trucks arrived at the camp, and into them were loaded the men with their supplies. McCabe instructed them to keep the covers secured over the end of each truck and to maintain silence during the long ride into Tashkent. The convoy delivered the men to the railroad yards, where three railroad coaches were waiting. Colonel Myakhotnik and his NKVD group of train attendants, all veterans of the February internee journey to Ashkhabad, were also there to supervise the men's transfer from truck to coach. Captain Kozlovski, having finished his assignment to assist in organizing the departure, was ready to return to Moscow.

One of the coaches was a soft-class car with compartments for the senior officers, including McCabe and Myakhotnik. The other two coaches were hard class—identical to the railroad cars used on the recent trans-Siberian journey from Khabarovsk to Tashkent, and in these the majority of the airmen were assigned.

It was now ten o'clock, and the men were advised to go to bed. Most of them did. Later, a locomotive shunted the cars from the railroad yards and coupled them to a train that departed Tashkent about midnight. The long trip "to the Caucasus" had begun.

December 7, 1944: After nearly two days of traveling in a southwesterly direction through Samarkand and Bukhara, the train was approaching Ashkhabad. There had been no unusual delays, and the rumor was circulating that the men would cross the Caspian Sea sometime on the following day en route to Tbilisi.

Unknown to the men, the execution of the NKVD master plan was on schedule. Shortly before midnight, when the train was a few miles east of Ashkhabad, a hotbox on one of the coaches was simulated according to plan, and the train switched all three coaches to a sidetrack, as previously rehearsed. McCabe and Myakhotnik continued to Ashkhabad on the train. McCabe promised the men that he would return within three or four hours.

December 8, 1944: McCabe did not return as promised. In his stead, a Red Army truck from Ashkhabad brought a hot meal to the waiting men. Having eaten, the anxious men waited again. They became ominously quiet because the feeling that "something was wrong" became contagious. The fact that dense fog limited visibility during the daylight hours did nothing to brighten their outlook.

In late afternoon a poker-faced McCabe brought word from Ashkhabad that there had been a change in plans and that the men would remain where they were until new orders were received from Moscow. "This is a hell of a way to spend my birthday!" John Ott, who just turned 26, fumed. "On a railroad siding in Russia!"

December 9, 1944: The siding on which the coaches were placed was on the semidesert. Eighteen miles to the south were rising mountain foothills where the boundary between Iran and the Soviet Union was located. Uncomfortable cold temperatures persisted, as did a light snow that was covering the ground. The restless, moody men paced the right-of-way beside the cars to pass the time. Some of them collected enough snow to build snowmen.

December 10, 1944: Dense fog returned to make the temperature seem even colder. After being delayed all day, McCabe arrived from Ashkhabad at 6:30 P.M. and asked the men to assemble so that he could make an announcement. McCabe's face was unsmiling. Standing on the steps of one coach, he grimly told them that Moscow had decided that all of the internees would be returned to the Tashkent camp.[6]

Two American newspapermen, he explained, had revealed the secret escape of the York crew. Moscow, he said, was waiting for Japanese reaction to the revelation. John Vivian, the former senior officer of most of the internees, believed that he knew the men well enough to be concerned about their acceptance of the bad news. His concern was justified.

The men did not make any demonstration when McCabe finished speaking. They stood in stunned silence. Then slowly they began to break away in groups, in pairs or singly. Some of them, taking whatever food they could stuff into their pockets, drifted from sight into the darkness.

Within two hours, 34 men, or roughly one-third of the internees, started an irrational attempt to escape. Wayne, now the responsible senior officer, vainly tried to persuade or order the men to stand fast. The 34, however, were past the point of listening to arguments or commands. Weakened by disease, they nevertheless were convinced that once they reached the border they would be free. Never mind the vigilant border guards. Never mind the roving mountain tribesmen who robbed and killed strangers for their clothing and food. Never mind the sand dunes and irregular dry streambeds that they would encounter. Never mind the lightly falling snow and the freezing temperatures.

The majority of the internees apparently felt as did John Mathers. Considering the obstacles, the effort to escape seemed futile to them and to him.

John Ott did not agree. He together with his army officer crew (Frank Perlich, Gilbert Arnold, and Raymond Shimer) and three navy officers (Kenneth Miles, Donnie Broadwell, and John Ehret) trudged through the cold night in the direction of the foothills. A few hours later when fatigue set in, they forced themselves to face the reality that they were physically unable to continue. They reluctantly turned back.

Three other navy officers (Byron Morgan, Thomas Edwards, and Eugene Dulan) walked along the railroad tracks to Ashkhabad, where they hoped to find the highway that led from the city through the mountains to Iran. They were quickly captured by an alert railroad guard, recognized as Americans, and marched to a local depot.

In the meanwhile, Red Army sentries began to report the interception of other Americans, and the Ashkhabad Soviet Command alerted local military authorities not to shoot but to seize any non-Russian speaking strangers and bring them also to the depot.

December 11, 1944: In all, 27 internees either returned voluntarily to the railroad cars (Ott and his companions among them) or were corralled by the alert Soviets. Not long after dawn several Red Army trucks arrived

6. War Department "EX Report No. 542, McGlinn, Richard M.," 10.

at trackside bearing both food supplies and the weary men from Ashkhabad. None of the men had suffered injury of consequence. Seven internees were still missing. In the afternoon, the three railroad coaches occupied by McCabe, Myakhotnik, and 93 demoralized American airmen were coupled to a Tashkent-bound train to commence the two-day return trip to the Vrevskaya internment camp.

December 12, 1944: The seven missing men were six navy aviators and a lone army flyer: Russell Manthie (Lindell's crew), John Rosa (McDonald's crew), Earl Mulford and Robert Baxter (Wayne's crew), Henry Pollard (Dingle's crew), Harold Toney (Cowles's crew), and Mike Losick (Jarrell's crew).

Although they were not well ("we were so sick," Manthie reported), without food, and half-frozen, the seven men managed to evade capture for nearly 24 hours. An experienced local tracker finally found them and took them to Ashkhabad, but by that time their companions had already departed. The bedraggled men were confined for three days in an unheated room and interrogated repeatedly, Manthie said.

December 13, 1944: The train with the three carloads of internees arrived at Tashkent in late afternoon. Trucks carried the silent men to the Vrevskaya camp, where the staff was being reassembled — with one change. Major Putakana would be replaced by Lt. Col. Ivan Siminov, a Cossack who, unlike NKVD colonel Myakhotnik, who also was a Cossack, made every effort to call attention to his heritage. He delighted in wearing shiny riding boots, black breeches with a wide red stripe down each side, a red tunic trimmed in black karakul fur, and a typical Russian hat of karakul to match. Frank Ogden recalled that Siminov, in contrast to the earlier commandant, "was an officer who was very understanding and tolerant and did his best to improve our lot." The men later learned that Siminov could speak a smattering of English, which he probably acquired during a peacetime mission to the United States to buy horses for the Red Army cavalry.

The internees returned to an icy barracks building. There still was insufficient fuel for the wall stoves. McGlinn, himself recuperating from his wilderness ordeal in Khabarovsk Territory, noticed that the health and morale of the Americans began to deteriorate the moment that they returned to the camp. The lack of heat was not necessarily a contributing reason. "The spirit of the men was at a very low ebb," McGlinn observed. "Sickness of one type or another was prevalent, and the men brooded, wondering whether they would ever get a chance to leave the Soviet Union alive."[7]

December 14, 1944: McCabe and Myakhotnik prepared to leave the camp

7. Ibid.

and return to Moscow. At McCabe's suggestion, the men wrote letters to their families so that he could take mail with him. In his final talk with the internees, he tried to assure the men that the situation was not hopeless, but according to Arnold, "he said little of cheer." Snow was falling when McCabe departed to go to the Tashkent railroad station. The departure marked McCabe's last contact with any of the internees. After three wartime years in the Soviet Union, he was reassigned in January, 1945.

December 15, 1944: Following the new snowfall, "this place is colder than hell," Arnold wrote. "I wear my coat and hat from morning till night and cover myself with all of my clothes during the night."

Wayne instituted a rigid and unpopular military disciplinary system designed to bring the dispirited, surly men under control. Extra guard-duty tours, solitary confinement, and bread and water diets were used to punish misconduct and mischief.

Disciplinary measures were not necessarily the answers for coping with frustration and despair. Since Christmas was near, the idea of having an organized major Christmas party was proposed by a group of officers. McGlinn personally discussed the idea with the commandant and pointed out to him that preparation for a party of this kind would be one good means of keeping many of the men mentally and physically occupied for several days. Siminov promised to present the proposal to NKVD and Red Army officials in Tashkent, where the results of the November 7 "party" had not been forgotten.

December 16, 1944: The camp's internee population was expanded by the arrival of 29 more men from the army B-29 crews of Weston Price and William Mickish and the army B-25 crew of William McQuillin. Siminov announced that the Tashkent officials not only agreed to the American proposal for a Christmas party but promised to provide special food rations for the occasion. The approval came as a surprise because of the internee pessimism that permeated the camp, and there was a perceptible change in the camp's general attitude. An organizational group began assigning individual and committee chores to prepare for the Christmas Eve event.

December 17, 1944: After a two-day railroad trip from Ashkhabad, the last seven of the men who attempted to escape were delivered to the camp. "They looked hard," Arnold wrote. Russell Manthie, one of the seven men, reported that the men probably had good reason for looking that way. Their experience during their hike toward the Iranian border, their confinement at Ashkhabad, and their return train trip to Tashkent "in a boxcar" were unpleasant memories, he said. The men at the camp observed that "the last seven" brought with them a souvenir — a puppy named "Gypsy," which they had found near Tashkent.

December 18, 1944: John Mathers was one of the internees who believed that "we were going to be a permanent fixture" in the camp. "Somebody, I can't remember who, drew a design for a group insignia," he wrote. "To keep occupied, why not embroider copies of the insignia?" Several men responded. The design consisted of a white heraldic shield on which were positioned the insignias of the Eleventh Air Force, the Twentieth Air Force, and the Navy's Fleet Air Wing Four. Nona helped the men to obtain sewing needles from the housekeeping staff. Once a week the men were issued clean cotton towels with red and blue stripes, from which colored threads were pulled. Using a piece of sheeting stretched over an embroidery hoop fashioned from a piece of wire, the men set to work on the tedious projects. Whether any of them finished an entire design was not recorded. Mathers himself was able to complete about three-quarters of his project.

December 19, 1944: Frank Perlich and Gilbert Arnold became involved in "a little trouble," Arnold said. Wayne accused them of stealing wood, but Arnold explained that he and Perlich thought that they were permitted to build their own heating fires but apparently misunderstood. Wayne confined them to quarters for two days.

December 21, 1944: Samuel Gelber was sufficiently recovered from his emergency surgery to rejoin his fellow internees at the camp. Meantime, preparation and rehearsal for the Christmas party continued. Leonard Karkoszynski (Ott's army crew) was painting an appropriate mural scene — an American soldier sitting on the edge of a foxhole and looking at the Christmas Star. Richard Johnson (Mahrt's navy crew) and Gebler organized the choral group. George Hummell (Jarrell's B-29 crew), using some of the special rations, volunteered to make cake and cookies. Edward Golden (also Jarrell's crew) collected writers to prepare the postdinner entertainment skits, mostly bawdy. Wayne released Perlich and Arnold from confinement and then put them on repeated tours of late-night guard duty.

December 24, 1944: The planning for the Christmas Eve party produced a climactic event that the depressed men desperately needed — a time to choke on tears and a time to laugh. The party began with formality in the dining room. The Soviet military commander and members of his staff from Tashkent, having accepted an invitation to attend, were ceremoniously seated. Table candles provided the lighting, carolers sang "Holy Night" and "Little Star of Bethlehem," and McGlinn recited a biblical Christmas reading. Then dinner was served — a piece of beef with a fried egg on it, rare side dishes including green onions, and Hummell's white cake for dessert. In addition, a small bottle of vodka and another of wine were at each man's place, and toasts proposed by Soviet and American alike followed one after another. The internees' nostalgia visibly began to fade.

The entertainment shattered the formality of the occasion: rollicking carols, humorous skits, barbershop harmony, and demonstration dances

The insignia designed by the internees of the aborted escape attempt in December, 1944. Drawing by John ("Butterfly") Mathers

such as jitterbugging, all of which created an atmosphere of temporary relaxation for the first time since the Ashkhabad fiasco.

December 25, 1944: Having arrived in Moscow, McCabe reported to General Deane the details of what happened when the Soviets decided to abort the NKVD escape plan at Ashkhabad. Deane immediately sent a message to Washington.

"I presume," Deane said, "the newspaper stories which caused the Soviet action were those of Pearson and Cassidy. . . . After the return to Tashkent," Deane concluded, "the Soviet officer in charge of the escape [NKVD colonel Myakhotnik] telephoned to Moscow. Later, when slightly intoxicated, he confided to McCabe that possibly the escape would be arranged again in about a month. I do not know how much credence to give this, but I shall of course see the General of the NKVD [Ivanov] who is in charge of the project in Moscow and try to have it arranged again."[8]

December 31, 1944: At the Vrevskaya camp another party was arranged, this time by the Soviets because New Year's was a major day of celebration in the Soviet Union. A banquet with extra food and ample amounts of vodka was served. John Vivian recalled that "efforts to get some entertainment going had no success." Nobody was in the mood, he said. Some of the internees, however, did remain in the dining room to drink vodka and sing until the new year arrived.

January 2, 1945: President Roosevelt sent a personal message to Ambassador Harriman: "The Director of Censorship has been directed by me to take steps to prevent publicity hereafter of any news regarding escape from neutral or Allied countries of interned Americans."[9] Harriman immediately made an appointment to see Foreign Minister Molotov and handed Roosevelt's communication to him. Harriman said that Molotov seemed pleased and remarked that the president's action would be helpful. Harriman told Molotov that he did not blame the Soviets for turning the group back and that it had been a very useful lesson.

In his diplomatic capacity, Harriman stressed the desirability of arranging for the group, now swollen to 130 internees, to escape soon. In a vague manner, it seemed to Harriman, Molotov promised to see what could be done.[10]

Molotov made no mention of any Japanese diplomatic reaction to the month-old American news leaks. Apparently there had been none of consequence because, after Harriman left the meeting, Molotov acted quickly, and the NKVD clandestine mechanism started turning again.

January 8, 1945: General Deane was informed by General Ivanov that

8. U.S. Embassy Moscow message M-22152 to Joint Chiefs of Staff, December 25, 1944, "Internees" files.

9. Lukas, "Escape," 16.

10. Ibid.

a representative of the U.S. Military Mission should go to Tashkent and proceed to execute the internee escape according to plan. [11]

January 11, 1945: An officer fluent in Russian, Maj. Paul Hall, had accompanied navy captain Felt during the latter's visit to the camp three months earlier. Deane now designated him to be the American representative for the role that McCabe formerly played in smuggling the internees into Iran. Hall departed for the six-day rail trip to Tashkent. Accompanying him were the two Soviet officers — NKVD colonel Myakhotnik and OVS captain Kozlovski — who had organized the two previous escape missions, one of which had been successful.

January 16, 1945: Word that a Soviet-American team was en route to Tashkent apparently filtered through Soviet channels into the camp because a rumor quickly spread that "we are going home." The same rumor of hope had circulated twice since January 1, so the current rumor was received with skepticism.

One of the earlier rumors had been cooled when several boxes of supplies, mostly winter clothing, had been received from the U.S. Miliary Mission. Why send such clothing to men who were leaving?

January 17, 1945: With sacks of mail in his care, Hall walked into the camp. Once recognized as an American officer, he immediately was the object of intense speculation. The men knew that Hall was not on a social visit.

Hall carried a letter from General Deane addressed to Wayne. [12] In the letter, Deane confirmed that the internees were being released, although the release would have the appearance of an escape. Deane expressed his worry about maintaining secrecy. "I can think of no better way to emphasize the necessity for secrecy on the part of your group than to point out how publicity concerning internees has affected each of you personally," he wrote. "For the sake of those internees who may come after you, it is imperative that no one, including your parents and closest friends, be given any of the circumstances concerning your release until after the conclusion of the war."

Deane offered the following option as a story to cover the initial phases of the escape: "If you and Major Hall think it wise," he wrote, "you can inform the group that you have received orders that they were to go to the American base at Poltava," a base in the Ukraine.

Hall immediately vetoed that idea. Since the previous attempt to exe-

---

11. Ibid., 17.
12. Letter, Maj. Gen. John R. Deane to Lt. Comdr. Charles Wayne, January 11, 1945, "Internees" files. In his concluding paragraph Deane stated: "I regret that we have been unable to do more for you during your stay in Tashkent, but I assure you that it was not because we did not have your welfare in mind. There are a great many administrative difficulties to be overcome each time we attempt to send you supplies."

cute the NKVD escape plan under the cover of false movement orders resulted in disappointment and chaos, Hall decided to end the speculation quickly by being frank. He was at the camp for one purpose, he told the men. He was there to take them out of the country. He provided no details. He would disclose parts of the secret plan as the operation unfolded, he promised.

January 22, 1945: Myakhotnik and Kozlovski days ago had completed the arrangements for the men's journey, arrangements that seemed not to require additional delays. And so the men waited impatiently day by day. The Soviet order to start the operation, however, was not promptly issued, and now Hall learned from Myakhotnik the reason. The NKVD plan called for the men to be trucked across the Iranian border and through the mountain passes south of Ashkhabad. Those passes were now closed by avalanches and snowdrifts, and the plan had to be modified to use a different route. The modifications were not simple. The logistics were different, and the changed border crossing required new precise scheduling.

January 23, 1945: Every detail seemed to be settled for immediate departure, and the men were ordered to be ready. Then the order was countermanded. The frustrated men were furious. Why the delay? No logical answer was offered.

January 24, 1945: One of the navy crewmen who had concealed his camera since his internment attempted to take a souvenir photograph of two of the waitresses. The girls loyally reported him to the commandant, who then suspected that other cameras were also hidden in the camp. Wayne agreed with the Soviets that all of them must be surrendered, and he ordered the men to comply. Arnold and Ott said that they believed that not one camera escaped the dragnet.

Later in the day, four internees pelted a passing Red Army officer with snowballs mixed with mud. The incident, McGlinn reported, was hushed up by the Soviets. In order to get to the bottom of the affair, Wayne wanted Siminov to bring the officer to identify the culprits in a lineup, but Siminov delayed doing so. The officer who had been the victim, Siminov said, could not be located. This led the Americans to believe that Siminov did not want to press the matter, especially since the internees were on the verge of leaving.[13]

January 25, 1945: Hall announced to the internees that they would depart after nightfall. Then, reflecting General Deane's worry about and the Soviets' concern for the need of absolute secrecy, Hall asked the men to sign individual pledges that they would not divulge the story of their escape from the Soviet Union.

The airmen were issued rations for five days. They carried most of the

13. War Department, "EX Report No. 542 (Incidental Intelligence)," 4.

same kinds of food that they had with them in December. The rations in-cluded raisins, but the boiled eggs and condensed milk were no longer available.

And they waited. Darkness came. And finally, at eight o'clock, it was time to go. Every one of the 130 internees departed. Only the puppy Gypsy remained, abandoned to whatever awaited puppies in wartime Soviet Union.

In most respects, the beginning of the internees' second trip from Tash-kent was identical to the first one—the same NKVD train personnel, the same kind of soft-class coach and two hard-class coaches, and the same train departure time at midnight. The major difference was that the in-ternee group now had 30 additional men, which meant that the coaches were more crowded than were the coaches in the December movement.

January 26, 1945: As a means of gaining the airmen's confidence and cooperation, Myakhotnik advised Hall to tell them about the plan for their escape. There would be no make-believe hotbox for causing the coaches to be sidetracked east of Ashkhabad. Instead, the train with the internees' coaches would continue to and through Ashkhabad and then westward. Eventually, the internees would be smuggled into Iran.[14]

January 27, 1945: During the second day, as the train drew closer to Ashkhabad, there were fleeting moments when some of the men "won-dered if all is well this time." There was an air of irritability as the men became more restless by the hour.

Arnold blamed his irritability on bedbugs. "I was eaten alive last night," he wrote. "It seemed that no matter where I was, it took the bedbugs about 12 hours to locate me."

The daylight hours finally merged into night. One hour before the sched-uled midnight arrival at Ashkhabad, the train passed the siding where most of the internees had been stalled in December. Fortunately, the men did not recognize the site of bitter memories because of darkness.

January 28, 1945: Following a routine stop at Ashkhabad, the train con-tinued for 150 miles toward the Caspian Sea. Shortly before daybreak, the train arrived at Kizil Arvat, where the internees' coaches were uncoupled and shunted to a remote siding.

At first daylight, NKVD lieutenant Nikitin, already an experienced con-voy commander in NKVD-planned escapes, guided ten Lend-Lease trucks alongside the coaches. Two of the tarpaulin-covered trucks carried con-tainers of fuel for the long journey to Tehran. The internees were assigned in units of about 16 men to each of the other eight vehicles. When the men boarded their trucks they found that straw covered the floor of each bed, but because of crowded conditions the straw provided little individ-ual comfort.

14. Lukas, "Escape," 17.

Specific orders were issued to each truckload of airmen. First, because each vehicle ostensibly was laden with cargo, the men must keep themselves concealed behind the closed tarpaulin canopy unless otherwise told. And second, they must not speak or smoke when the truck was not in motion.

By 8:30 A.M. the loading was completed, and Nikitin in the lead truck started the convoy, devoid of human sound, on its way. The trip was first interrupted at the Soviet-Iranian border crossing point and later at several road checkpoints in the Soviet occupation zone in Iran, but Nikitin skillfully passed the convoy through the obstacles by adhering to prearranged schedules and using falsified papers.

January 29, 1945: The route from Kizil Arvat ran toward the southeastern rim of the Caspian Sea at Bandar-e Shah and then across the Elburz Mountains to Tehran. The road was dusty and rough by day and frigid and rough by night, and the Americans suffered from both dirt and chill. Short rest stops were frequent, but the drivers had only one opportunity for a brief nap. At noon the trucks were halted long enough for the men to wash themselves in the waters of the Caspian Sea.

With little rest or sleep, the airmen and drivers were numb with exhaustion when the convoy began its last leg of the trip. Nikitin had a schedule to meet, and he led the convoy into the mountains for a night crossing.

January 30, 1945: The trucks one after another arrived at Camp Amirabad at 8:00 A.M., 48 hours after leaving the train at Kizil Arvat. The secret escape was finally completed, seven weeks after it was first attempted.

When the vehicles discharged their human cargo at the back entrance of an empty hospital wing, Hall's mission was completed. The men were now former internees under control of American security personnel in civilian dress.

As each man entered the building, he was greeted by a medical corpsman who told him, "Loosen your collar and shirt sleeves, please," and then sprayed him with delousing powder. Next, the men were told to take a shower. Their clothing was taken from them and later destroyed, but they were permitted to keep their souvenirs such as the lighter and Uzbek headgear. A few of the men scrambled to save their diary notes. They were issued fresh underclothing and a new uniform. Each man, army and navy officer and enlisted man alike, was dressed identically in a plain army enlisted man's uniform. On the record, the army flyers themselves were identified as being members of War Department Special Group No. 2.[15]

15. Designated as members of this special unit from the time of their coming under American control at Tehran, the army men continued to be so identified after they arrived at the New York Port of Embarkation. When they fanned across the United States for further disposition, the various Army Reception Centers were instructed to handle the men as personnel of "War Department Special Group No. 2."

Afterward, food was brought to them. White bread, butter, and coffee seemed to have the greatest appeal. "They ate it as though it were angel food cake," Richard McGlinn reported. And then "a beautiful white, clean bed" was waiting, John Vivian remembered. In the meanwhile, an army finance officer gave each man a partial payment of $200.

The repatriates were kept completely isolated. They quickly discovered that they were "not free" but were in effect prisoners of "our own people." The segregation for the sake of secrecy continued until they reached the United States five weeks later.

January 31, 1945: After being rested by hours of sleep, the men were prepared to leave. In the early afternoon their air transports were airborne from the Tehran air base bound for Cairo. However, a sandstorm blocked their approach to Cairo, so the planes were diverted to Abadan. The former internees spent their second night of freedom in an army barracks under guard.

They were escorted to the mess hall to eat at off-hours. Because of the guards and the unusual identical plain uniforms, "the men serving us at the mess hall were really confused," Vivian related. "They decided that a carrier had gone down in the Persian Gulf and that we were the survivors."

February 1, 1945: Late in the day the loaded airplanes departed Abadan and landed the men at the Cairo air base as midnight neared. The airplanes taxied to the far side of the field, where the men were herded into trucks — tarpaulin-canopied trucks, the likes of which the former internees thought they had seen the last. An armed military policeman sat in the rear of each vehicle. "If the trucks stopped, our instructions were to remain quiet — and no smoking," Vivian said. Old stuff to them!

February 2, 1945: The men were trucked to an army rest camp located at the edge of the Gulf of Suez. There they were informed that they would remain until a ship was available to transport them to the United States.

The waiting period under military restrictions would be eight more days. "Three good meals a day," Gilbert Arnold said, "and baseball in the afternoons, with the enlisted men beating the officers every game."

February 10, 1945: In the predawn darkness the jammed air transports left Cairo and turned toward the west. Because of the night arrival and departure at the Cairo air base, the men were unable to glimpse the pyramids at any time.

The aircraft, pausing once to refuel at Benghazi, flew all day along the northern edge of Africa and then across the Mediterranean Sea to Naples. When the planes landed, a group of curious American officers were waiting to greet them. When one of the senior officers asked where the men had been, Charles Wayne, the ranking former internee, explained that he was under orders not to reveal that information.

Armed guards immediately escorted the men to open trucks. The airmen were divided among the trucks. Then the vehicles, with the guards seated at the tailgates, took the men through the city to the Naples dock area. There they boarded the army transport *John L. Sullivan.*[16]

February 11, 1945: The *Sullivan* had been used in recent voyages for transporting German and Italian prisoners of war to camps in the United States. For this voyage, however, the ship had been reserved exclusively for the 130 former internees.

The men had the run of the ship. "The upper cargo spaces in the hold were all equipped with tiers of bunks for the enlisted men," John Mathers remembered. "There were some small staterooms for the officers. We ate on folding tables in the hold."

A tug pushed the *Sullivan* into the bay, and the ship sailed without convoy or escort for Oran, Algeria.

February 14, 1945: After a three-day voyage from Naples, the *Sullivan* was anchored among other ships in the Oran harbor. Soon other ships gathered until 36 vessels were ready to sail.

February 16, 1945: The convoy of slow-moving cargo vessels and frisky armed escorts steamed toward the Strait of Gibraltar and the Atlantic Ocean. "Out in front rode two destroyer escorts, one on each side and two more in the rear," Vivian noted. "After watching for awhile, I discovered that it [sailing in convoy] was similar to flying in formation . . . similar in that the ships were slowly opening and closing on their position and that the convoy leader was exhorting the ships to keep closed up." Arnold explained that the convoy was traveling at about ten knots, "which to a flyer is comparable to walking."

Once the convoy was under way, a casino was organized to exploit the gambling instincts of the homeward-bound airmen. Mathers remembered that one of the B-29 crewmen had worked in the Nevada casinos before the war. "This guy and some of his buddies set up the casino operation on the folding tables in the hold every evening," he said. After the men had been given partial pay at Tehran, they had a total of $26,000 in their pockets, and their only opportunity to spend any of the money was for souvenir items while at the Suez rest camp. Speaking of the casino operators, Mathers said, "I know that they took most of my $200. If they averaged only $50 from each of the other men, it was a pretty profitable trip for somebody."

According to Arnold, the *Sullivan*'s crewmen "were going mad trying to learn our identity, but so far they have had little luck in finding out."

February 17, 1945: At noon the convoy sailed past the Rock of Gibraltar and entered the Atlantic Ocean to begin a 16-day crossing. The convoy came under submarine attack almost immediately. One tanker was re-

16. War Department, "EX Report No. 542," 12.

ported to have been torpedoed, and the escorts and overhead PBY aircraft counterattacked with depth charges. The lurking submarine remained in the area for 24 hours, during which time the convoy commander ordered the *Sullivan* to move from its tailing position to the more secure center of the convoy.

February 23, 1945: Except for one more call to general quarters because of the suspected presence of a stalking submarine, the *Sullivan*'s voyage was one of monotony. To fill the long daylight hours, the men turned to reading, sunbathing, and playing listless card games. In the evening, there was the waiting casino.

February 26, 1945: High winds and rough seas. Since the *Sullivan* was riding high in the water because of empty cargo holds, the vessel pitched and rolled. Seasickness was expected, and the expectations were fully realized. The men's discomfort was also compounded by attacks of suspected food poisoning.

March 3, 1945: The storms seemed to worsen until the convoy swept past Cape Hatteras, after which the sea began to calm. As the storms diminished, the men waited impatiently for the *Sullivan*'s arrival in New York City.

March 6, 1945: The *Sullivan* anchored off Staten Island the night before, and fog delayed its docking at Brooklyn Port of Embarkation until nearly noon. Before the men were allowed to leave the ship, security officials came aboard to remind them of their obligation not to disclose the information that they had been interned in or escaped from the Soviet Union. Then the men were separated, the navy flyers going to the naval air station at Floyd Bennett Field, New York, and the army airmen of War Department Special Group No. 2 going to Fort Hamilton, New York.[17]

Souvenirs and any other items such as clothing that indicated their presence in the Soviet Union were immediately impounded for the duration of the war. Some of the men reported that their confiscated property was returned to them in later years, but others said that they never saw their articles again. Finally, representatives of the director of Naval Intelligence and the War Department's assistant chief of staff G-2 requested that the men sign similar oaths of secrecy binding them to silence.

Another surreptitious odyssey across and from the Soviet Union was ended.

17. Ibid.

9

The Fourth Escape
May, 1945

*Today is the forty-second anniversary of our belly land-
ing in Kamchatka. I still visualize the ground coming up
so fast, and no wheels down. Seems like only yesterday.*
— John R. Smith, November 18, 1986

Within two weeks after the last American internees had been removed from
Kamchatka on November 7, 1944, the stage in neutral country was being
set for the internment of still another goup of American airmen. The
American bomber harassment of Japan's northern Kurile Islands installations and shipping in the winter of 1944–45 was as unrelenting as flying
conditions would allow. Some aircrews were lost, and others sought survival in Kamchatka. The army's 404th Bombardment Squadron supplied
most of the future internees, and the navy provided one crew — its last.

November 17, 1944: Six B-24s departed from their Shemya base to strike
two enemy air bases on Paramushiro.[1] One of the bombers soon returned
to base because of engine trouble, but the other five, flying through wors-
ening fog, continued the mission.

Donald Taylor and 11 other airmen were aboard one of the raiding
B-24s. It was their third combat mission as a crew — and their last.

November 18, 1944 (Kamchatka time): The five bombers reached the
target area. While maneuvering to start the bomb run, Taylor's plane was
suddenly attacked by fighters that raked the bomber with machine-gun and
small-cannon fire. (The crew later counted 75 holes in the plane.) The bomb-
bay doors were jammed, two of the bomber's four engines were struck,
the hydraulic system and some of the electrical circuits were damaged, and
the radar was destroyed. Taylor and Edward Wheeler (navigator) were

---

1. John H. Cloe, *Top Cover for America* (Missoula, Mont.: Pictorial Histories Publishing, 1984), 133.

wounded. An explosive shell mangled Taylor's left foot, and Wheeler's left leg and hand were hit.

Taylor managed to turn the bomber northward and into cloud cover before Lester Yelland (copilot) took the controls. By the time the bomber had managed to fly to the vicinity of Cape Lopatka, Taylor's bloody foot had been bandaged and Taylor insisted on retaking control of his crippled aircraft. The plane headed into a Siberian blizzard that was sweeping across the lower portion of Kamchatka. Fortunately, Taylor found a hole in the storm through which he threaded the bomber and was then able to locate and follow the coast of Kamchatka to the north. Taylor planned to go to Petropavlovsk, but he soon realized that the bomber could not stay aloft much longer.

Through the curtain of falling snow Taylor glimpsed a flat beach area and made the decision to crash-land on the sand. Because of the jammed bomb-bay doors, the load of bombs could not be jettisoned.

"We bellied in to a nice soft landing," John Smith (radar operator) said. The crewmen crossed their fingers and waited for the skidding bomber to come to rest. The aircraft remained intact, and there was no fire. Gasoline fumes, however, temporarily filled the wreck, and any attempt to notify the Shemya base of the crew's whereabouts by radio was postponed because of the danger that a spark might ignite an explosion.

The snowstorm raged all night while the men huddled in the plane. Taylor and Wheeler were in considerable pain, but the other ten men were unhurt.

November 19, 1944: At daybreak the men began removing the heavy blanket of snow that covered the plane so that the wreck could be seen by search aircraft. Bernard Bendorovich (radio operator) tried to make radio contact with the bomber base on Shemya, but the signal was too weak. He discovered that a switch had been accidentally turned on in the cockpit, and the battery that powered the transmitter had been partly drained. Bendorovich said that when the battery, now turned off, had rested, it would regain some of its strength.

The men had no idea where they were. Some of the crew even speculated that they had become disoriented and crashed on the edge of a Japanese-held island. Taylor ridiculed that idea. The wrecked plane contained little emergency food and scant medical supplies. Help from any source was essential, so Taylor asked for three volunteers to search for civilization. Leo Lodahl (bombardier), Billy Burnett (nose gunner), and John Smith prepared to leave at first light the next morning. Smith at age 24 was the "old man" of the crew not only because he was oldest in years but also because he was a veteran of earlier missions in both B-25 and B-24 bombers. He therefore felt an obligation to "mother-hen" the crew.

November 20, 1944: Equipped with two small hatchets from the bomber's inadequate survival kit, the three men left the crash site and trudged southward through deep snow. Their movement was blocked by a swift-flowing stream. After deciding to return to the aircraft, the men were suddenly engulfed in freezing rain. They found partial shelter for the night under a pile of utility poles. Cutting fuel wood from one of the poles, they kindled a fire for warmth. "We also thought that the fire would serve as a signal," Smith said. The men continued to hope that the Soviets somehow would become aware of the American crew's crash.

November 21, 1944: Bendorovich's faith in his battery's revitalization was justified, and his urgent signal, although faint, was received on Shemya before it failed altogether. The 404th Squadron immediately passed the information to the Eleventh Air Force, and attempts were initiated to contact the Soviets at Petropavlovsk through the ALSIB weather-reporting radio circuit.[2] Separate actions were also taken to inform the U.S. Military Mission in Moscow about the plight of the stranded crew.

When Bendorovich's signal was heard, a radio-directional bearing on the signal's origin was made from Shemya, so the location of the crashed plane was generally known to be less than 100 miles up the Kamchatka coast from Cape Lopatka. Because of the stranded crew's critical situation, Capt. William Beale and his B-24 crew were directed to fly a mercy mission in order to drop emergency supplies.[3] Such a mission meant entering the Soviet Union's airspace, but from the Eleventh Air Force's point of view, the violation was warranted.

Later in the day on Kamchatka, the three cold, damp, exhausted men returned to the crash site to report their inability to cross the stream that blocked their route. Plans were made to renew the effort to find help the next day. This time, the men would take an inflatable raft from the bomber.

November 22, 1944: Four men departed at daybreak to retrace the path through the snow to the south. Even with the inflated raft to cross the stream, their progress was again blocked, this time by a cliff. Discouraged, they also turned back.

On Shemya, Beale's B-24 was loaded with medical supplies, food, clothing, shelters, and tools, all packaged for parachuting. Then, after a flight of nearly five hours, Beale made the Kamchatka landfall and began searching the coastline at an altitude of 300 feet.

"Shortly after Cape Zhelty was rounded," Beale later reported, "the missing plane was seen. . . . It was intact, with the left wing low, and pointed in a north-northwest direction. Snow obliterated any marks made in the landing." The bomber, he said was about 100 yards above the water-

2. Ibid.
3. Intelligence Summary No. 431, 404th Bombardment Squadron, November 21, 1944, U.S. Air Force Historical Research Center.

line. Between the plane and the water the message "4 men south" had been spelled out, partly by trampling the snow and partly by the use of red material. Beale could see two tarpaulin shelters under the left wing, and six men, arms waving, were observed near the wreck.

Beale made five low passes over the wreck to parachute the supplies, most of which landed within 300 yards of the men. (One 24-volt battery for the radio, however, was never recovered.) Then he turned south to "search for the four men mentioned in the message spelled in the snow. They were seen walking northward toward the plane," he said. Having accounted for 10 of the 12-man crew, Beale assumed that the two missing men were the ones whom Bendorovich had originally reported as wounded.

Beale circled his B-24 offshore for 90 minutes while he tried to contact the marooned crew by radio. Even a walkie-talkie radio that was dropped to the men produced no communication. His mercy mission otherwise completed, Beale veered away and commenced the long flight back to Shemya.[4]

"The food and medical and survival equipment probably saved our lives," Smith wrote. "Needless to say, we ate that night, and we slept in sleeping bags."

November 23, 1944: If the men were to resume communication with their Shemya base, a source of electrical power was needed. With ingenuity born of desperation, Bendorovich and others recovered the bomber's damaged auxiliary generator, which had been buried beneath the wreck, and successfully repaired it. This source of emergency power for the radio enabled Bendorovich to establish a communication link with the Shemya base. The stranded men learned that the Soviets at Petropavlovsk were now aware of their crash landing and that a rescue party would reach the men eventually.

"With plenty of food and medicine, we decided to sit and wait," Smith said. "Our morale rose 110 percent! Taylor, for the first time since the crash, smiled, even though he still was in severe pain."

November 30, 1944: The "sitting and waiting" continued day after day — seven of them. Then a small Soviet ship, bobbing in the rough sea, appeared offshore during the morning. The ship's crew attempted to launch a boat, but the turbulent waters discouraged them. The ship vanished to the north.

Later in the afternoon, Smith recalled, a small Soviet plane flew overhead and dropped a can of Spam with a note tied to it: "Watch to the north for three flares and answer with two of your own."

At dusk the three flares burned as promised, and so did the American responses. At about nine o'clock a Red Army lieutenant and six armed

4. Ibid.

soldiers with two small horses arrived at the crash site. The long waiting period was over.

Bendorovich wanted to notify the Shemya base of the rescuers' arrival, but one of the soldiers refused to allow it. Except for denying them access to their radio transmitter, "the rescue party treated us well," Smith said. Taylor, drugged with morphine to deaden his pain, was put on one of the horses, and Wheeler on the other. With the men's supplies piled on the rubber raft that they pulled behind them, Taylor's crewmen and their Red Army escort began walking northward along the coast. In the darkness the shadowed outline of the canted B-24 wreck on the beach slowly faded behind them. The men's memories of the aircraft that sheltered them for two weeks were later kept alive by a blurred photograph that Smith had the forethought to make. Years later, Taylor said that if a wish could be fulfilled, his wish would be to fly once again over the lonely Kamchatka beach where his crash-landing occurred.

December 1, 1944: After walking all night, the party of rescuing and rescued men reached a military outpost where they paused to rest and eat. The journey resumed. In the afternoon the men arrived at a cove where a small naval vessel was waiting for the Americans. Their boarding was made difficult because of the rough seas that drenched the men. Once the men were aboard, the ship commenced its voyage to Petropavlovsk.

The two wounded men were taken to the ship's dispensary, and the other ten men were moved below deck to eat and then to be questioned. The interrogation, Smith remembered, continued for hours, "but all they got were our names, ranks, and serial numbers."

December 2, 1944: The ship entered Avacha Bay and docked at Petropavlovsk. Taylor and his crew were now officially interned in the Soviet Union.

From the ship the interned flyers were taken ashore and served breakfast, the first of the meals offering the "different" diet of their future. They also met the frail interpreter Mike Dondekin, who became a familiar daily visitor during their confinement at Petropavlovsk.

After breakfast both Taylor and Wheeler were taken to the military hospital. Taylor underwent two operations on his injured foot during the following weeks.

The remaining ten men of the crew were driven northwest of the town to the rustic former schoolhouse that only recently had been vacated by previous American internees. The men inherited the beds with wooden boards for springs, straw-filled mattresses, and thin blankets, one per man. Each flyer, however, possessed a personal second blanket, which had been among the supplies that had been dropped at the beach wreck. In the building the men also inherited the bedbugs that had plagued the earlier internees.

A few Red Army soldiers provided an informal guard. Bitter winter gripped Petropavlovsk. The internees ventured outside only to go to the outhouse, to wash in the snow, or to use the steam bathhouse. "We had nothing to do," Smith said. "Just played cards."

December 6, 1944 (Shemya time): Robert Weiss and a crew of 12 from the 404th Bombardment Squadron flew toward the northern Kurile Islands on a weather reconnaissance mission. Near Kamchatka, Weiss reported by radio that his B-24 had lost an engine. The situation was worsened by a fuel leak.[5]

December 7, 1944 (Kamchatka time): The disabled B-24 had enough fuel to permit its reaching Petropavlovsk for a safe landing. Because the Soviet practice in receiving and handling American intruders at Petropavlovsk seemed to have settled into a routine activity, Weiss and his oversized crew were not delayed in joining Taylor's men.

The two bomber crews were from the same 404th Squadron and therefore were not strangers. Although the 23 men were beginning to crowd the limited space in their temporary barracks, Taylor's crewmen especially enjoyed some of the following days. After two weeks of isolation on the beach and a week of boredom at Petropavlovsk, they now had a new audience to whom to relate the details of their crash-landing experience. Morale improved.

Because Taylor was in the hospital, Weiss was the remaining able-bodied first pilot among the internees. He assumed temporary command of the flyers.

December 24, 1944: The two crews were the only American internees to be in Petropavlovsk during any of the wartime Christmas seasons. As Christmas Eve approached, they did not plan nor did they want any kind of formal observance. They did not expect the Soviets to appreciate the day's significance. To their surprise, when the Christmas Eve meal was served, the Red Army guard officer provided vodka for the occasion.

After eating the unappetizing meal, the men spent the remainder of the evening singing familiar Christmas carols and recalling past holidays with family and friends. One man wrote, "This was no big deal, but it helped us to cope with the fact that we were half a world from home."

January 15, 1945: The men of the two crews were ill from colds and dysentery and were losing weight. Their impatient waiting since Christmas was finally rewarded with the announcement that they were leaving Petropavlovsk, and quickly. En route to the airfield the 23 men were joined by Taylor and Wheeler from the hospital. At the airfield they found a DC-3 type transport fitted with skis ready to fly them to Magadan. During the flight across the Sea of Okhotsk, the temperature steadily dropped. When

5. Eyewitness statement, December 6, 1944, Missing Air Crew Reports, no. 12427.

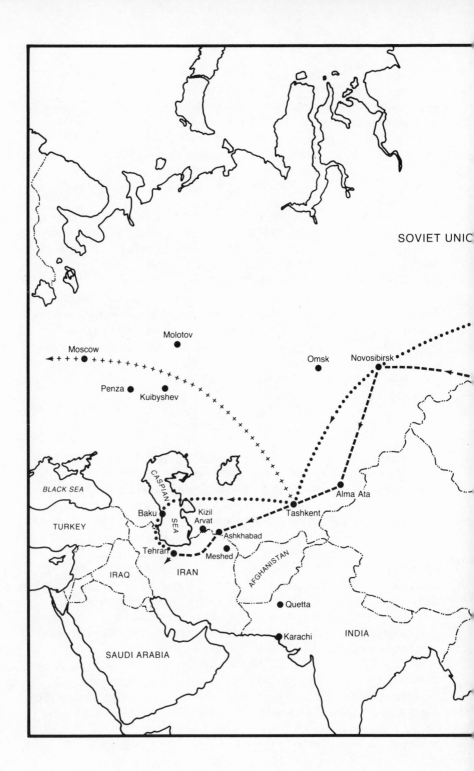

SOVIET UNION

Molotov

Moscow

Omsk   Novosibirsk

Penza

Kuibyshev

Alma Ata

BLACK SEA

CASPIAN SEA

Tashkent

Baku

Kizil
Arvat

TURKEY

Ashkhabad

Tehran   Meshed

AFGHANISTAN

IRAQ   IRAN

Quetta

SAUDI ARABIA

Karachi   INDIA

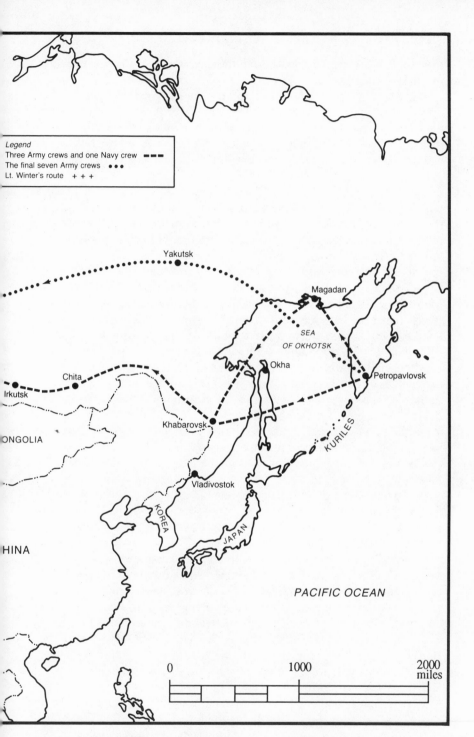

Yakutsk

Magadan

*SEA
OF OKHOTSK*

Okha

Petropavlovsk

Chita

Irkutsk

Khabarovsk

KURILES

ONGOLIA

Vladivostok

KOREA

JAPAN

HINA

PACIFIC OCEAN

0   1000   2000
miles

MAP 4. Route of internee groups 4 and 5

they landed at Magadan, Smith said, the men were told that the mercury stood at 70 degrees below zero.

Their layover in Magadan was memorable for two reasons. Despite the deep-freeze temperature outside and the hungry bedbugs inside, they were more comfortably housed. And then, for the first time since being interned, their meals were varied and more enjoyable. Completely unremembered was the mass of chained prisoners, the sight of which had horrified earlier Americans who passed through Magadan.

January 17, 1945: The internees were flown to Khabarovsk, where they were lodged in the Red Army rest camp. Like most of the internees before them, their brief residence in the rest camp would be recalled as being a pleasant interlude because of the contrast in conditions here with those in remote Petropavlovsk.

January 18, 1945: Only three days after the Taylor and Weiss crews were flown from Petropavlovsk, the Soviets interned the B-24 crew of Kenneth Elliott. The 404th Squadron flew eight missions during January, and two B-24s were lost. One was shot down. The other was Elliott's damaged bomber, which managed to make a landing at Petropavlovsk.[6]

January 24, 1945: Put aboard a hard-class coach, the Taylor and Weiss crews began their long trans-Siberian railroad trip that would deliver them to Tashkent. Their heating, eating, sleeping, and bedbug problems were similar to those reported by earlier internees who made the Siberian transit in November and December. Their train was frequently delayed, the men said, because it was sidetracked so that eastbound freight trains could have the right-of-way. These trains, they said, were laden with heavy military equipment apparently destined for the Red Army in the Soviet Far East.

According to rumor, the internees were being moved to Tashkent. John Smith was not certain where he was going, but he assumed that sooner or later he would come to the place where he could meet some of his friends. Smith said that he had flown 25 missions with 77th Squadron crews before transferring to the 404th Squadron, so he was acquainted with many of the members of lost B-25 and B-24 crews, some of whom were believed to have crashed or landed in Kamchatka. He was especially anxious to determine whether the crews of the most recent missing army bombers (Head and McQuillin's B-25s and Ott's B-24) were alive and interned.

February 5, 1945: When the internees arrived at Vrevskaya near Tashkent, the camp was empty. Evidence that Americans had been there was everywhere: graffiti, some athletic equipment, a six-band radio receiver, and some dog-eared English-language publications.

Both Colonel Siminov, the commandant, and Nona, the interpreter,

6. Eyewitness statement, January 18, 1945, Missing Air Crew Reports, no. 12428.

were waiting to greet the internees. Taylor had tolerated the hardships of the trip across Asia, but he required further hospitalization. He was promptly sent to the Tashkent military hospital, where he would undergo still another operation on his foot.

In Taylor's absence, Weiss continued to act as the group's American commander, through whom Siminov exercised his control over the behavior of the internees. Shortly, however, Weiss was replaced by Albert Miller (weather observer aboard the Weiss B-24) because Miller, although not a regular member of the bomber crew, was senior in rank.

Nona busied herself with the established routine of getting the new arrivals settled in the camp. She issued orders to the men in English and to the staff personnel in Russian, and she soon had the camp organized in an orderly manner.

Nona was conspicuous in the camp not only because of her facility in English but also because she was physically attractive and well dressed. She had recently acquired a white poodle, and the men from the first hours identified the dog with Nona.

Nona made no secret of the fact that she had worked with many Americans in the camp. In her excellent English she announced that she had been "mama" to 200 airmen. What happened to them? Where had they gone? According to rumor, Nona was overheard to say that she knew of an escape route, but whether she was implying that the earlier American internees had followed that route was never clear. Whatever were her remarks, however, they may have had a bearing on immediate events in her life.

February 8, 1945: Nona disappeared without a trace.[7] No American saw her again. Inquiries about her absence brought shrugs from the Soviet staff. In a few days her white poodle also vanished.

Nona's replacement was Tamara Guscova. The only thing she had in common with Nona was her fluency in using the English language. Tamara was at least 15 years younger than the nearly middle-aged Nona. Compared to the slender, fair-faced Nona, Tamara was heavy and had pockmarked skin.

The new internees never had the opportunity to become dependent on Nona, but Tamara quickly won their confidence and cooperation and even admiration. When Leo Lodahl returned to the United States and later became the father of a daughter, he named her Tamara.

February 14, 1945: At Petropavlovsk, the Soviets arranged for Elliott and his crew to be flown from Kamchatka. They eventually arrived at Khabarovsk, where they were taken, as were most of the internees before

---

7. Seventeen years later, Byron Morgan received an unexpected Christmas card from Nona. At that time she apparently was living in Naro-Fominsk, southwest of Moscow.

Tamara Guscova, who demonstrated her fluency in English by autographing her portrait "To a good American boy I've known in Russia." Photograph courtesy Robert Wolbrink

them, to the Red Army rest camp to wait for the next leg of their odyssey across Asia.

February 20, 1945: On Attu, Navy Squadron VPB-131 assigned four bombers to attack enemy shipping in the Kurile Islands waters and cannery and fishing installations on Shumushu.[8]

8. Charles L. Scrivner, *The Empire Express* (Terre Haute, Ind.: Historical Aviation Album, 1976), 36.

February 21, 1945 (Kamchatka time): No enemy shipping was located. Turning to Shumushu, the four navy raiders attacked the secondary targets with rockets.

One of the bombers was manned by John Powers and his crew of five. After leaving the target area, Powers reported by radio that he was in trouble with a damaged engine and was heading for Soviet territory. Powers believed that his engine had been hit by flak. However, photographs taken of Powers' plane during his rocket run indicated that the damage may have been caused by flying debris from his own rocket hits.

The other three bombers escorted Powers along the coast of Kamchatka to Petropavlovsk. The landing site, however, was hidden by frontal weather. Powers turned back toward Cape Lopatka. Meanwhile, the fuel limitations of the three escorts forced them to abandon Powers and fly back toward their Attu base.

Powers sighted the lighthouse at Cape Lopatka, but the terrain was not suitable for an attempted landing. His final message stated: "Bailing out over Lopatka."[9] All six men landed safely in deep snow.

February 22, 1945: The American Embassy in Moscow reported to the chief of naval operations, "Soviets advise crew of six located evening of February 21. All safe. Crew bailed out and plane continued north on automatic pilot. Plane not yet located."[10]

The rescued Powers crew was subsequently removed to Petropavlovsk. During the ensuing ten weeks, the six navy airmen were routed westward via Khabarovsk in accordance with Soviet scheduling. Their ultimate destination, of course, was the Vrevskaya internment camp near Tashkent.

February 26, 1945: The most recent arrivals at the Vrevskaya camp were four-legged. "Little Red" and her two fuzzy pups found an entry hole at the base of the camp's fence, and thereafter she defended her domain from any other canine intruder. Red looked like a miniature Irish setter, but none of her coloring was perpetuated in her offspring, one of which was black and white and the other, black and brown. After Red weaned the pups, the men allowed them to sleep in the recreation room, where they could be protected. Inevitably the men developed a sentimental bond with the pups. The bond became stronger as the pups grew.

March 12, 1945: When Elliott and his B-24 crew, coming from Khabarovsk, walked through the camp's gates, the surprised internees recognized and welcomed them. The Taylor and Weiss crews had not been forewarned that another B-24 (or any American bomber, for that matter) had followed them to Petropavlovsk.

9. Ibid., 37.
10. Appendix 9, "VPB-131 Squadron History," from January 1, 1945, to March 1, 1945, U.S. Naval Historical Center, 3.

Elliott, a former college basketball star, quickly found the camp's make-shift basketball court and thereafter spent most of his waking time there. His admirers, watching Elliott's concentration and ability, reported, "He was good!"

The three B-24 crews, all from the same squadron (404th), raised the camp internee population to 36 (plus Taylor, who still remained in the Tashkent hospital).

March 22, 1945: Among the emergency supplies that had been dropped to the Taylor crew on the Kamchatka beach in November were individual army-issue flashlights. John Smith, who took the photograph of the wrecked B-24, said that the crew was determined that the exposed film would not be confiscated by the Soviets. From the time that the crew was rescued, the film was secreted in the barrel of first one flashlight and then another. Each man, as if he was playing a game, took his turn in hiding the film. The film was smuggled successfully across Asia, then through Iran, and finally to the United States, where the out-of-focus photo was developed and printed a year later. Other items were also smuggled in the flashlights, including at least one set of diary notes.

Smith had another use for the flashlights, this time with the knowledge of Colonel Siminov. By early spring, frogs in one of the irrigation ditches were loudly croaking each night. Smith recalled that as a boy he had gone frog hunting at night, using a flashlight and a stick to hypnotize and stun the frogs.

A group of the men asked the camp commandant for permission to conduct a nocturnal hunt. Siminov was skeptical at first. Then he agreed and assigned two guards to go with the hunters. Later, the men returned with a sack of frogs that they dressed to obtain the legs.

"What a feast!" Smith said as he remembered the scene in the camp kitchen where the legs were fried and the men enjoyed the snack. "It took some doing, but we talked the commandant into tasting a couple of legs. That was a mistake," he said, "because Siminov wanted us to hunt for more frogs. But we convinced him that we got all of the big frogs and we would have to let the little ones grow."

March 30, 1945: Time dragged. "We didn't bother to keep track of dates," one internee remarked. "Each day was just another day. They all ran together."

The routine of playing ball, checkers, or cards was somewhat varied when Siminov asked the men to help with food preparation by peeling potatoes. Since the potatoes were usually small in size and they appeared on almost every meal's menu, one internee remembered that "it took a lot of potato peeling to meet the daily need."

April 7, 1945: Edward Wheeler, Taylor's navigator, who had been wounded during his last mission in November, was now recovered. Bored by the camp's monotony, Wheeler impulsively allied himself with a fellow crewman, Quitman Newell (waist gunner). The pair evaded the guards and went to Tashkent. They were quickly intercepted and returned to the camp. Siminov, with the approval of Miller, put the men in solitary confinement.

April 13, 1945: A few days earlier, Siminov arranged for the internees to be escorted to Tashkent for a ballet troupe's performance on April 13. Shortly before leaving the camp, the men learned from an announcement on the camp's shortwave radio that President Roosevelt had suddenly died on April 12. The sympathetic housekeeping staff members hastily cut black material into armbands for each of the men to wear. At the theater before the ballet began, the Soviets offered a moment of silence out of respect for the deceased American leader.

April 15, 1945: On the day of the burial of President Roosevelt, the internees organized a memorial service to be held at the camp. At the conclusion of the service a member of Elliott's crew volunteered to sound taps on a bugle that Siminov obtained for the occasion.

April 20, 1945: Edgar Bacon (Elliott's copilot) unexpectedly developed violent abdominal pains. By midnight his condition worsened, and a doctor who responded to an emergency call ordered him to the Tashkent hospital. The diagnosis was acute appendicitis, requiring immediate surgery. As in the case of Samuel Gelber, Bacon's surgery was reported to have been performed without the use of general anesthesia. Bacon later recovered from the ordeal with a souvenir, an "ugly nine-inch scar." There were no other complications.

April 22, 1945: Donald Taylor returned from the hospital to the camp, where he rejoined his crew. He still retained some metal in his ankle and lower leg.

May 2, 1945: John Powers and his navy crew finally arrived at the camp, and the American command responsibility automatically passed to Powers because of his seniority. The army/navy internee ratio (37 to 6) was so uneven that Powers would have preferred that the army retain the command authority. It was not to be. Powers took charge and became an effective leader.

May 8, 1945: The internees learned of the end of the war with Germany when they heard Churchill's announcement on the camp's shortwave radio. The men's immediate reaction was to ask the inevitable questions: What now? How does the German surrender affect me? Tamara said that she did not know, and Siminov could not or would not respond.

May 15, 1945: In Moscow, OVS general Kutuzov informed General Deane that arrangements had been made for the escape of the 43 Americans who had been concentrated at Tashkent. The escape project, he said, would start as soon as General Deane named the American escort.[11]

May 18, 1945: Major Paul Hall again was given the American assignment to oversee the escape. Accompanied by NKVD lieutenant colonel Cherimisinov and OVS major Ogorodnik (who once before had traveled with an American doctor to the camp in December, 1943), Hall boarded a Soviet plane for a same-day flight to Tashkent. Hall's two previous trips to Tashkent by rail had been seven days long.[12] At NKVD insistence, the escape was planned to be executed in precisely the same manner as the two earlier group evacuations from the camp.

May 19, 1945: The Soviet-American team of officers was motored to the camp after breakfast. Hall was wildly greeted not only because he was the first American that the internees had seen in the Soviet Union but also because he brought four sacks of mail—their first. Unfortunately, the mail was addressed only to members of the Taylor and Weiss crews. The Elliott and Powers crews had been identified as being "in a neutral country" too late for any of their families' letters to be delivered by Hall at this time.

At lunch, Hall announced that the group "would very shortly move to a new location." For some of the officers who recalled Nona's comment about the American internees who were no longer in the camp, Hall's statement instantly caught their attention. Speculation, always an essential conversation ingredient among the idle men, was freshly fueled. A new location? To meet the other internees?

May 20, 1945: As preparations continued for departure to the "new location," Hall had an opportunity to talk with the internees and to assess the conditions under which they had lived. "There were a few complaints over so-called restrictions. Some officers wanted freedom of the town, for example," he wrote. "However, in view of the circumstances, Soviet administration of the camp was excellent. After three trips to Tashkent, we are firmly convinced that the Soviets are doing everything in their power to make our people comfortable during their temporary stay in the Soviet Union."[13]

May 21, 1945: Siminov, dressed as usual in his immaculate uniform, assembled the internees so that the camp staff could distribute souvenir cigarette lighters of the small round design identical to the lighters that were given to the previous group of escapees.

May 22, 1945: Departure day was tomorrow, May 23, according to Hall. The arrangements, he said, were now complete. Some of the men asked Hall if they could take their mascots with them. "What mascots?" Hall

11. Richard C. Lukas, "Escape," *Aerospace Historian,* Spring, 1969, 17.

12. Paul S. Hall, undated official summary, "Escape of Internees, May, 1945," "Internees" files, 1.

13. Ibid.

asked. "The two pups," the men said—the two pups that were playing at their feet. Hall's answer was short and decisive. No!

May 23, 1945: The Soviet-American team inspected the two coaches— one soft class and one hard class—and found them to be disinfected and satisfactory. (On the subsequent journey there were few complaints about bedbugs.) At 9:30 P.M. the entire group of 43 men boarded the coaches, which later were coupled to a train bound for Ashkhabad.

Unknown to Hall, the two frisky pups were slipped aboard the hard-class coach and into the compartment reserved for the coach attendants. The American dog-smugglers did not know that the attendants were NKVD personnel, who, for some reason, kept the men's secret. The pups were safe all the way to Ashkhabad.

May 24, 1945: During the morning, Hall, Cherimisinov, and Ogorod-nik revealed the plan of escape to Tehran. "At this time," Hall wrote, "we warned them not to disclose a word as to where they had been or how they had gotten out. They were told of a previous party whose escape had been delayed because of a security leak. We believe," Hall added, "that they thoroughly understood the importance of absolute secrecy, both as a necessary condition for future escapes and as a solemn obligation to the United States and the Soviet Union."[14]

At the same time, General Deane in Moscow sent an "eyes only" top-secret message to General Booth in Tehran and General Bissell in Washington to provide the Persian Gulf Command and the War Department with a complete roster of the internees involved in the planned escape.[15]

May 25, 1945: The NKVD escape plan had one variation—this time there would be no make-believe breakdown to be used as an excuse to sidetrack the coaches. Instead, when the train arrived at Ashkhabad in midafternoon, the coaches were switched to an inconspicuous siding where the men were kept aboard until 8:00 P.M.

Four tarpaulin-covered trucks arrived under the supervision of NKVD lieutenant Nikitin, who had controlled the intricate truck-convoy schedul-ing on the two earlier mass escapes. While the men (and the two pups) were being divided among the trucks, General Velikanov appeared to con-firm that his border troops would play their usual clandestine roles in pass-ing the convoy across the border into Iran. Cherimisinov assured Hall that Nikitin and his NKVD drivers would pass the various highway checkpoints in the Soviet occupation zone on schedule.

Leaving Velikanov, Cherimisinov, and Ogorodnik at the railroad sid-

14. Ibid., 2.
15. U.S. Embassy Moscow unnumbered message to Tehran, Cairo, and War Department, May 24, 1945, "Internees" files. Because of past problems in confirming the identities of American internees, Deane's message was qualified: "Following is list of personnel known to be in Tashkent and presumably will be in Major Hall's group."

ing, the convoy with Hall and the 43 internees started south on the road
that would take them across the border, through the lofty mountains,
and eventually across the desert flatlands of northern Iran. The path that
they would follow was the same one used by the second escape group—
Ashkhabad, Quchan, Sabzevar, Semnan, and thence to Tehran.

May 26, 1945: By daylight the most dangerous part of the trip—the
border crossing and the tortuous road over the mountains—had been completed. The convoy entered a hot, treeless, dusty wasteland. "The journey
was rough, long, and tiring," Hall reported. "We thought it best to have
a rest every four or five hours." The rest stops were usually made at one
of the infrequent oases, where there was sufficient water at least to wash
some of the dust from mouths and noses.[16]

At the second rest stop, Hall discovered the two pups. Hall was instantly
upset. His fury over being disobeyed, however, rapidly cooled. He acknowledged that he could not abandon the two helpless animals in the desert.
He took one of the pups to ride with him in his truck cab, and the other
finished the trip to Tehran with one of the internees.

"We distributed and collected secrecy oaths," Hall said. "Each member
of the party pledged his absolute silence in regard to all aspects of his escape," Hall reported. "These oaths were numbered and labeled 'Top Secret' and were enough to throw a good scare into anyone." Unknown to
the men, the oaths were later destroyed.[17]

May 27, 1945: Between midnight and daylight the convoy was halted
in order to allow the drivers to sleep. Thereafter, except for unscheduled
short rest stops, the convoy moved steadily toward and through Tehran
and entered Camp Amirabad shortly before 5:00 P.M.

The reception at Camp Amirabad, Hall reported, was perfect as usual.
The men were isolated in two wards of the camp hospital and were deloused as the introduction to the established clandestine procedure for
handling escaped internees. The two pups were also deloused and then
taken to the mess hall for adoption. The American soldiers who inherited
them never knew that the dogs had been smuggled hundreds of miles from
within the Soviet Union.

The 37 army flyers, now designated as members of "AAF Special Group
No. 3," together with the six navy airmen, were again reminded that complete secrecy was mandatory. At this point, Major Hall quietly took his
leave, and the men saw no more of him. His job done, Hall eventually
returned to Moscow.

May 28, 1945: The uniforms that the flyers had been wearing were discarded and burned, and a complete army enlisted man's clothing issue was

16. Hall, "Escape of Internees, May, 1945," 3.
17. Ibid.

provided to each former internee. Well fed and clean, the men felt relaxed for the first time in months. Their assigned security escort, who would accompany them to the United States, gave the men another security briefing so that the need for secrecy was kept uppermost on their minds.

May 29, 1945: Because of the small number of escaped men at Camp Amirabad, the American authorities decided to fly the group directly to the United States at once.[18] In the early afternoon, the rested men were put aboard two transport planes and started on their way home.

June 1, 1945: The 43 repatriated men landed at Washington, D.C. after flying across North Africa and the Atlantic Ocean via the Azores and Bermuda. For them the odyssey at last was over. But not the secret.

18. Lukas, "Escape," 17.

10

Release of the Last Internees
August, 1945

In the closing months of World War II, the War Department reported on the continuing air strikes by U.S. flyers in the North Pacific.

> The Eleventh Air Force has been busily knocking away on Japan's well-guarded back door up in the barren, fog-bound Kuriles. The hot spot of these islands is Shumushu and Paramushiro. There, perhaps to protect themselves from the potential threat of their Russian neighbors on Kamchatka, the Japs have concentrated more air facilities and ground defenses than anywhere else in the whole northern chain. . . . Severe flak and aggressive interception . . . in May alone, accounted for two B-24s and five B-25s.[1]

As in previous years, some of the crews found refuge in Soviet territory. As one of the diplomatic preparations for the Soviet entry into war with Japan, Moscow served notice on April 5, 1945, that the Soviet Union "makes known to the Government of Japan its wish to denounce" the April 13, 1941, Neutrality Pact between the Soviet Union and Japan. Foreign Minister Molotov, speaking to Japan's Ambassador Sato, justified the denunciation by reviewing the radically changed international situation since the pact was originally signed: the Soviet Union was invaded by Germany, Japan was an ally of Germany, and Japan was waging war with allies of the Soviet Union — the United States and Great Britain. The denunciation, however, simply confirmed what everybody knew: the Soviet Union no longer feared an attack by Japan. Furthermore, until the Soviet Union fulfilled its secret pledge to declare war on Japan, the Soviet Far East was still "neutral country," and American flyers landing there were still interned.

By mid-May, the first of 52 American airmen began arriving in Kamchatka to form the nucleus of the final group of internees to be held by

---

1. Assistant Chief of Staff, Intelligence, War Department, "11th AF Keeps Knocking at Jap's Back Door in Kuriles," *Impact,* August, 1945, 61.

the Soviet Union. For whatever reason, the Soviets received and treated these latest internees in exactly the same manner as they did the 239 Americans who came to "neutral country" in 1942, 1943, 1944, and early 1945.

May 11, 1945 (Kamchatka time): Richard Kleinke's B-24 was the first American plane to reach the Petropavlovsk landing field in four months. While involved in a massive strike by 404th Squadron's heavy bombers against the northern Kuriles, Kleinke's plane "lost two engines over the target and fell behind the rest of the formation," Navigator John ("Jack") Smith said. The crew members knew that the badly damaged aircraft could never return to its Shemya base, so "we headed north."[2]

The crippled bomber was soon intercepted by Soviet fighters. Escorted by them, Kleinke reached Petropavlovsk and managed a safe landing. Soldiers surrounded the crew, then took the Americans and their possessions to a nearby dugout. Later they were joined by an interpreter — round-faced Pavel ("Paul") Trukhachev, who, since the earlier American encounter with him in 1943, had been promoted from lieutenant to captain. Paul's use of English was still imprecise and his smile still frozen when he struggled with the alien language.

The Kleinke crew, Smith recalled, was treated quite well at the landing field. Paul, he said, even arranged for the new arrivals to have vodka to drink "so that we could forget home."

On the same day, a flight of B-25 bombers from the 77th Squadron was assigned a separate mission: a hazardous attack on shipping and naval vessels in the strait between Paramushiro and Shumushu. Hubert Winter was pilot of one of the bombers. With him were his regular crew plus an extra officer, Ernest Stifel.[3] "This type mission previously had been considered too risky," Winter said. The strait was only a mile wide with gun batteries on both shorelines, and the naval ships in the area were also heavily armed against air attack.

"We planned to go in low beneath their radar," Winter recalled, "and then get out fast." The plan failed because of weather. Unable to approach the strait at low altitude because of a dense cloud cover, the raiders climbed to get above it. When they abruptly broke through a hole in the clouds, they were directly over the strait. The enemy's fire was immediate and intense. "The planes in front of me quickly peeled off on either side to find cover in the clouds," Winter said. "Fearing collision in the clouds, I elected to hold my course and complete the mission by dropping bombs and strafing one of the ships in the water below. This was not because I wanted to be a hero, but I had little other choice."

2. Radio communication was also maintained until the B-24 landed at Petropavlovsk. The Soviets confirmed the crew's internment five days later.

3. Stifel was the 77th Bombardment Squadron's gunnery officer. He volunteered to fly the mission.

Henry Hobson and Leonard Kupersmith, pilots of the two nearest B-25s, later reported what happened to Winter.[4] Hobson watched as Winter dived on a freighter in the strait. "He was bracketed for several seconds by machine guns and a number of bursts from antiaircraft," Hobson said. Winter's bomber was obviously hit. Kupersmith was able to fly alongside Winter's plane and contact him by radio. "Winter said that Lt. Stifel and his radio operator were badly wounded and that he was losing fuel rapidly out of the left side," Kupersmith said. "He also stated that he was going into Petropavlovsk." According to Kupersmith, both engines on Winter's plane seemed to be running normally, but he observed a large hole on the right side of the bomber just below the waist window. His last sighting of the plane was when Winter was about 50 miles north of Cape Lopatka.

The hole was caused by a shell that entered one side of the bomber's midsection and exploded when it exited the other side. The explosion mortally injured Paul Wutchic and severely wounded Stifel. Stifel's flak jacket saved his life, but his right leg from hip to ankle was riddled with shrapnel.[5] Jackson Babb (engineer) and Robert Davis (navigator) cut away some of Stifel's bloody clothing, dusted his multiple wounds with sulfa powder, and tried to make him more comfortable.

About 30 minutes before reaching Avacha Bay and Petropavlovsk, Winter was aware that two Soviet fighters had appeared and were flying beside the B-25, one on each wing. The fighters led Winter to the landing field.

The time was now nine o'clock in the evening of the long subarctic day. After the battered bomber rolled to a stop, Stifel remembered being lifted from the plane. A doctor who spoke some broken English and who was later identified as Major Golosofsky quickly examined both Stifel and Wutchic. He told Stifel that he would live. The unconscious Wutchic was beyond help and died within minutes. Stifel was put in a truck and, attended by Golosofsky, who mercifully gave him morphine, was taken to the military hospital.

The Kleinke crew that had been held in the dugout at the airfield now joined the survivors of Winter's crew. The 17 men surrendered their side arms and underwent a preliminary interrogation, after which they were trucked to the rustic former schoolhouse where they would be domiciled during their long internment at Petropavlovsk. The barracks arrangement had not improved since the departure of the last of the earlier internees — the same springless cots with the straw-filled mattresses, the same primitive outhouse, the same steam bathhouse.

---

4. Eyewitness statements, May 11, 1945, Missing Air Crew Reports, no. 14409.
5. A further complication was a severed sciatic nerve in Stifel's hip. Despite his wounds, he never lost consciousness.

"I should mention here," Winter said, "that the Soviets had nothing better to offer." Petropavlovsk was one of the most distant outposts in Siberia. Even by the time that the American crews arrived in May, 1945, the living conditions at remote Petropavlovsk were still crude in every aspect for Soviet and American alike. "We ate what they ate," Jack Smith said.

May 12, 1945: The tired men were again questioned, this time more intensively. The main thrust of the interrogation was aimed at learning the bomber strength at the American bases on Shemya and Attu.

After the unproductive interrogation, the Soviets and Winter made arrangements for Paul Wutchic's burial near the hospital. The members of the combined crews of Kleinke and Winter (except Stifel) and a Red Army honor guard were present for the brief graveside service.[6] A Soviet photographer captured the somber moment, and later a copy of the photograph was given to each of the Americans.

Paul Trukhachev used his limited English skills to prepare the list of American names for transmittal through Moscow to Washington.[7] Paul moved into the internees' barracks and lived with the Americans during their long residence at Petropavlovsk.

At the hospital Stifel himself was being prepared to undergo the first of many operations designed primarily to save his life and later to save his leg. The surgeon and commander of the hospital was Lieutenant Colonel Keechieff. He probably was the same doctor whose compassionate care of earlier internees had earned American gratitude. He quickly established a close doctor-patient relationship with Stifel. Obviously a dedicated man of medicine, Keechieff did not perform many basic medical procedures to which Americans were accustomed partly because of a shortage of medical supplies, medications, and modern surgical equipment. After taking X rays of Stifel's leg, Keechieff used ether to anesthetize his patient and then probed for most of the shrapnel fragments.

May 13, 1945: For Stifel, the days now would begin to blur because of recurring fever. His knee and ankle were badly swollen. Morphine or pantopon was used in trying to ease his unrelenting pain.

From the time Stifel arrived at the hospital, Keechieff's nurse Vera conscientiously attended him. She was a small dark-haired woman who had served on the German front in the Black Sea area, even though she had a husband and two children. The Americans never learned what set of circumstances had caused her to be sent to the distant shores of the Bering Sea, but they were thankful that she was at Petropavlovsk to care for Stifel.

---

6. Thomas Ring's grave was nearby, but these latest American internees were not aware of Ring's death and burial in 1943.

7. Probably because of a translation error, Stifel was reported on May 18 to have been "slightly" wounded. As a result, his family never knew the seriousness of his wounds until they met him in a Richmond, Virginia, hospital after the end of the war.

Members of Winter's B-25 crew and of Kleinke's B-24 crew at Paul Wutchic's burial in Petropavlovsk. *Identified, left to right:* Paul Galleron, Carl Stella, John S. Smith, Jackson Babb, Floyd Sargent, Yorke Smith, Robert Davis, Hubert Winter, Raymond Cutler, John Tyler, Sam Zakoian, Richard Kleinke, and Robert Jolly. Not identified or missing were four members of Kleinke's crew. The Red Army honor guard is on the right. Photograph courtesy of John S. Smith and Hubert Winter

Vera and Stifel used a system of signs and key words so that she could understand his needs. She tried to make him as physically comfortable as possible. At the same time she helped Stifel's morale simply because he knew that she was near or could be called quickly. During his worst periods she was by his side day and night, and as he improved, she brought him special items of food from her home.

May 14, 1945: Although the stench was only barely noticeable in Stifel's bed, Keechieff and Vera knew instantly what it meant. A quick examination of Stifel's leg revealed the cause of the odor—gangrene. Stifel was too ill to realize the significance of their discovery.

May 15, 1945: In Stifel's second operation, Keechieff slashed Stifel's leg from hip to foot. The exposed incisions, the doctor later explained, would allow circulating air to combat the gangrene. Vera sat beside Stifel, holding his hand and wiping his clammy face.

Five miles separated the hospital from the internment area. Hubert Winter assumed that the distance and lack of transportation (horse-drawn wagons) were the reasons for his not being permitted to visit Stifel, and he relied on Paul Trukhachev for reports on Stifel's condition. For medical reasons, Keechieff may have wanted his patient isolated. Stifel himself believed, however, since the hospital was located on high ground overlooking the Petropavlovsk harbor, that the Soviets did not want visitors to observe the accelerated military activity there.

"The Americans were told almost daily that we were likely to be leaving the next day," Jack Smith said. The jaded airmen gradually learned to ignore empty promises and to avoid further groundless speculation. "Next day" for the internees extended over two additional months until it finally arrived in late July.

May 16, 1945: When the 404th Squadron sent virtually its entire fleet of B-24 bombers against Paramushiro targets, two of the aircraft were damaged by antiaircraft fire, one so severely that it too sought haven at Petropavlovsk.[8] The pilot was William Blakeway, and he brought with him his crew of 11 to add to Petropavlovsk's new internee population.

While Blakeway's B-24 crew was involved in the battle to survive over Paramushiro and later en route to Petropavlovsk, Keechieff and Vera waited tensely as they monitored Stifel's reaction to Keechieff's desperate surgical gamble.

May 17, 1945: With the arrival of the additional airmen, the internees' barracks was beginning to fill. Despite the confined living conditions, Jack Smith recalled, the men managed to control their restlessness. They loafed, he said. Or they played cards or chess. The nearby Red Army soldiers challenged the Americans to volleyball games, and the Americans consistently beat them.

At the hospital, Keechieff discovered that his most recent surgery had not been successful. Stifel's putrefying flesh continued to defy him. He planned still another operation on the weakening American. If this failed, then amputation of the leg would be the last resort to save Stifel's life.

May 18, 1945: Once again, with Vera beside him, Stifel went under Keechieff's knife. Stifel bore scars from this thrice-repeated surgical treatment until the day he died 35 years later, in 1980.

May 19, 1945: Keechieff carefully checked Stifel's incisions. He faintly smiled. Vera, bleary-eyed from her all-night vigil at Stifel's bedside, patted Stifel's arm. So far, so good.

---

8. John H. Cloe, *Top Cover for America* (Missoula, Mont.: Pictorial Histories Publishing, 1984), 136.

Stifel was alert and feeling better, especially after a note from Hubert Winter was delivered to him.

Dear Stife:
    Couldn't talk them into letting anyone come in. . . . Don't know what the deal is. Hope everything's okay. Expect a good report. . . . You probably heard of this other B-24 crew that came here day before yesterday. We have a pretty full house out here now. Makes 29 (& an even 30 counting you). May speed our getting out of here if you recuperate soon enough, but that can't be rushed. . . . Hope to see you again soon. The boys say hello & good luck. (Signed) Hub"

May 20, 1945: Seven B-25s from the 77th Squadron were sent to raid northern Kurile enemy installations, including a radar station and a cannery. Only four returned to Attu.[9] The raiders met antiaircraft fire so intense that one bomber fell in flames, another was seen to crash-land on Shumushu, and a third, piloted by Harold Beever, was badly crippled but managed to reach Petropavlovsk safely.

At the Petropavlovsk hospital, Stifel continued to be in constant pain, and Vera kept seeking ways to make him feel more comfortable. Two days had elapsed since the last operation, and there still was no sign of recurring gangrene. Keechieff was pleased, but he also was concerned about Stifel's loss of blood and state of depression.

May 21, 1945: There were frictions and petty personal problems to be resolved when so many men were living in such a small space. Now that Beever's crew had increased the number of internees to 35, the airmen sought new means of activity and diversion to relieve tensions. Neighboring Red Army soldiers may have replanted the idea, but Jack Smith said that the men found " a fire pit with logs for seats placed around it" and initiated an evening ritual of sitting, talking, and singing around the campfire. The internees as well as the guards and soldiers took turns in gathering wood to burn. Smith remembered the time when "Paul Galleron [Kleinke's copilot] and I spent three days secretly cutting down a large tree. At the campfire one night we announced that it was our turn to get the wood. We showed our little pocketknives to the guards and then walked into the woods. Five minutes later we came back, dragging that big tree behind us. The men were suddenly laughing, and even the guards enjoyed our joke."

May 23, 1945: Winter wrote to Stifel again:

Dear Stife:
    How's my boy? Hope OK. Have heard good reports every day of your progress, and we are all hoping it continues.
    Have been trying to get them to let us come to see you but as yet, no

9. Ibid.

luck. Don't know what the deal is, but they say "soon I can go see you." Will come as soon as I can.

Am sending this Red Cross kit, and inside is your wife's picture and the money from your jacket. Think this kit contains everything you will need or that we can give you. This toilet paper is a valuable luxury. Use it sparingly.

We . . . are living well but miss all the luxuries of Attu. . . . Hoping to see you soon. (Signed) Yours, Hub

May 25, 1945: Finally, to Stifel's delight, Keechieff agreed that his patient could have visitors. Winter and members of his crew were brought to the hospital for a brief reunion. Keechieff was pleased with his decision because Stifel seemed to rally from his depression and became more animated. Faced with this reaction, Keechieff further agreed with Winter that a member of the crew should stay at the hospital on a rotation basis. Stifel never again felt abandoned.

May 26, 1945: In Moscow, the Red Army's General Slavin responded to General Deane's inquiry about the condition of the internees. Slavin assured Deane that Kleinke's, Winter's, and Blakeway's crews were well, with the exception of Stifel ("lightly" wounded) and Wutchic (killed in action). He made no mention of Beever's crew, which had been interned a week earlier. He did volunteer the information, however, that "all crews will be sent by the usual means to the camp in the region of Tashkent."[10]

At Petropavlovsk, Harold Beever and his copilot, Cecil Osburn, came to the hospital to bring Stifel news of the rising number of lost crews in the 77th Squadron. Later, as other 77th Squadron crews arrived at Petropavlovsk, they reported that for every crippled 77th bomber that managed to reach neutral country, an additional B-25 crew usually failed to return to Attu.

May 27, 1945: Colonel Keechieff apparently had won his gamble to rid Stifel's leg of gangrene, but there were other complications. Surgery of the type that Keechieff performed on Stifel had been a costly one in blood, and controlling Stifel's bleeding by means of dressing changes had been a continuing problem. The supply of fresh bandages was so scant that makeshift dressings were often supplemented by an outer layer of newspaper coverings. On Keechieff's order, Major Golosofsky began a quick series of transfusions by using both American and Soviet donors. Jackson Babb (Winter's engineer) had a blood type that most nearly matched Stifel's, but in general the transfusions—ten of them—were made without close matching, Stifel later wrote. As a result, he suffered chills and other unpleasant reactions after each transfusion.[11]

At one point, Stifel developed influenza, which worsened into pneumo-

---

10. Letter No. 75, Assistant to the Chief of the Red Army General staff, Moscow, to Chief, American Military Mission USSR, May 26, 1945, "Internees" files.

11. After the war, Stifel joked that he contained more Russian blood than American.

nia. Golosofsky used "cupping," an ancient treatment that was performed by placing glass cups (which had been heated to create a semivacuum) on Stifel's back. Because of or despite the treatment, Stifel recovered.

June 10, 1945: Eight B-25 bombers from the 77th Squadron were ordered to strike at Araito Island west of Shumushu in order to divert enemy attention while an American naval task force approached to shell installations on the south end of Paramushiro. The eight aircraft were divided into two flights of four bombers each. Pilots in the first flight were Edward Irving (the flight leader on his first mission), John Tidball, Robert Talley, and Robert Wolbrink.

"The second flight lost contact with us almost immediately due to very low visibility," Tidball recalled. "We four continued 'on the deck' for the entire trip. I remember vividly at one point maintaining contact with Irving by watching the wake in the water from his props."

When Irving led the flight across Cape Lopatka, Talley broke radio silence to remind Irving that "this is Russia and we don't do this." Irving's response: "Maintain radio silence and your position."

"It was most interesting to see the cape from sixty feet," Talley said. "It was flat plowed ground and included one old fellow with a wooden plow and one horse. He never looked up." Talley told his crew that there would be no firing toward the ground under any circumstances.

The four B-25s unloaded their bombs over Araito and then made a sweeping turn to head back to Attu. By that time, however, enemy fighters were swarming and chased the flight, led by Irving, toward the cape again. "The fighters began their attack as we were over the cape," Talley said.

A quick glance by Talley revealed that the plowed field that he had earlier observed "had opened up. There was a deep trench filled with men and equipment.

"I was flying on Irving's left wing," he reported. "It was then that I believe that I saw tracers from Irving's right waist gun fire toward the ground. . . . I have wondered if Irving ever told his crew that they were crossing Russian territory. A gunner could have seen troops in that trench and just automatically fired at them."

Why did Irving intrude over Soviet territory a second time? "I can only guess," John Tidball said, "that it was pressure from the Japanese fighters that caused him to lead the flight over the tip of Lopatka again. At any rate, we were being shot at by the Japs from above and the Soviets from below. It was not a good place to be."

Soviet antiaircraft guns had been firing warning shots regularly at straying American intruders since the Kurile raids began 1943. This time, however, the guns found a target.

According to Talley, Irving was under 100 feet altitude when ground fire hit Irving's bomb-bay fuel tank. The explosion shattered the top gun turret, and flames erupted from the cavity. Talley said that he urgently told Irving by radio "to turn left" toward the water, and he thought that Irving was trying to comply. Then Irving's bomber went out of control, dived into a fog bank, crashed, and exploded.

In the meanwhile, Robert Wolbrink's B-25 was raked by Japanese fighter machine-gun fire.[12] The turret gunner, Matthew Glodek, was killed instantly by a bullet through his head, Wolbrink said, and the bomber's right engine was damaged at the same time.[13] Wolbrink feathered the propeller. Tidball made radio contact with Wolbrink, who reported his situation and said that he was "heading north for a landing in Russia."

En route to Petropavlovsk, Wolbrink discovered that the landing gear's hydraulic system had been wrecked. He alerted his crew to prepare for a "wheels up" arrival in the Soviet Union. The subsequent belly landing on the grassy field at Petropavlovsk was made without injury to the surviving crewmen.

June 11, 1945: The Red Army detachment organized a burial ceremony for Matthew Glodek, "which I appreciated," Wolbrink stated. Together with a Red Army honor guard, the crewmates of Glodek were taken to the small burial ground near the hospital. The service was brief and simple.[14]

Wolbrink and Jerry Kroot (Wolbrink's copilot) went to the hospital to visit Stifel and report to him the latest actions in which their mutual parent unit, the 77th, had engaged. While there, Kroot met one of Stifel's doctors, Golosofsky, and discovered that they spoke a common language— Yiddish. As a result, they were able thereafter to help in closing the communication gap at the hospital.

A strange fungus that Kroot had discovered on his hands seemed to be spreading. Experimental treatment was begun at the hospital while Kroot acted as an interpreter.[15]

June 20, 1945: The standard black bread that was provided to the internees was delivered regularly in a two-wheeled, horse-drawn cart. The bread was stacked in the cart like wood, Jack Smith said.

One day in mid-June the same cart arrived at the barracks. This time the cart contained shoes instead of bread. "We wore our flying suits during the entire time that we were in the Soviet Union," Smith recalled. "The only item of clothing that the Soviets offered to each of us was a pair of shoes to replace our flying boots." The cart was heaped with canvas-

12. Robert Talley, eyewitness, recently reported that he saw the burst of a Soviet artillery near-miss not far from the right side of Wolbrink's bomber.

13. Cloe, *Top Cover,* 137.

14. In September, 1945, after his release and return to the United States, Wolbrink went to Buffalo, New York, to visit Glodek's parents in order to express his condolences. To his dismay, he discovered that the parents had never been notified of their son's death. Their last information was that Glodek was "missing in action" following his June 10 mission.

15. Treatment at Petropavlovsk, however, failed to cope with the fungus.

topped, hard-soled foot gear. Selecting a suitable pair was not difficult because "one size would fit all."

June 26, 1945: It now had been six weeks since the first crews had arrived and a month since General Slavin had assured General Deane that the airmen would be transferred to Tashkent. Yet nothing had happened. Were the Soviets waiting for Stifel to be well enough to travel? Or perhaps the internees' situation had slipped from the attention of the Soviet bureaucracy involved in preparing for the Soviet entry into the war with Japan? The reason for the endless delay was never revealed.

The internee colony at Petropavlovsk had now increased to five crews (41 airmen). The continued inactivity was having a noticeable effect on the men. They were alternately quarrelsome and listless. They had tired of beating the Soviets in their daily volleyball games, and they no longer paid any attention to the recurring rumors that war between the Soviet Union and Japan was "very soon."

July 4, 1945: The American holiday did not go unobserved. The Soviet military command arranged for several old movies to be shown in conjunction with a visit by two of the senior Red Army officers in the area. And there was vodka, of course. The Soviets also arranged for two special Red Army athletes to be flown to Petropavlovsk for the occasion. (From where, nobody recalled.) These men, Jack Smith said, wore numerous medals for volleyball championships. Beaten so often by the Americans, the Soviets now had their satisfaction. "With the two players," Smith admitted, "they beat our team every game!"

At the hospital, Stifel was included in the celebration as well. The Soviets, he discovered, would seize any opportunity to propose toasts, and he could not refuse to participate in the ritual, especially on this special day. "I was lucky that I was already lying down!" he later confessed.

By this time in early July, Stifel's spirits were obviously rising. It was the sight of a bat appearing in and flying through his hospital ward, he said, that unaccountably snapped him out of his depression and helped him to regain his sense of humor. He still was in constant pain, but with Vera's assistance, he was exercising in bed and gaining strength. He could feel that he was suddenly improving, and Keechieff agreed.

July 10, 1945: Under the doctor's anxious eye, Stifel was able to leave his bed long enough to stand on crutches for a short time. Stifel asked Keechieff "to tell me the truth about my leg." The doctor admitted that he gambled on Stifel's survival when he decided not to amputate Stifel's leg when gangrene was discovered. About 35 percent of such patients die before amputation, he said. Another 50 percent die as a result of the amputation ordeal, and 15 percent survive. And so Stifel was fortunate still to have both his life and his leg.

July 17, 1945: Four B-25 bombers from the 77th Squadron flew to Shumushu and Paramushiro to strike enemy shipping along the coasts of the islands.[16] Eleven crewmen from two of the bombers were later added to the internee colony at Petropavlovsk.

After completing the coastal sweep of bombing and strafing runs, George Wampler realized that his left engine was losing power. Wampler by radio asked fellow pilot John Tidball to fly near Wampler's left wing and make a visual inspection of the engine. Tidball reported that he thought that he could see two small holes in the nacelle but no other unusual conditions. "Wampler then lowered and raised his landing gear to check the hydraulic system, and it appeared to be operating normally," Tidball wrote. Two minutes later "Wampler informed me that he was losing fuel from his left engine and would proceed to 'Apron' (Petropavlovsk)."[17]

Wampler never reached Petropavlovsk. Unable to keep his bomber aloft, he was forced to make an emergency ditching in the icy Bering Sea off the Kamchatka coast. Hubert Winter surmised that "Wampler would have tried to make a landing at Petropavlovsk if at all possible because one of his crewmen, Orville Judd [gunner], was deathly afraid of water."

The floundering bomber skipped across the water, and then the sea came rushing in. After the emergency raft was inflated and launched from the rapidly sinking airplane, five of the struggling airmen swam toward it. Fear of the ocean seemed to petrify Judd, the sixth man. He did not respond to shouts of encouragement and sank from sight. Wampler himself was almost drowned before he could reach and be pulled aboard the raft.[18]

The five men might never have been found alive. Within two hours, however, one of the rare Soviet ships to ply that sea route arrived by chance on the scene of the ditching and rescued the wet, shivering men.

Later, when the ship docked at Petropavlovsk, Wampler was taken to the hospital, where Stifel reported that "they got the water out of him." Wampler's four surviving crewmen were sent to join the other Americans at the internee barracks.

In its attack on an enemy vessel three miles off Paramushiro, the B-25 piloted by Robert Terris skimmed over the water with the bomb-bay doors open. According to Edward Sorenson (engineer/gunner), the bomber was so low when the train of bombs was released that the propeller turbulence

16. Cloe, *Top Cover,* 137.
17. Eyewitness statement, July 17, 1945, Missing Air Crew Reports, no. 14762.
18. Robert Talley, one of Wampler's close friends in the 77th Bombardment Squadron, recalled that Wampler also had a fear of water and often discussed his ironic predicament. At least 99 percent of the 77th Squadron's combat missions were flown over the deadly waters of the northern Pacific Ocean and the Bering Sea.

made whirlpools on the surface of the sea. In some unexplained manner, Sorenson said, the last bomb in the train apparently bounced back into the bomb bay and hung there. L. J. Vaughn (gunner) was splashed with seawater. His first reaction was that the liquid was blood, and he screamed that he had been hit.

Sorenson recalled that the floorboards had been dislodged and jumbled by the erratic bomb, but he managed to push them back into some semblance of order. Terris then left the cockpit and came to survey the situation. Nobody, however, dared to touch the bomb, which was lodged precariously in the bomb bay. The bomb was armed and ready to detonate.

John Tidball received a radio call from Terris, who told him that "he had an armed bomb hung up and that he planned to fly to 'Apron' and bail out rather than risk a landing." Tidball said that Terris "apparently was very alarmed."[19]

The "flying bomb" approached Petropavlovsk from the sea and turned inland. At about 3,500 feet, between the town and the landing field, Terris ordered his men to jump. Hubert Winter said he remembered that "we watched the parachutes after they opened and drifted into the valley beyond the knoll where the internees' barracks was located." Soon there was an explosion, "which we assumed was the crash of the aircraft."

Unfamiliar with parachute-landing technique, Sorenson did not know how to control his canopy. He saw small trees immediately below him, and then, he said, "I hit the ground violently on my butt. I was knocked out." When he revived, a Red Army soldier was watching him from where he stood about 30 feet away. Beyond the soldier was an ancient truck. Sorenson and the soldier, reacting to hand signals, together helped one another to retrieve the parachute from a tree and carried it to the truck. Sorenson's tobacco pipe had been broken during the landing, and he raised his arm to throw it away. The soldier stopped him with a hand motion, so Sorenson handed him the pieces. Perhaps, Sorenson thought, the soldier wanted to repair the pipe for his own use, or perhaps he suspected that the pipe contained secrets of some sort.

Sorenson was driven in the truck to a nearby farmhouse where he was united with the other five airmen, all uninjured. Terris and his crew, the last American crew to enter the Soviet Union as a neutral country, in a few hours were added to the crowded internment barracks area.

July 20, 1945: At last, Moscow made a decision to move the internees to Tashkent. As usual the decision was closely held, with neither the Red Army's OVS nor the American Embassy being informed of the impending transfer.

Paul Trukhachev told the internees that two aircraft were being made

19. Eyewitness statement, July 17, 1945, Missing Air Crew Reports, no. 14763.

available for the flight from Kamchatka. The men reacted to a rumor that they were departing the very next day, and excitement soared. As was the case with all hope rumors among the American internees on Kamchatka, dating from 1943, this rumor was false. Final departure was nearly a week away.

July 27, 1945: Confirmation of the travel arrangements — the routings to be followed and the overnight stops — were completed at last. A shortage of available interpreters posed a problem. It was solved, however, by Paul Trukhachev's making the trip with one of the planeloads of internees.

For Stifel, leaving Petropavlovsk was the one thing he wanted above all, yet he regretted cutting the emotional cord that tied him to Colonel Keechieff. During his long recovery period, he and the doctor frequently played chess (although an excellent player, Stifel quickly learned that he must *never* beat his opponent), and during these times Stifel developed a personal relationship with the doctor. Stifel had a genuine liking for Keechieff, and the feeling seemed to be mutual. During one of the final days Keechieff confided to Stifel that he was dying of cancer caused by radiation from X-ray equipment.

The doctor gave Stifel his photograph, which he autographed in Russian: "to Mister Stayfel, for Good Memories — Lieutenant Colonel Keechieff, 21 July 1945." In turn, Stifel gave his watch to the doctor. Keechieff promptly presented it to Vera because the watch had a sweep-second hand, which Vera needed for taking patients' pulse counts. Stifel then enlisted Hubert Winter's help in a last-minute fruitless canvass of the internees to find another watch for Keechieff. Stifel learned of Winter's failure in a note: "I haven't been able to do much about the watch. They are quite scarce and therefore almost invaluable to the owners. Will keep trying to swing the deal."

Because of the moral support that Vera had given him when he needed it most, Stifel was saddened when it was time to leave her. "What can I send you when I go home?" he asked. "Shoes!" she immediately responded.[20]

July 28, 1945: All 52 men, most of them in various stages of exuberance because of the abundance of farewell vodka, were taken to the airfield, where two transports were ready for them to board and leave Kamchatka permanently.

For Hubert Winter, however, a pall was cast over his preparation for departure. One of the Red Army officers handed him a billfold belonging to Edward Irving, whose bomber was shot down over southern Kamchatka on June 10.[21]

20. When Stifel and his wife planned to send useful items to Vera after the war, Stifel was advised that his generosity might cause problems for Vera.

21. Winter delivered Irving's billfold to an official in the Pentagon in early September, 1945.

Lieutenant Colonel Keechieff (Kichaev), the Soviet doctor at the ill-equipped hospital in Petropavlovsk. Photograph courtesy Mrs. Ernest A. Stifel, Jr.

July 30, 1945: After three days of flying with overnight stops at Yakutsk and Novosibirsk, the internees were delivered to Tashkent, then to the vacant camp at nearby Vrevskaya. The trip was remembered as being boring. There were no major incidents, and Stifel withstood the exhausting journey surprisingly well but complained of stiffness and a sore back. The flight route bypassed Khabarovsk completely, probably because that Soviet Far Eastern rail hub and logistic center was jammed with the flow of military reinforcements and equipment for the approaching Soviet entry into hostilities with Japan.

Jack Smith's most vivid memory of the trans-Siberian flight was the pot-bellied stove that had been installed, complete with a pipe through the top of the cabin, in the transport in which he was a passenger. A supply of fuel wood was also in the cabin, "but we wouldn't let them light the fire," he said.

At the internment camp a Soviet staff had been assembled. The internees did not recall having a designated commandant, although an unidentified colonel was present behind the scenes. They well remembered Tamara, however. Having already served as the principal interpreter for the fourth group of internees, Tamara enthusiastically entered on similar duties for this final group. Even though the men would rely on her for only three weeks, Tamara also gained their confidence and admiration. Hubert Winter saw ample evidence that other Americans had been in the camp in recent times because of the presence of names written on the walls, a shortwave radio receiver in working condition, and odds and ends of American army uniforms.

July 31, 1945: Ernest Stifel was promptly moved to the Tashkent military hospital, where the doctors changed bandages and put his leg in a cast. Stifel was more comfortable, he said, but he was appalled by the breakdown in sanitary conditions at the hospital. En route to Tashkent he had expressed hope that he could be medically evacuated to an American hospital soon. Now, depressed by his current surroundings, he clung to the idea of evacuation. If that were not feasible, perhaps he could be moved to the camp.

Jerry Kroot also became a hospital patient because of the condition of his hands. Unfortunately, the fungus on them was persistent, and any encouraging treatment would await his return to America. In the meantime at the Tashkent hospital, Kroot's unique language capability was recognized quickly and put to use.

August 1, 1945: Winter wrote Stifel a note.

. . . Haven't heard how they were treating you or anything about you. . . . Can't tell yet about chances of getting you evacuated but have taken measures to get you out. What results we will get is a question but am fairly optimistic. We wrote to the U.S. Military Mission in Moscow trying to speed things up for you. . . . Paul [Trukhachev] is still here and his personal belief is that they will evacuate you soon. Said that he would try to see you before going back.[22]

22. Capt. Pavel Trukhachev, having completed his assignment as an English-language voice of authority during the internees' long journey from Kamchatka to Tashkent, had no opportunity to compare Tashkent's "luxury" with Petropavlovsk's frontier life. He departed on his return trip to the Soviet Far East without being able to visit Stifel at the hospital.

... We have a comparatively good set-up here, however we naturally are eager to get out of here ourselves. Think you would like our place better than the hospital if they have no specific reason for keeping you there. Our interpreter mentioned her trying to get you settled here if you wish it that way. . . .

Adios, Hub

Some of the men began to develop diarrhea at the camp. Winter reminded Stifel to "beware of water — best use Halazone [water purification] tablets." In addition to diarrhea, malaria in varying degrees of seriousness swept through the camp during the men's short confinement there.

George Wampler also wrote to Stifel.

Hi ya, Stif: . . . I've been thinking a lot about you and wondering how you are. Hub and I wrote a letter to Moscow about you with hopes it would hurry up your removal to the States. I'm also going to try to send a telegram if possible.

Everything is swell out here. Hub and I are in charge and the initial headaches are almost over. We have quite an organization.

We all think it would be swell if you could come out here. I think you would like it a lot better. . . .

George W

August 2, 1945: In a Moscow meeting called by the Red Army's OVS with representatives of the U.S. Military Mission, Major Ogorodnik reported that seven airplane crews (52 men) had arrived at the Tashkent internment camp. Major Ogorodnik further stated that there were no other American flyers either in the Far East or en route. OVS, the major said, was not aware of the internees' transfer to Tashkent until July 31, two days ago.[23]

August 6, 1945: Men in the camp recreation room, while listening to English-language broadcasts, heard an Indian station announce the news about "the big bomb that had been dropped on Japan," Jack Smith recalled. The news did not excite the men. Japan was now thousands of miles away, and so was the big bomb. Moscow was closer. In Moscow's hand was their future.

August 9, 1945: Following the Soviet Union's declaration of war against Japan, the 52 American flyers lost their status as internees. In a letter to Molotov, Ambassador Harriman reminded the foreign minister that there was no longer any need for the NKVD to organize an escape because these men could now be openly returned home as allies. Molotov responded that the appropriate Soviet authorities had already been given instructions re-

23. Informal unsigned memorandum, "Notes on Meeting at OVS (Moscow), 2 August 1945, 1330 Hours," "Internees" files. Present at the meeting were Major Ogorodnik (OVS), Lieutenant Colonel Andersen, and Major Hall (U.S. Military Mission).

garding the liberation of all American airmen formerly interned in the Soviet Union.[24]

August 10, 1945: Unaware of the Soviet Union's entry in the war and of the changed status of the Americans at the camp, Winter wrote to Stifel.

> Hello Stife: Well, 3 months in Russia behind us. Here's hoping we are in the States in another month.
>
> Glad to hear from you. Sorry to hear conditions aren't so favorable there. We, George [Wampler] and I, talked to the colonel last night & asked him to do what he could to get you out right away. We got the same story — we'll have to wait for word from Moscow & not much can he do about it.
>
> After thinking it over, I think you are better off where you are. The colonel said he would allow visitors to come in more often, so think I shall be in soon. . . .
>
> Hub

August 12, 1945: Tamara demonstrated her use of written English in a personal note to Stifel. "Hello Stifel. Wanted to come and see you very much. But the truck will be in town for 6 hours getting products and I won't be able get back soon. The boys send you books and writing table [tablet?] for letters. I hope I'll be able to get to the hospital soon and find out everything about your situation. But if you need me quicker you let me know and I'll come. Sincerely Tamara." Tamara later delivered food and cigarettes to Stifel.

August 13, 1945: OVS general Kutuzov informed General Deane that the U.S. Military Mission could send a representative to Tashkent in order to complete the arrangements to fly the 52 Americans to Tehran.[25]

August 14, 1945: As a result of a diplomatic overture initiated by Ambassador Harriman and approved by President Truman and Stalin, Gen. Dwight Eisenhower arrived in Moscow on August 11 for a four-day visit of pomp and ceremony. After a glittering formal dinner at the Kremlin on August 12, Eisenhower and Stalin conversed through interpreters in a more relaxed atmosphere. During this informal period with Stalin, Eisenhower suggested that he would like a picture of Stalin.[26] Stalin would not forget the suggestion.

On Eisenhower's last day in Moscow, Harriman organized an evening reception on August 14 for the Eisenhower party. Harriman was abruptly called from the reception on urgent business, and when he returned he dramatically announced the surrender of Japan.[27] World War II was over.

August 17, 1945: Tamara told Hubert Winter that a Red Army officer

---

24. Richard C. Lukas, "Escape," *Aerospace Historian,* Spring, 1969, 17.
25. Ibid.
26. Dwight D. Eisenhower, *Crusade in Europe* (New York: Doubleday, 1948), 464.
27. John R. Deane, *The Strange Alliance* (New York: Viking Press, 1946), 219.

from Moscow wanted to talk with him. In the meeting that Tamara attended, the officer told Winter that he would take Winter and only Winter to Moscow the following morning. The officer did not offer any explanation. Winter wondered if the letters that had been written concerning Stifel's medical evacuation could be the reason for his summons to Moscow.

Winter's clothing was in poor condition after three months of internment. In order to have a presentable appearance for his flight to Moscow, he needed some sort of uniform. Surveying the military clothing items that earlier American internees had abandoned in the camp, Carl Stella (Kleinke's bombardier) selected some pieces and made hasty alterations with the help of a sewing kit. The result was a makeshift uniform that, together with his fleece-lined flying boots, Winter could wear until he located better attire. "I was far from presentable, however," Winter said.

August 18, 1945: "I left Tashkent on some kind of day honoring Soviet airmen," Winter said. "The pilot of our plane flew only a short day on the way to Moscow because of the holiday. We landed near a small town so that he and the crew could celebrate." Winter and his Red Army escort were quartered that night in a huge room with about 30 other men. "I couldn't sleep much," Winter recalled, "because every one of the 30 men was snoring. It sounded like a big pond of bullfrogs!"

August 19, 1945: From the U.S. Military Mission in Moscow, General Deane sent the following personal message to General Eisenhower at his U.S. Forces headquarters in Frankfurt, Germany: "Have received a framed portrait of Stalin endorsed 'To the famous strategist General of Armies D. Eisenhower with very best wishes. Signed I Stalin.' Am forwarding this to you by first safe means."[28]

Late in the afternoon, Hubert Winter and his escort arrived in Moscow, and Winter was taken to the U.S. Military Mission offices. There he was told that the Red Cross reported his father to be gravely ill and that emergency arrangements had been made to send Winter home. The mission officers were surprised that the Soviets had not already told Winter about his father's condition.

General Deane and his staff were also guilty of being close-mouthed. They did not inform Winter that Lt. Col. James D. Wilmeth was flying to Tashkent to arrange the final evacuation of the 51 Americans remaining there.[29] In effect, although the participants were not aware of it, a race was under way. Who would reach the United States first: Winter, or his fellow former internees?

August 20, 1945: "My travel orders issued by the Military Mission called

28. U.S. Embassy Moscow message M-25353 to USFET Main (personal for Eisenhower), August 19, 1945, in Dwight D. Eisenhower Library archives, Abilene, Kansas.
29. Lukas, "Escape," 17.

for high priority transportation and should have taken me back to the States in a matter of a couple of days," Winter said. "That, however, was not to be the case."

When he departed the American Embassy in early morning to go to the Moscow airport, Winter was handed a small wooden crate to carry to Berlin. On the crate were markings in Russian and English indicating that it contained a portrait of Stalin that was a personal gift from the generalissimo to Eisenhower. Winter was unaware that he was the "first safe means" that Deane had mentioned in his earlier message. "I guess that I was designated a courier because I was going that way," he said, "and I could make delivery to General Eisenhower's Berlin headquarters."

Winter recalled that "my orders were of no help in boarding an Aeroflot plane at the airport. It took almost one hour for the airport officials to clear me. They were suspicious of my orders and therefore were being cautious. But when I called the markings on the wooden crate to their attention, things suddenly started to happen." Winter was convinced that the crate and not his orders was his real ticket that allowed him to leave the Soviet Union.

Winter and an American navy officer traveling companion were squeezed aboard a jammed plane. "We were so heavily laden that the aircraft could hardly lift off the ground," he said.

After a refueling stop in the war-demolished city of Pinsk, the plane continued to East Berlin, where it landed in late afternoon. Winter's navy companion could speak Russian. Telling Winter to wait, the navy officer took a Red Army soldier with him and went to look for a telephone.

Hours later, after nightfall, the navy officer returned with an American military vehicle and driver, and together they began to search for the route to the American sector in West Berlin. Because the driver was not familiar with the designated roads in East Berlin and it was very dark, the trip developed into a harrowing experience. "Soviet sentries would shoot at us as we drove through unlighted areas that were probably restricted, but we did not stop for fear of having to spend hours and hours undergoing interrogation," Winter said.

After midnight, having finally navigated through and from East Berlin, Winter and his companion were safely delivered to a West Berlin hotel that served as an American officers' quarters. And so to sleep "in my first good bed in months."

At the camp and in the Tashkent military hospital, excitement exploded as word spread rapidly that Colonel Wilmeth, accompanied by a Red Army representative, would arrive from Moscow in a few hours. Stifel noted in his diary, "Hub is in Moscow, but nobody knows why."

Paul Galleron and Jack Smith carried some melons from the camp kitchen supply tunnel and put them to cool in the irrigation ditch that bordered the camp. While wading in the water, Galleron stepped on a sharp object and gashed his foot badly. He resisted any suggestion that he go to the hospital. He was able to hobble on crutches after a doctor from Tashkent stitched and bandaged the deep wound.

August 21, 1945: Winter took the crated portrait to Eisenhower's Control Council headquarters, where he hoped to hand it personally to the general. On arrival, however, Winter was informed that Eisenhower was not in Berlin at that time. Instead, Winter delivered the crate to a duty officer.[30]

He then began the tedious and frustrating process of finding air transportation to the United States. At the military air booking office, Winter's high-priority travel orders were noted, and he was told, "We will call you when a seat is available." Because of the confusion in Berlin so soon after the war's end, Winter waited in vain for the promised telephone call.

Winter had no opportunity to buy a new uniform until he later arrived in Washington. In commenting about his mixed and ill-fitting attire, Winter said, "It's surprising that I wasn't picked up and put in jail for vagrancy or some such charge, but everyone overlooked my appearance because, I presume, of the widespread feeling of exhilaration at the end of hostilities."

Back at Vrevskaya, Colonel Wilmeth arrived with bags of mail and packages for the former internees. This first communication from home since their arrival in the Soviet Union helped the men to control their anxiety and impatience until the final arrangements for their departure from the Soviet Union were completed.

August 22, 1945: Eisenhower acknowledged his receipt of Stalin's portrait by sending the following message to Moscow: "For Ambassador Harriman, from Eisenhower. At your first opportunity may I ask you to pass to the Generalissimo my profound thanks for the trouble he took in sending me a photograph and my humble appreciation of the generous terms in which he autographed it to me. Thank you very much."[31]

August 23, 1945: At the Tashkent hospital, Stifel had been assured that he and Kroot would be evacuated with the other Americans. The tentative plan for departure called for the trucks carrying the men from the camp to be routed via the hospital, where Stifel and Kroot would join them, then the entire group of 51 men would go directly to the Tashkent airport.

In a hasty note Tamara announced that the plan had been modified. "Hey, Boys! They changed their mind and decided to bring you to the airdrome by the hospital truck. We send you clothing and you must be ready

---

30. The autographed portrait of Stalin is now in courtesy storage at the Eisenhower Library.
31. USFET Main message S-18789 to U.S. Embassy Moscow, August 22, 1945, in Eisenhower Library.

by four o'clock in the morning. . . . Hope to see you in the plane. Love, Tamara."

George Wampler also reassured the anxious men at the hospital with a note referring to the men's clothing. "Dear Stifel & Kroot. . . . What we don't send, we'll bring along with us. We have it all together except your left shoe, Kroot. Perhaps it is in the hospital. We'll see you at the airport early tomorrow morning. Wamp."

While the men in the camp waited restlessly, one of the Soviet staff members gave a puppy to Jack Smith. The puppy, Smith said, was a black and white miniature husky type with a tail that had a double curl. Smith and Carl Stella succeeded in smuggling the animal inside their jackets or shirts from Tashkent all the way to Washington.[32]

August 24, 1945: Colonel Wilmeth assembled his 51 men at the airport and divided them between two Soviet air transports. Forty-eight of the men were able-bodied. Stifel was a litter patient, and both Kroot and Galleron, the latter on crutches because of his slashed foot, were listed as ambulatory ones.

The two aircraft were flown directly to Baku on the Caspian Sea, where they landed at lunch time. Because the Americans lacked passports or other official clearance papers, the Soviet authorities at Baku were reluctant to allow the aircraft to resume their flights until they were ordered by radio from Moscow to do so. Then, on to Tehran and Camp Amirabad for a cordial American reception. Since the war was over, there was no attempt to keep the men's presence in Tehran a secret, nor were secrecy pledges ever mentioned.

August 25, 1945: The men were paid, bathed, physically examined, and issued items of fresh clothing. While Stifel was having his bandages changed and a new cast put on his leg, the other men indulged themselves in a spending spree at the Post Exchange and were taken on a tour of Tehran's Underground Market.

Some of the men were eager to find an audience and talk about their unique experiences but encountered disinterest. The impact of the indifference caused the former internees to begin to realize for the first time that the war was indeed ended.

August 26, 1945: Traveling on Persian Gulf Command orders, the 51 men were now identified as an AAF Special Project. Despite this careful identification, however, the administrative planning for the continued evacuation of the project men was not well coordinated. Confusion caused an all-day delay until the group was finally airborne from Tehran at dusk.

32. Carl Stella later reported to Smith that the dog had been killed by an automobile at Stella's home.

August 27, 1945: The evacuation aircraft landed briefly at Cairo in the predawn hours then flew westward across North Africa. The men arrived at Casablanca as the sun was setting.

August 28, 1945: At Casablanca, Stifel was scheduled to complete his journey to the United States on a medical air-evacuation plane. Separated from Stifel, his 50 companions were transferred to transatlantic aircraft for their long flight to Washington. They were officially logged as having arrived at Washington National Airport late on August 28, some 60 hours after having departed Tehran.

But where was Hubert Winter? And where was Ernest Stifel?

August 31, 1945: After four days of waiting in his Berlin hotel room for a telephone call from the air booking office, Winter decided that he could wait no longer. He found an American soldier to guide him to an army airfield. From here Winter began hitchhiking by air across Western Europe.

From Berlin to Nancy, France. Then, from Nancy to Paris. Later, from Paris to the Azores. From the Azores he found a plane that was flying to New York via Newfoundland. He arrived in New York on August 31, some ten days after he had delivered the famous crated portrait in Berlin. He immediately booked a commercial flight to Washington and reached his destination about midnight. Had Winter remained with his crew at Tashkent, he would have arrived in Washington three days sooner.

September 1, 1945: When Ernest Stifel last saw his companions at Casablanca on August 28, he expected to follow them within hours. Again, administrative disarray interferred. For three days Stifel waited for the military bureaucracy to clear the way for his transatlantic flight. Finally, at three o'clock in the morning, he was once more airborne, on the final leg of his odyssey.

When Stifel's litter was carried from the medical evacuation plane at New York many hours later, the last interned American airman to be repatriated from the Soviet Union during World War II was home.[33]

33. Ernest Stifel eventually lost the battle to save his leg; it was amputated in 1949.

Postscript

Half of the world's northern hemisphere was the stage for the airmen whose travels ranged over Japan and China across vast areas of the Soviet Union and into Iran and even India. The prominent actors were, of course, Americans, but behind the scenes were Soviet bureaucrats, soldiers, and civilians. Both Americans and Soviets were caught in the imbroglio of wartime international law and manipulation. If the Soviets opened fully their records of this aspect of Soviet-American wartime collaboration, there probably would be minor variations and explanations, but the basic story concerning the American internments and escapes would remain unchanged.

Once repatriated, the men responded to the Soviet Union experience in different ways. Some, faced with the realization that there was no glory in having been sequestered in the heart of a strange land, were embittered — and report that they still are. They regard themselves as having been prisoners of war and have continued to reject any argument to the contrary.[1] Many of the former internees, however, expressed more reflective views. They concluded that they were treated as well and as fairly as could be expected in a country preoccupied by total war in the West and trying desperately to avoid a simultaneous war in the East.

Reacting to pleas from former internees, in 1988 Congress passed and the president signed legislation that reclassified their status so that they also qualified for Veterans Administration disability compensation and other benefits to which former prisoners of war have been entitled.[2] Unlike traditional prisoners of war, who were forcibly detained by an *enemy* government, the internees were held by a neutral government. The congres-

---

1. Another man expressed a less caustic view: "Our treatment was one of neglect rather than meanness."

2. Remedial legislation applicable to the internees was incorporated into the Omnibus Veterans Benefits and Services Act of 1988.

sional legislation recognized that the internees, having been forcibly detained by a *foreign* government, were entitled to prisoner-of-war status, therefore enabling the Veterans Administration to extend benefits to the men with health problems traceable to the internment experience.

Only three of the airmen reported that they have visited the Soviet Union as tourists since World War II. In 1986–87, Byron Morgan, a navy flyer in the third group of internees, attempted to stimulate interest in an "internee reunion" to be held in Tashkent. A travel agency organized an itinerary and sought to recruit prospective reunionists. Unfortunately, only eight men reacted favorably to the idea of a sentimental return to the Soviet Union. The small number was insufficent to justify any further planning, and the notion was abandoned.

Appendix A
Interned Crews, by Unit

Unit (and type of aircraft flown)	No. of crews interned
Army Doolittle raid (B-25)	1
Army Eleventh Air Force (Aleutian bases)	
77th Bombardment Squadron (B-25)	12
404th Bombardment Squadron (B-24)	9
Army Twentieth Bomber Command (China bases; B-29)	
395th Bombardment Squadron	1
771st Bombardment Squadron	1
794th Bombardment Squadron	2
Navy Fleet Air Wing Four (Aleutian bases; PV-1, PV-2)	
VB-135 Squadron	6
VB-136 Squadron	4
VPB-131 Squadron	1
Total	37

Appendix B
Interned Crews, by Release Group

Group No. 1. One crew (5 men); "escaped" May 11, 1943

Parent Unit	Crew (pilot's name in italics)	Landed	Date Interned (USSR time)
Doolittle	*York,*[a] Emmens, Herndon, Laban, Pohl	Vladivostok	Apr. 16, 1942

Group No. 2. Eight crews (61 men); "escaped" Feb. 18, 1944

1. Army 404th	*Pottenger,* Filler, Hanner, Wiles,[b] Homitz, Dixon, Ring,[c] Bernatovich, Day, Dimel,[b] Varney[b]	Kamchatka	Aug. 12, 1943
2. Army 404th	*Putnam,* A. T. Miller, Amundson, Dyxin, George, Albert, Bryson, Doyle, H. M. Hammond, Goode, Gross	Petropavlovsk	Sept. 12, 1943
3. Army 77th	*Savignac,* Keithley, Hodges, Fawcett, Vickers	Petropavlovsk	Sept. 12, 1943
4. Army 77th	*Rodger,* Fry, Eastmoore, Overby, Green	Petropavlovsk	Sept. 12, 1943
5. Army 77th	*Salter,*[d] E. H. Taylor, Koepp, Wiar, Graham, Lans	Petropavlovsk	Sept. 12, 1943
6. Army 404th	*Wagner,* Vandiver, Black, Corbett, Marx, Kerns, Waid, Saugestad, Carter, Everett, Vasquez, Daniels, Fuller	Petropavlovsk	Sept. 12, 1943
7. Army 77th	*Hurst,* J. M. Taylor, O'Dair, Wilcox, Huber, C. H. Field	Petropavlovsk	Sept. 12, 1943
8. Army 77th	*Marrier,* Sabich, Hahn, Billingsley, Dunwoody	Petropavlovsk	Sept. 12, 1943

Group No. 3. Seventeen crews (130 men); "escaped" Jan. 30, 1945

1. Navy VB-135	*Bone,* Mantle, Stevens, Sommers, Gelber, Crow, Horvath	Petropavlovsk	June 15, 1944

2. Navy VB-135	*Schuette,* Brassil, Morgan, Duna- way, Jage, Beggin, Morris	Petropavlovsk	June 15, 1944
3. Navy VB-135	*Mahrt,* Johnson, King, Dickson, Patzke, Strom, Everard	Kamchatka	June 20, 1944
4. Navy VB-135	*Clark,* Miller, Mathers, Simes, Brennan, Rowe	Petropavlovsk	July 23, 1944
5. Navy VB-135	*Vivian,* Wilson, Edwards, An- derson, Schasney, Virant, Nommensen	Petropavlovsk	July 24, 1944
6. Army 771st	*Jarrell,* Kirkland, Ogden, Golden, Losick, Earley, R. Price, Zuercher, Bailey, Hummell, Bost	Vladivostok	July 29, 1944
7. Navy VB-136	*Lindell,* Head, Richardson, Wil- liamson, Brown, Manthie	Petropavlovsk	Aug. 13, 1944
8. Army 395th	*McGlinn,* Caudle, Turner, E. C. Murphy, Conrath, Webb, Stocks, Robson, Childs, Mannatt, Beckley	Khabarovsk Territory	Aug. 20, 1944
9. Navy VB-136	*Cowles,* Panella,[b] Parker, Toney, J. R. McDonald	Kamchatka	Aug. 20, 1944
10. Navy VB-136	*Dingle,* Petterborg, Dulan, Henry, Pollard, Leintz	Petropavlovsk	Aug. 28, 1944
11. Army 77th	*Head,* R. W. Hammond, Mc- Intosh, Lawton, Carr, Crowell	Petropavlovsk	Sept. 10, 1944
12. Navy VB-135	*D. F. McDonald,* Miles, Broad- well, Ross, Rosa, Nicodemus	Petropavlovsk	Sept. 11, 1944
13. Navy VB-136	*Wayne,*[d] Murphy, Ehret, Mul- ford, Baxter	Kamchatka	Sept. 17, 1944
14. Army 404th	*Ott,* Perlich, Arnold, Shimer, Martel, Clark, Petersen, Saigh, Austin, Shelton, Kar- koszynski	Petropavlovsk	Sept. 25, 1944
15. Army 77th	*McQuillin,* D. A. Ward, Voland, Brishaber, Sylvester, Her- mansen, Horin[e]	Petropavlovsk	Nov. 1, 1944
16. Army 794th	*W. H. Price,* Flanagan, Scherer, Morrison, Rutherford, Larkin, Pletter, Weed, Bar- dunias, Stavinski, Cook	Vladivostok	Nov. 11, 1944
17. Army 794th	*Mickish,* Schaefer, Diamond, Rutledge, J. W. Ward, Arent- sen, Mann, Brownwell, Mertz, Sigrist, Hassinger	Vladivostok	Nov. 21, 1944

Group No. 4. Four crews (43 men); "escaped" May 27, 1945

1. Army 404th	*D. H. Taylor,*[e] Yelland, Wheeler,[e] Lodahl, J. R. Smith, Ruh- man, Bendorovich, Burnett, Lakin, Divoky, Lutton, Newell	Kamchatka	Nov. 18, 1944

2. Army 404th	*Weiss,* R. C. Murphy, Michael, Bechtel, A. R. Miller, Wil- liamson, Bingold, Reed, Kimsey, Leighton, Shuping, Centore, Herron	Petropavlovsk	Dec. 7, 1944
3. Army 404th	*Elliott,* Bacon, Bingham, Cohen, Schwierjohn, Hamann, Harri- son, Wyberg, Fallows, Koller, Morris, Roth	Petropavlovsk	Jan. 18, 1945
4. Navy VPB-131	*Powers,*[a] Thomas, Pleasant, Timperman, Mann, Hosner	Kamchatka	Feb. 21, 1945

Group No. 5. Seven crews (52 men); released Aug. 24, 1945

1. Army 404th	*Kleinke,* Galleron,[f] J. S. Smith, Stella, Zakoian, Neet, Y. H. Smith, Raymond, Cutler, Jolly, Stakshus, Nutley	Petropavlovsk	May 11, 1945
2. Army 77th	*Winter,*[g] Tyler, David, Stifel,[e] Babb, Sargent, Wutchic[i]	Petropavlovsk	May 11, 1945
3. Army 404th	*Blakeway,* Kuehner, Hand, Potter, Cayon, Stevenson, Gleason, Burgess, Schwerdt- man, Lokey, Folkman, Leatherwood	Petropavlovsk	May 16, 1945
4. Army 77th	*Beever,* Osburn, Olah, Nichols, Jonasen, Parrish	Petropavlovsk	May 20, 1945
5. Army 77th	*Wolbrink,* Kroot,[h] B. F. Field, Caris, Glodek,[i] Dehaven	Petropavlovsk	June 10, 1945
6. Army 77th	*Wampler,*[g] Millar, Scherl, Prosuk, Judd,[j] Curley	Kamchatka	July 17, 1945
7. Army 77th	*Terris,* Earnheart, Drynan, Kurczak, Vaughn, Sorenson	Kamchatka	July 17, 1945

[a]Commanding officer of the group.

[b]Injured in crash.

[c]Died as a result of crash injuries.

[d]Commanding officer of the group and also commander of the parent squadron.

[e]Wounded.

[f]Injured in internment camp.

[g]Alternative commanding officer of Group No. 5. Later, Winter was released separately through Red Cross Action.

[h]Disabled.

[i]Dead on arrival at Petropavlovsk.

[j]Lost at sea when bomber ditched off Kamchatka.

Appendix C
Alphabetical Roster of Internees

Name	Grade when interned
1. Albert, Myron M.	Technical Sergeant
2. Amundson, Floyd A.	2nd Lieutenant
3. Arentsen, William R.	2nd Lieutenant
4. Arnold, Gilbert S.	2nd Lieutenant
5. Austin, Carl W.	Staff Sergeant
6. Babb, Jackson L.	Sergeant
7. Bacon, Edgar	2nd Lieutenant
8. Bailey, Merl A.	Sergeant
9. Bardunias, John	Staff Sergeant
10. Bechtel, John C.	Flight Officer
11. Beckley, John G.	Sergeant
12. Beever, Harold V.	2nd Lieutenant
13. Bendorovich, Bernard P.	Corporal
14. Bernatovich, Peter J.	Staff Sergeant
15. Billingsley, John A.	Staff Sergeant
16. Bingham, Perry G.	2nd Lieutenant
17. Bingold, Leonard J.	Staff Sergeant
18. Black, Benson H., Jr.	2nd Lieutenant
19. Blakeway, William D.	2nd Lieutenant
20. Bost, Herbert A.	Corporal
21. Brishaber, Joseph R.	Corporal
22. Brownwell, Frederick D.	Staff Sergeant
23. Bryson, Ernest A., Jr.	Staff Sergeant
24. Burgess, Carlton P.	Sergeant
25. Burnett, Billy J.	Corporal
26. Caris, Roy C.	Corporal
27. Carr, John F.	Staff Sergeant
28. Carter, David L.	Sergeant
29. Caudle, Ernest E.	1st Lieutenant
30. Cayon, Edward S.	Flight Officer
31. Centore, Anthony	Sergeant

32.	Childs, Otis L., Jr.	Sergeant
33.	Clark, Charlie H.	Technical Sergeant
34.	Cohen, William A.	2nd Lieutenant
35.	Conrath, Almon W.	1st Lieutenant
36.	Cook, Millard S.	Staff Sergeant
37.	Corbett, Thomas A.	Staff Sergeant
38.	Crowell, William C.	Staff Sergeant
39.	Curley, Bernard T.	Sergeant
40.	Cutler, Raymond E.	Corporal
41.	Daniels, Robert L.	Corporal
42.	Davis, Robert E.	2nd Lieutenant
43.	Day, Charles R.	Staff Sergeant
44.	Dehaven, Roy A.	Corporal
45.	Diamond, Jack A.	2nd Lieutenant
46.	Dimel, Donald L.	Staff Sergeant
47.	Divoky, Charles E.	Corporal
48.	Dixon, James P.	Technical Sergeant
49.	Doyle, Edward D.	Staff Sergeant
50.	Drynan, Arthur W., Jr.	1st Lieutenant
51.	Dunwoody, Joseph A.	Staff Sergeant
52.	Dyxin, Robert W.	2nd Lieutenant
53.	Earley, Lewis A.	Technical Sergeant
54.	Earnheart, Philip R.	2nd Lieutenant
55.	Eastmoore, Norman E.	2nd Lieutenant
56.	Elliott, Kenneth E.	2nd Lieutenant
57.	Emmens, Robert G.	1st Lieutenant
58.	Everett, Henry C., Jr.	Sergeant
59.	Fallows, John A.	Sergeant
60.	Fawcett, James A.	Staff Sergeant
61.	Field, Byron F., Jr.	2nd Lieutenant
62.	Field, Charles H.	Sergeant
63.	Filler, Richard E.	Flight Officer
64.	Flanagan, John E.	1st Lieutenant
65.	Folkman, Vance L.	Corporal
66.	Fry, Loyal W.	Flight Officer
67.	Fuller, Howard C.	Corporal
68.	Galleron, Paul L.	2nd Lieutenant
69.	George, Mahfooz A.	Technical Sergeant
70.	Gleason, George P.	Sergeant
	Glodek, Matthew M.[a]	Corporal
71.	Golden, Edward J.	2nd Lieutenant
72.	Goode, Nathan S.	Sergeant
73.	Graham, Paul H.	Staff Sergeant
74.	Green, Gerald J.	Staff Sergeant
75.	Gross, Charles C.	Private
76.	Hahn, Albert W.	2nd Lieutenant
77.	Hamann, Merle H.	Sergeant
78.	Hammond, Hutchen M.	Staff Sergeant
79.	Hammond, Ralph W.	2nd Lieutenant
80.	Hand, George S.	2nd Lieutenant
81.	Hanner, Charles K., Jr.	2nd Lieutenant

82.	Harrison, Zeph J.	Sergeant
83.	Hassinger, Therman	Staff Sergeant
84.	Head, William W., Jr.	1st Lieutenant
85.	Hermansen, Norman	Corporal
86.	Herndon, Nolan A.	2nd Lieutenant
87.	Herron, Edmond J.	Corporal
88.	Hodges, Harold R.	2nd Lieutenant
89.	Homitz, Anthony S.	Technical Sergeant
90.	Horin, Nicholas	Corporal
91.	Huber, Harry B.	Staff Sergeant
92.	Hummell, George	Sergeant
93.	Hurst, Russell K.	2nd Lieutenant
94.	Jarrell, Howard R.	Captain
95.	Jolly, Robert M.	Corporal
96.	Jonasen, Leif O.	Sergeant
	Judd, Orville K.[b]	Sergeant
97.	Karkoszynski, Leonard R.	Staff Sergeant
98.	Keithley, John L.	2nd Lieutenant
99.	Kerns, Joseph P.	Staff Sergeant
100.	Kimsey, Vernon J.	Staff Sergeant
101.	Kirkland, John R.	1st Lieutenant
102.	Kleinke, Richard B.	2nd Lieutenant
103.	Koepp, Harry J.	1st Lieutenant
104.	Koller, Glenn T.	Sergeant
105.	Kroot, Jerry M.	2nd Lieutenant
106.	Kuehner, Gordon V., Jr.	2nd Lieutenant
107.	Kurczak, Edward	Sergeant
108.	Laban, Theodore H.	Staff Sergeant
109.	Lakin, Martin	Corporal
110.	Lans, Irwin L.	Private
111.	Larkin, Donald J.	Master Sergeant
112.	Lawton, Warren G.	Technical Sergeant
113.	Leatherwood, Roy T.	Corporal
114.	Leighton, Walter M.	Sergeant
115.	Lodahl, Leo C.	Flight Officer
116.	Lokey, James T.	Corporal
117.	Losick, Mike, Jr.	Master Sergeant
118.	Lutton, Bert	Corporal
119.	McGlinn, Richard M.	Major
120.	McIntosh, John B.	2nd Lieutenant
121.	McQuillin, William L.	2nd Lieutenant
122.	Mann, William P.	Technical Sergeant
123.	Mannatt, Louis M.	Sergeant
124.	Marrier, Wayne A.	2nd Lieutenant
125.	Martel, Arthur G.	Technical Sergeant
126.	Marx, Lawrence E.	Staff Sergeant
127.	Mertz, Edward J.	Staff Sergeant
128.	Michael, Edward R.	2nd Lieutenant
129.	Mickish, William J.	1st Lieutenant
130.	Millar, Richard H.	2nd Lieutenant
131.	Miller, Albert R.	1st Lieutenant

132.	Miller, Allen T.	2nd Lieutenant
133.	Morris, Sterling C.	Sergeant
134.	Morrison, Edwin	2nd Lieutenant
135.	Murphy, Eugene C.	1st Lieutenant
136.	Murphy, Richard C.	2nd Lieutenant
137.	Neet, Kenneth J.	Sergeant
138.	Newell, Quitman U.	Private
139.	Nichols, Charles, Jr.	Sergeant
140.	Nutley, John W., Jr.	Corporal
141.	O'Dair, James R.	2nd Lieutenant
142.	Ogden, Frank C.	2nd Lieutenant
143.	Olah, George W.	2nd Lieutenant
144.	Osburn, Cecil M.	2nd Lieutenant
145.	Ott, John E.	1st Lieutenant
146.	Overby, Clarence H.	Technical Sergeant
147.	Parrish, Albert S.	Corporal
148.	Perlich, Frank J.	2nd Lieutenant
149.	Petersen, Robert H.	Staff Sergeant
150.	Pletter, David	Technical Sergeant
151.	Pohl, David W.	Corporal
152.	Pottenger, James R.	2nd Lieutenant
153.	Potter, Richard T.	2nd Lieutenant
154.	Price, Roy	Staff Sergeant
155.	Price, Weston H.	Captain
156.	Prosuk, Albert	Sergeant
157.	Putnam, Roger K.	2nd Lieutenant
158.	Raymond, Gordon R.	Corporal
159.	Reed, Robert H.	Staff Sergeant
	Ring, Thomas E.[c]	Technical Sergeant
160.	Robson, Charles H.	Staff Sergeant
161.	Rodger, John T.	1st Lieutenant
162.	Roth, Morton H.	Sergeant
163.	Ruhman, Louis H.	Corporal
164.	Rutherford, Eugene P.	2nd Lieutenant
165.	Rutledge, James R.	1st Lieutenant
166.	Sabich, Vladimir P.	2nd Lieutenant
167.	Saigh, Dean P.	Staff Sergeant
168.	Salter, Richard D.	Major
169.	Sargent, Floyd E.	Sergeant
170.	Saugestad, Arnold M.	Sergeant
171.	Savignac, Norman R.	2nd Lieutenant
172.	Schaefer, John K.	2nd Lieutenant
173.	Scherer, Melvin E.	1st Lieutenant
174.	Scherl, George J.	2nd Lieutenant
175.	Schwerdtman, William E.	Sergeant
176.	Schwierjohn, Theodore I.	Staff Sergeant
177.	Shelton, Thomas B.	Staff Sergeant
178.	Shimer, Raymond W.	2nd Lieutenant
179.	Shuping, J. W.	Sergeant
180.	Sigrist, Herman K.	Staff Sergeant
181.	Smith, John R.	Sergeant

182.	Smith, John S.	Flight Officer
183.	Smith, Yorke H., Jr.	Corporal
184.	Sorenson, Edward F.	Corporal
185.	Stakshus, Alfred F.	Corporal
186.	Stavinski, Henry J.	Staff Sergeant
187.	Stella, Carl F.	2nd Lieutenant
188.	Stevenson, Parmer W.	Technical Sergeant
189.	Stifel, Ernest A., Jr.	1st Lieutenant
190.	Stocks, William T.	Staff Sergeant
191.	Sylvester, Robert L.	Corporal
192.	Taylor, Donald H.	2nd Lieutenant
193.	Taylor, Edward H.	2nd Lieutenant
194.	Taylor, John M.	2nd Lieutenant
195.	Terris, Robert W.	Flight Officer
196.	Turner, Lyle C.	2nd Lieutenant
197.	Tyler, John W.	2nd Lieutenant
198.	Vandiver, Winfred H.	2nd Lieutenant
199.	Varney, Richard T.	Corporal
200.	Vasquez, Margarito	Sergeant
201.	Vaughn, L. J.	Corporal
202.	Vickers, Grady	Sergeant
203.	Voland, Charles E.	2nd Lieutenant
204.	Wagner, Carl G.	Major
205.	Waid, Charles L.	Sergeant
206.	Wampler, George L.	1st Lieutenant
207.	Ward, Donald A.	Flight Officer
208.	Ward, James W.	1st Lieutenant
209.	Webb, Melvin O.	Staff Sergeant
210.	Weed, Frank A.	Staff Sergeant
211.	Weiss, Robert A.	2nd Lieutenant
212.	Wheeler, Edward H.	Flight Officer
213.	Wiar, Kenneth I.	Staff Sergeant
214.	Wilcox, Robert W.	Staff Sergeant
215.	Wiles, Robert W.	2nd Lieutenant
216.	Williamson, James E.	Staff Sergeant
217.	Winter, Hubert B.	2nd Lieutenant
218.	Wolbrink, Robert B.	2nd Lieutenant
	Wutchic, Paul W.[a]	Sergeant
219.	Wyberg, Vaughn C.	Sergeant
220.	Yelland, Lester R.	2nd Lieutenant
221.	York, Edward J.	Captain
222.	Zakoian, Sam G.	Staff Sergeant
223.	Zuercher, Jerome C.	Sergeant

U.S. Navy Personnel

224.	Anderson, Kenneth G.	AMM 2nd Class
225.	Baxter, Robert P.	ACRM
226.	Beggin, John F.	AMM 2nd Class
227.	Bone, Russell P.	Lieutenant
228.	Brassil, John E.	Lieutenant (jg)
229.	Brennan, John	ARM 2nd Class

230.	Broadwell, Donnie L.	Ensign
231.	Brown, Cyril J.	ARM 3rd Class
232.	Clark, Jackson W.	Lieutenant (jg)
233.	Cowles, Jack R.	Lieutenant (jg)
234.	Crow, Frank L.	AMM 3rd Class
235.	Dickson, William E.	AMM 2nd Class
236.	Dingle, John A.	Lieutenant (jg)
237.	Dulan, Eugene F.	Ensign
238.	Dunaway, Willie A.	AMM 1st Class
239.	Edwards, Thomas H.	Ensign
240.	Ehret, John E.	Ensign
241.	Everard, Richard T.	AOM 2nd Class
242.	Gelber, Samuel	ARM 2nd Class
243.	Head, James S.	Ensign
244.	Henry, Charles D.	AMM 3rd Class
245.	Horvath, Joseph P.	AOM 3rd Class
246.	Hosner, Francis P.	AOM 3rd Class
247.	Jage, Edward J.	ARM 3rd Class
248.	Johnson, Richard H.	Ensign
249.	King, William A.	Ensign
250.	Leintz, Daniel	ARM 3rd Class
251.	Lindell, Carl W.	Lieutenant
252.	McDonald, Darryl F.	Lieutenant (jg)
253.	McDonald, John R.	AOM 3rd Class
254.	Mahrt, George A.	Lieutenant
255.	Mann, Ralph H.	ARM 2nd Class
256.	Manthie, Russell L.	AOM 3rd Class
257.	Mantle, Glenn W.	Ensign
258.	Mathers, John F.	Ensign
259.	Miles, Kenneth G.	Ensign
260.	Miller, Berwyn J., Jr.	Ensign
261.	Morgan, Byron A.	Ensign
262.	Morris, Walter H.	AOM 2nd Class
263.	Mulford, Earl A.	AOM 2nd Class
264.	Murphy, John W.	Lieutenant
265.	Nicodemus, William F.	ARM 2nd Class
266.	Nommensen, Emil A., Jr.	AOM 2nd Class
267.	Panella, Leonardo	Ensign
268.	Parker, Millard B.	Ensign
269.	Patzke, Clifford C.	ARM 3rd Class
270.	Petterborg, Emil M.	Ensign
271.	Pleasant, Wiley E.	Ensign
272.	Pollard, Harvey H.	AOM 2nd Class
273.	Powers, John W.	Lieutenant
274.	Richardson, Murlin K.	Ensign
275.	Rosa, John W.	AMM 1st Class
276.	Ross, Jack C.	AOM 3rd Class
277.	Rowe, Herbert C.	AOM 2nd Class
278.	Schasney, Paul J.	AMM 2nd Class
279.	Schuette, Howard P.	Lieutenant
280.	Simes, Hoyle A.	AMM 1st Class

281.	Sommers, Lawrence E.	AMM 1st Class
282.	Stevens, Ralph W.	Ensign
283.	Strom, William D.	AMM 2nd Class
284.	Thomas, Charles M., Jr.	Lieutenant (jg)
285.	Timperman, Robert G.	AMM 3rd Class
286.	Toney, Harold R.	ARM 1st Class
287.	Virant, Frank A.	ARM 2nd Class
288.	Vivian, John P.	Lieutenant
289.	Wayne, Charles	Lieutenant Commander
290.	Williamson, Harry H.	AMM 1st Class
291.	Wilson, David R.	Ensign

[a]Dead on arrival at Petropavlovsk.
[b]Lost at sea when bomber ditched off Kamchatka.
[c]Died as a result of crash injuries.

Bibliography

Assistant Chief of Staff, Intelligence, War Department. "11th AF Keeps Knocking at Jap's Back Door in Kuriles." *Impact,* August, 1945, 61.

Cassidy, Henry C. "'Escape' of Tokyo Raid Crew from Russia Revealed." *St. Louis Post-Dispatch* (Washington dateline), December 2, 1944.

Cloe, John Haile, with Michael F. Monaghan. *Top Cover for America.* Anchorage, Alaska: Anchorage Chapter, Air Force Association; Missoula, Mont.: Pictorial Histories Publishing, 1984.

Deane, John R. *The Strange Alliance.* New York: Viking Press, 1946.

Eisenhower, Dwight D. *Crusade in Europe.* New York: Doubleday, 1948.

Emmens, Robert G. *Guests of the Kremlin.* New York: Macmillan, 1949.

Gamarekian, Barbara. "Ex-Ambassador Flies World War II Route." *New York Times* (Washington dateline), July 21, 1987.

Garfield, Brian. *The Thousand-Mile War.* New York: Doubleday, 1969.

Glines, Carroll V. *The Doolittle Raid.* New York: Crown Publishers, 1988.

Harriman, W. Averell, and Elie Abel. *Special Envoy to Churchill and Stalin, 1941–1946.* New York: Random House, 1975.

Hoover, Herbert, *The Memoirs of Herbert Hoover, 1920–33.* New York: Macmillan, 1952.

Jones, Robert Huhn. *The Roads to Russia: United States Lend-Lease to the Soviet Union.* Norman: University of Oklahoma Press, 1969.

Keefe, Eugene K., Arsene A. Boucher, Sarah J. Elpern, William Giloane, James M. Moore, Terrence L. Ogden, Stephen Peters, John P. Prevas, Nancy E. Walstrom, and Eston T. White. *Area Handbook for the Soviet Union,* Foreign Area Studies, American University, DA Pam 550-95. Washington, D.C.: GPO, 1971.

Knightley, Phillip. *The Second Oldest Profession.* New York: Norton, 1987.

Lukas, Richard C. "Escape." *Aerospace Historian* (Air Force Historical Foundation), Spring, 1969, 14–17.

Mazuruk, Ilya. "Alaska-Siberia Airlift." *Soviet Life,* October, 1979, 30.

Merrill, James M. *Target Tokyo: The Halsey-Doolittle Raid.* Chicago: Rand, 1964.

Pearson, Drew. "Washington Merry-Go-Round." Syndicated newspaper column (United Feature Service) released November 30, 1944. The complete collection of Pearson's syndicated columns is now held in the archives of the Lyndon Baines Johnson Library, Austin, Tex.

Reynolds, Quentin. *The Curtain Rises.* New York: Random House, 1944.

Scrivner, Charles L. *The Empire Express.* Terre Haute, Ind.: Historical Aviation Album/Sunshine House, 1976.

Sherl, David Smoilovich. "Let's Meet Again!" *Soviet Life,* April, 1988, 56–59.

Standley, William H., and Arthur A. Ageton. *Admiral Ambassador to Russia.* Washington: Regnery, 1955.

Unterberger, Betty M. *Intervention against Communism: Did the United States Try to Overthrow the Soviet Government, 1918–1920?* College Station: Texas A&M University Lecture Series, 1986.

Wheeler, Keith, and editors of Time-Life Books. *Bombers over Japan.* Alexandria, Va.: Time-Life Books, 1982.

White, W. L. *Report on the Russians.* New York: Harcourt Brace, 1945.

Index

Home from Siberia was composed into type on a Compugraphic digital phototypesetter in ten point Times Roman with two points of spacing between the lines. Times Roman was also selected for display. The book was designed by Jim Billingsley, typeset by Metricomp, Inc., printed offset by Thomson-Shore, Inc., and bound by John H. Dekker & Sons, Inc. The paper on which this book is printed carries acid-free characteristics for an effective life of at least three hundred years.

TEXAS A&M UNIVERSITY PRESS : COLLEGE STATION